AN ECONOMIC HISTORY OF MODERN SPAIN

Map 1 Spain: general

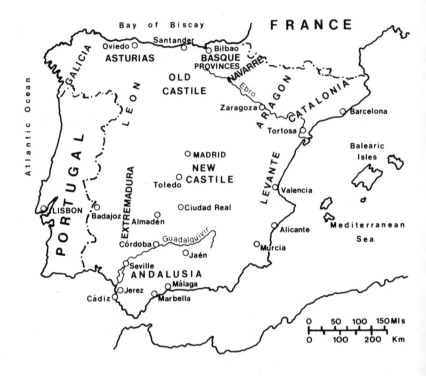

JOSEPH HARRISON

An economic history
of modern Spain

HOLMES & MEIER PUBLISHERS, INC.
New York

First published in the United States of America 1978 by
HOLMES & MEIER PUBLISHERS, INC.
30 Irving Place, New York, N.Y. 10003

Copyright © 1978 by Joseph Harrison

Library of Congress Cataloging in Publication Data

Harrison, Joseph.
  An economic history of modern Spain.

  Bibliography: p. 175.
  Includes index.
  1. Spain – economic conditions. I. Title.
HC385.H33   1978   330.9′46   78–9560
ISBN 0–8419–0411–1

PRINTED IN GREAT BRITAIN

CONTENTS

TABLES AND MAPS

TABLES

MAPS

PREFACE

This book sets out to examine the economic and social development of Spain since the beginning of the eighteenth century. With a few notable exceptions, British and American scholars have devoted relatively little attention to the specific problems of Spain since the nation's decline in power and fortunes following the Golden Age of the sixteenth and early seventeenth centuries. The author is therefore fully conscious of the enormous debt of gratitude which he owes to a remarkable school of Spanish historians who in the last two decades have sought to reach an understanding of the more recent past of their economy and society. Unlike many during the Franco era, the best of Spain's economic and social historians were far from inward-looking and have endeavoured to place a backward and underdeveloped Spain in the general context of an expanding European capitalism.

The present author has also rejected the view that Spain is different, divorced from developments elsewhere. Her recent history will be shown to be closely linked to that of her more advanced neighbours. In the middle of the last century, for example, foreign companies plundered the Spanish subsoil for precious mineral resources, pouring in capital to facilitate this process. British, French and German firms later sent to the backward Spanish nation goods that were manufactured from raw materials produced within her own frontiers. Nor was Spain isolated from the social and political ideas of the times. The Spanish Enlightenment and later her attempts at agrarian reform were both pursued in imitation of outside developments. In the last quarter of the nineteenth century French and Italian orators spread the gospels of Marxism and anarchism among a dissatisfied urban and rural proletariat. The Russian revolution of 1917 and Italian fascism had no little impact on certain sections of the Spanish population.

Even so, not all economic and social developments south of the Pyrenees can be explained largely in terms of external factors and ideas. It will be the author's contention that the origins of the brutal and costly civil war of the 1930s are to be found less in the international economic depression of that era than in the frustrated efforts of a reformist regime to tackle some of the many structural problems endemic to early twentieth-century Spanish society, such as the excessive influence of the Church, the armed forces and centralising administrators. In similar vein, the bottlenecks to production in the early years of the Franco period, which brought great hardship to millions of Spaniards, will be seen in part as the misconceived search for self-sufficiency by Falangist politicians and bureaucrats who rejected outside help when it was offered.

The discerning reader may well detect that the author is more familiar with original sources in some parts of the book than others. My investigations were originally confined to those areas covered in the middle passàges of the work. Above all I was interested in the attempts of the regions of the periphery to industrialise. However, the business communities of Catalonia, Asturias and the Basque region had increasingly to come to terms, as I had, with the policy makers in central government dominated by southern landlords and Madrid financiers who constituted the ruling oligarchy. The heavy industrialists of Oviedo and Bilbao were constantly dependent on State patronage for orders for their products and for a protective tariff to keep out more enterprising foreign competitors from the Spanish market. The textile manufacturers of Barcelona, suffering from an extraordinarily low demand for their cotton and woollen goods from an impoverished rural population, looked to Madrid both for a guaranteed home market and the added incentive of the markets of the American colonies. Like the mill owners of Catalonia before me, I soon became aware of the deficiencies of the mid-nineteenth-century agrarian reforms which manifestly failed to increase the spending power of rural consumers after the wars of independence in Spanish America.

My knowledge of social movements and of their roles in the Second Republic, together with a profound respect for the reformist politicians of that period, was developed over the years through my teaching commitments in the Universities of East Anglia and Manchester. I should like to thank students taking my courses there for many fruitful hours of discussion and argument although by their standards they must have considered me a dreadful reactionary.

Finally, I must express my gratitude to those colleagues and friends who have offered help and encouragement, among them Professor Alan Milward, Professor William Callahan, Dr Richard Griffiths, Dr Paul Preston, Dr James Chandler and Mr Derek Gagen; also to Professor W. H. Chaloner for his advice on the Spanish monetary system. I have likewise benefited from correspondence and discussions with a number of distinguished Spanish economic historians, including Professors Jordi Nadal, Josep Fontana, Gabriel Tortella and Gonzalo Anes. Special thanks are also due to don Juan Fco. Palomar, librarian of the *Fomento del Trabajo Nacional* in Barcelona. It goes without saying that any errors and omissions are entirely my own responsibility.

                                                                                          J. H.

CURRENCY AND UNITS OF MEASUREMENT

A NOTE ON THE SPANISH CURRENCY

Until the early nineteenth century various types of gold and silver money circulated in Spain without there existing a true monetary system. It is known that there were ninety-seven different types of money in circulation at the beginning of the nineteenth century, including British and French currencies.

After 1812 the main unit of currency in Spain was the *real de vellón* valued at about 2½ English pence or approximately one hundred reales to the pound sterling.

Following the creation of the Latin Monetary Union in 1865 by France, Italy, Switzerland and Belgium the Spanish Finance Minister, Figuerola, created a new monetary system in 1868 based on the peseta, equivalent to four *reales de vellón*. Although the exchange rate fluctuated during the late nineteenth and early twentieth centuries the theoretical rate was 25 pesetas to the pound sterling. During the inter-war period the peseta fell on world exchanges, dropping to 39 to the pound or 11·69 to the dollar in January 1940. After the Second World War the peseta dropped sharply against the main currencies, falling to 100 against the pound and 25 against the dollar in January 1949. Since 1959 the peseta has been devalued on four separate occasions. At the end of the 60's it stood at about 167 to the pound or 70 to the dollar.

TABLE OF MEASUREMENTS

fanega	1·5 bushels
hectare	2·471 acres
hectolitre	22·0 imperial gallons (liquid measure)
kilogram	2·204 lb
kilometre	0·621 miles
metric ton	2,204 lb
quintal	100 kg

CHAPTER 1

The economy of the *ancien régime*

After a long and painful phase of stagnation and decline, Spain at long last began to show signs of economic revival in the course of the eighteenth century. No clearer indication is there of that country's changing fortunes than the fate of the Spanish population. Compared with the seventeenth century, when the number of Spaniards fell by approximately one-fifth, during the eighteenth century Spain experienced something of a demographic revolution. The deciding factor which allowed for population expansion was the disappearance of plague from the Peninsula after the last major outbreak from 1648 to 1654. According to the estimate of the economist Gerónimo de Ustáriz made in 1724, Spain had seven million inhabitants at the beginning of the eighteenth century. The first official census was not carried out until 1768 and showed that the population had risen to 9,307,804. Two further censuses were taken before the century was out; the widely accepted Floridablanca census of 1787 and the less reliable Godoy census of 1797, which put the Spanish population at 10,409,879 inhabitants and 10,541,221 inhabitants respectively. The probable under-estimate of Godoy's census is partly corrected by the Antillón census of 1808, which calculated that Spain had 12 million inhabitants at the time of the Napoleonic invasion. Despite the lack of reliability of much of the evidence, it is reasonable to conclude that the Spanish population rose by about one-half during the eighteenth century. With such a rate of demographic expansion Spain would have been more or less in line with the European average, although worse off than England and Wales, which doubled their population from 5 million inhabitants in 1700 to nearly 10 million in 1800. The probability is that Spain was also slightly outpaced by France, whose population increased from 18 million in 1714 to 27 million in 1800.[1]

Global figures, however, disguise a considerable regional imbalance in the rate of expansion of the Spanish population during the eighteenth century. The most marked disparity was between the centre and the periphery. While contemporaries lamented the depopulation of the interior, parts of the periphery enjoyed a population growth as high as that of England and Wales. Catalonia doubled its population between 1718 and

1787 from approximately 400,000 (or at most 500,000) to about 900,000. Galicia, Asturias, Murcia and the two Andalusian provinces of Granada and Seville also increased their share of the Spanish population. But the most astonishing rate of demographic increase occurred in Valencia, where the number of inhabitants nearly quadrupled between 1718 and 1794, rising from 255,080 to 934,724, giving the region the highest density of rural population in Europe. In contrast, the interior provinces of Soria, Guadalajara and La Mancha experienced no more than a modest increase in population, while the number of inhabitants in Extremadura scarcely surpassed ten per square kilometre throughout the century.[2]

Another distinctive feature of the Spanish population in the eighteenth century was the overwhelming predominance of the countryside over the towns. Only two cities had more than 100,000 inhabitants: Madrid, the Spanish capital, which expanded from 130,000 inhabitants in 1723 to 167,607 in 1797, and the Catalan capital, Barcelona, which more than trebled its population, from 35,000 in 1718 to 115,000 in 1797. Three towns were approaching 100,000 inhabitants by 1800: Valencia, Granada and Seville, all capitals of expanding agricultural provinces. Next in size came Cádiz with 70,000 inhabitants, followed by Málaga and Saragossa with 50,000. The historic cities of Castile were in frank decline. Valladolid, once the home of 100,000 people, saw its population reduced to 20,000, while a similar fate overtook the cities of Burgos, Salamanca, Segovia, Avila and Toledo. There were no sizable towns at all in the north. At the end of the eighteenth century Bilbao had no more than 12,000 inhabitants, Vigo and Gijón 6,000 and Santander only 2,000.[3]

A breakdown of the 1797 census into occupational groups by Antonio Domínguez Ortiz shows quite clearly that despite the substantial demographic rise of the preceding years the old economic order prevailed at the end of the century, although national figures obscure important regional developments. Out of the 10½ million Spaniards in 1797, one-quarter were classified as active. The peasantry constituted by far the largest category, with 1,677,172 persons, further subdivided into 364,514 peasant proprietors, 507,423 renters and 805,235 day labourers. The Godoy census also disclosed that Spain contained 403,382 nobles (considerably fewer than in 1768), 182,564 members of the secular and regular clergy, and 25,685 tradesmen. Servants accounted for about 280,000 people, while another 170,000 found employment in the military and the bureaucracy. This pre-industrial society also contained a large number of vagrants and paupers variously estimated at between 100,000 and 140,000 persons.[4]

Census evidence concerning the number of Spaniards engaged in industry is much less trustworthy, although there is little doubt that industrial workers formed a much smaller proportion of the total active labour force than agricultural workers. The censo de frutos y manufacturas of 1803 puts the number of Spaniards employed in industry in 1799 at 269,781, yet it unfortunately does not distinguish between domestic and manufacturing industry. Yet, if this census is guilty of underestimation, the 1808 census almost certainly errs on the side of exaggeration, claiming an industrial labour force of 100,000 for Catalonia, dispersed in 2,000 establishments.[5]

Whatever the exact figures, it is clear that Spain's population increase in the eighteenth century did not spring from a global transformation of the economic and social structure. With one of the lowest population densities in Europe, the country was making up for its disastrous demographic performance under the Habsburgs, when over-ambitious political policies left Spain with a smaller population than might have been expected. The economic recovery of the *ancien régime* was largely confined to a restricted part of the periphery, in particular the prosperous agricultural region of Valencia and the industrialising region of Catalonia.

THE ROLE OF AGRICULTURE

The general trend of economic development in eighteenth-century Europe was towards the transformation of a frequently regionalised and often feudal agricultural economy into one where commercial agriculture on a national scale, internal and overseas trade, and industrial capitalism assumed ever greater importance. An increase in food production, the result of ploughing up more land, brought about and was encouraged by an expanding population—one which was less likely to succumb to such contagious diseases as the plague. In the long run the main beneficiaries of the rise in the number of inhabitants were the landlords, who drew advantage in three main ways: if they farmed their lands themselves they paid lower wages to a growing agricultural labour force while profiting from higher prices because of increased demand for their produce or, if they chose to rent out their lands, were in a position to charge higher rents. The landlord class thereby accumulated large amounts of capital which they could later reinvest in improving their estates, building themselves country houses or financing trade and industry. The increased production of foodstuffs, and in some cases the greater productivity which resulted from the improvement of the land, allowed for the release of labour to the factories, above all from marginal lands. As for the early industrialists, they were able to take advantage of ready supplies of labour and capital together with extended home and overseas markets in which to sell their goods.

Eighteenth-century Spain was not exempted from such developments. Landlords did indeed benefit from increased prices, profits and rents. However, agrarian reformers were conscious of a number of major obstacles blocking the path to what they saw as economic progress. To begin with, large amounts of land were held in mortmain or 'dead hands'. Vast tracts of fertile soil were given over to the pasturing of transhumant flocks

Map 2 Agricultural regions of Spain

- – – – Provincial Boundaries
- ━ ━ ━ Regional Boundaries

of sheep belonging to the anachronistic guild of the Mesta which had long since served its purpose of providing a near bankrupt Spanish Exchequer with funds. Except for Catalonia and Valencia, precious little of the income derived from the soil was channelled into the formation of commercial and industrial capital.

THE REGIONAL DISTRIBUTION OF LAND HOLDINGS

The most striking characteristic of Spanish land holdings, as remarkable today as in the eighteenth century, is the predominance of diminutively small or excessively large units of production, and the relative insignificance of medium-size holdings which offer a peasant family an adequate livelihood. Small holdings of less than ten hectares (one hectare = 2·47 acres) occupy nearly half the Spanish land surface and produce three-fifths of agricultural income. In the north they occupy over 60 per cent of the land surface and earn more than 70 per cent of agricultural income. The north-west corner of Spain contains tens of millions of tiny plots of land, with holdings of less than one hectare constituting more than 50 per cent of all small holdings. Large holdings are most common in the south of Spain. In the 1930s holdings of over 100 hectares occupied twice as much of the southern land surface as holdings of less than ten hectares. Large holdings were traditionally less efficient than small plots; only in Extremadura and western Andalusia did large holdings produce more income than small holdings. Medium-size holdings of ten to 100 hectares nowhere constitute a majority of all holdings. They occupy about one-quarter of the Spanish land surface and produce a little over one-fifth of total agricultural income. Only in Catalonia, the south-east and the two northern provinces of Alava and Navarre do they make a significant contribution to regional agriculture.[6]

The classic example of an area of small holdings is Galicia in the north-western corner of the Peninsula, whose land surface is divided into 15 million parcels. A government commission set up in 1907 to study the extreme fragmentation of land found in the district of Vera in the province of Corunna a plot of land measuring thirty-two square metres which had three owners: one owned the ground, another the only chestnut tree on the ground, while the third had a right to six eggs per annum. In Vigo the commission found numerous plots of thirty, twenty and even ten square metres—a holding of one hectare was considered by many to be a vast domain. In Santa María de Ordax it was not uncommon to find a single farmer in possession of 80 to 120 individual plots which comprised a total area of no more than seven hectares and were up to five kilometres distant.[7]

Since the Middle Ages most of the land in Galicia belonged to the Church and the nobility, who let it out on a special lease known as the *foro*. The tenant or *forero* paid a quit rent to the owner or *forista*, usually as little as 2 per cent of the capital value of the holding. In return the tenant was given a long lease on all land and farm buildings, usually for 'three lives and twenty-nine years more'.[8] The object of such favourable terms was to induce free peasants to settle on the land, much of which was no more than bare rock or scrubland. This type of settlement worked well for both parties until agricultural prices started to rise in the eighteenth century. The *foreros* now began to sub-let their holdings at a much more lucrative sum than they themselves paid the *foristas*. At the same time the Church and the nobility also attempted to cash in on the new situation by asserting their traditional rights of eviction and raising rents. In 1763 the Council of Castile resolved the matter in favour of the *foreros*, a decision which was to prove something of an obstacle to the development of Galician agriculture. Assured possession of their lands at very low rentals, the *foreros* continued to sub-lease at more and more speculative rates, thus bringing about the creation of the multitude of small plots or *minifundos*. Farms became so subdivided that the Galician peasant found it increasingly difficult to grow enough maize, rye, chestnuts and potatoes to provide for the scant needs of his family and at the same time raise a few scraggy cattle and pigs which he sold off to pay his taxes. By the middle of the nineteenth century this most primitive system of subsistence farming was manifestly incapable of feeding the growing population of the region. When the potato crop failed in 1853–54, Galicia experienced a famine of 'Irish' dimensions for which the only possible remedy was massive migration, both within the Peninsula and to Latin America. While the men offered themselves as seasonal labourers at harvest times and performed all kinds of manual jobs in the towns, from waiters to water carriers, thousands of young girls went into domestic service.

To the east of Galicia, along the Biscay coast to the Pyrenees, are the regions of Asturias, Santander, the Basque provinces and Navarre. The distinguishing feature of this northern area is a system of mainly small holdings which traditionally gave rise to a more prosperous class of tenant farmer than in Galicia. Except for parts of western Asturias and the coastal zone of the Basque province of Vizcaya, the *foro* was far less in evidence. In consequence, the whole of the northern belt was characterised by a far more stable community life. Basque inheritance laws encouraged the peasant farmer to hand over the whole of his land to his chosen heir, while younger sons were frequently encouraged to seek their fortunes in the New World. The wealthy *indiano*, the man who returned from the colonies with enough money to buy himself a plot of land, was a much revered member of Basque society. The preservation of the traditional aspects of rural life was embodied in the local customs or *fueros*, which were vigorously defended by the peasantry. Another feature of the Basque provinces of Guipúzcoa and Vizcaya, much admired by eighteenth-century travellers and reformers, was the homestead or *caserío*, which distinguished this area from the rest of Spain, where agricultural villages were the rule.[9] In the provinces of Alava and Navarre the *caserío* begins to give way to the farming village, and medium-size holdings form a greater proportion of total holdings.

One of the more prosperous agricultural regions of eighteenth-century Spain was Catalonia in the north-east. The basis of the region's agricultural fortunes were the cultivation of wheat and the vine in the central and coastal zones. It was the increased yields of foodstuffs which helped to feed the expanding population of Catalonia in the first two-thirds of the century, although as the eighteenth century drew to a close increasing resort had to be made to cereal imports. Part of the explanation of this development lay in the growing importance of the vine, which expanded rapidly in such districts as El Penedès and El Priorato, from where large quantities of wines and brandies were exported to northern Europe and Spanish America. In addition, the mountainous interior of Catalonia contained large tracts of marginal land which soon began to yield diminishing returns. It was from this barren and isolated area, where the peasantry scratched a meagre living from the soil, that Catalan industry was to recruit its early proletariat. This accounts for the apparently paradoxical situation whereby eighteenth-century Catalonia was manifestly incapable of feeding its own population yet provided the genesis of modern Spanish capitalism.

Among the wine growers of Catalonia the economic resurgence of the eighteenth-century gave rise to a new class of peasants known as the *rabassaires* who rented their land from the landlords and municipalities, who in turn saw renting as the most effective means of increasing their incomes. The length of the lease was indefinite and could be passed from father to son. The *rabassaire* paid the landowner a fixed proportion of the value of his crop and could not be evicted until half the vines which he had planted were dead, a period usually of between forty and fifty years. For most of the century the landlords and the *rabassaires* were content with the terms of their leases. Disputes appeared only in the 1760s, when a number of leases came up for renegotiation following the death of half the vines that were planted in the boom years of the 1720s.[10] Yet so successful did the *rabassaire* system of leaseholding appear outside Catalonia that Jovellanos, Campomanes and other Ministers of the Enlightenment hoped for its extension to the rest of Spain.

To the south of Catalonia the eastern littoral, known as the Levante, constituted another area of great constrasts. A contemporary account of the late 1790s highlighted the great difference between the barren and unproductive mountainous zone of the north and west and the irrigated *huertas* of the coast, with their thrice-yearly harvests.[11] In the eighteenth and nineteenth centuries the coastal plains of the Levante developed a thriving and varying agriculture which yielded rich harvests of wine, brandy, fruits and rice. The rows of mulberry trees provided the basis of the principal industry of the region—silk. A prosperous export trade in agricultural produce, moreover, led to the accumulation of considerable wealth.

The predominant form of holding in the Levante was the small holding. Since the expulsion of the Moriscos from 1609 to 1614, Valencian peasants rented plots of land on leases known as *censos* for which they paid a fixed sum. Yet far more crucial to the prosperity of regional agriculture than the size of holdings or the terms of the lease was the regulation of water supply. In Valencia water was sold with the land but owned by the community. Disputes among Valencian farmers about the al-location of water were settled by a medieval institution known as the Cort de la Seo, or Water Tribunal, which met at regular intervals on the steps of the cathedral. The fact that the judgements of this archaic body were never contested testified to the basic conservatism of the Valencian peasantry.

In pronounced constrast to the dynamic and wealthy districts of the eastern littoral, the central tableland of Castile appeared a stagnant back-water to the agrarian reformers of the *ancien régime*. In the middle of the eighteenth century Campomanes estimated that in Old Castile alone there were 1,500 deserted villages which had once contained 30,000 inhabit-ants.[12] The increase in agricultural prices brought about the ploughing up of large areas of marginal land and led to the repopulation of many of the deserted villages. However, the majority of developments concerned the extension of land under the plough rather than the use of more intensive methods of cultivation. In addition, poor soils and summer droughts gave rise to a system of monocultures based on wheat, wine and olives.

The system of land holdings in Castile was the product of the reconquest of the region from the Moors, a process which for the whole of Spain took nearly eight centuries to complete. The recapture of the lands which were to comprise the kingdom of Castile and León took place in the first stage of the Reconquest during the ninth and tenth centuries. In order to defend the previously underpopulated region against further Moorish attack the Crown offered small plots of land to free peasants with additional grants to religious foundations and noble supporters. Under the threat of further Moslem assaults on their new lands the free peasantry frequently sought the protection of the local *seigneur*. What arose, however, was not feud-alism but an institution known as *behetría* by which the peasants them-selves elected the *seigneur* and also had the right to replace him should they decide that he was not serving the community.

The second stage of the Reconquest occurred during the eleventh cen-tury, when the frontiers of Castile were pushed southwards from the Duero to the Tagus. This stage was completed with the occupation of Toledo in 1085. The territory captured comprised the southern portion of Old Castile and the western part of New Castile. In the northern half of this zone from the Duero to the central mountains the pattern of land holdings was similar to the previous resettlement. South of the central mountain range the role of the nobility in directing resettlement was greater, yet they were still not sufficiently strong to impose a feudal structure. However, the belligerence of the Moslems during the twelfth century led to the creation between the years 1164 and 1183 of three powerful military orders, Calatrava, Santiago and Alcántara, to whom the Crown of Castile would be deeply endebted in any future campaign.

The pattern of land holding in the Spanish south has its origins in the third stage of the Reconquest in the thirteenth century, when the whole of southern Spain fell to the Crown of Castile, with the exception of the Moorish kingdom of Granada. Faced with the problem of redistributing vast tracts of recaptured land, Ferdinand III and Alfonso X rewarded the military orders and individual nobles with grants of large estates known as *latifundios*. These great estates specialised in the production of wool from merino sheep which was sold to the markets of northern Europe, and the extensive cultivation of wheat and olives with very low yields.

In Extremadura herds of wild bulls were allowed to pasture freely over vast areas of land. Neither arable nor pastoral farming supported a large peasant population. Moreover the local unit of exploitation, the *cortijo*, was worked by men who lived little better than slaves. Writing in the 1760s, the intendant of Seville, Pablo de Olavide, referred to the agricultural labourers of that province, the *braceros*, as 'the most unfortunate men I know in Europe. They work in the *cortijos* and the olive groves when the overseers summon them. Then, although nearly naked, with only the ground for a bed, they at least live on the bread and soup they are given: but when the bad weather stops work, starving, homeless and hopeless, they are forced to beg. Half the year these men are labourers and the other half beggars.'[13] Through the centuries this brutal and inefficient system perpetuated itself. As corporate bodies the Church and the military orders could not sell their lands, while the nobility, seeking to maintain the family title and estates intact, entailed their estates.

Not all southern estates were farmed directly by the landowners. The *latifundistas* frequently let their estates to tenant farmers or *labradores* who themselves engaged the hapless *braceros* at planting and harvest time. Furthermore, the *labradores* sub-let marginal land to a class of small farmers known as *pelentrines* who, despite their superior social status, were often little better off than landless labourers. In parts of Extremadura there existed another group of tenant farmers known as the *yunteros*, so called because they owned a team of mules or *yunta* which they used in ploughing.

In the second half of the eighteenth century all these groups of tenant farmers were threatened with eviction by the landowners, who, in common with their counterparts throughout the Iberian Peninsula, hoped to benefit from the rise in wheat prices. In the 1760s the landlords made a systematic attempt to increase rents. Olavide described the situation in Andalusia in 1768 in the following manner. 'At each extirpation of the lease the owner demands a higher rent from the tenants and threatens to lease to another if he meets with refusal, knowing full well that with the lack of farm land and with the excess of farmers, he can always find someone ready to rent. The tenant, who has sunk his supply of animals, feed and other provisions into the farm and stands to lose everything if he loses his lease, finds himself in the sad necessity of signing the terms that the tyranny of the owner has set out for him, and every year the owner raises the prices until they become intolerable.'[14]

THE ECONOMIC SOCIETIES

The rise in agricultural prices and the increased rents which resulted from the population expansion of the eighteenth century were an incentive to landlords to find ways of raising additional revenue from their estates. The majority of noble landlords rented out their lands, while the main source of income of the Church was the diezmo, a tithe of one-tenth of the yields. Thus it was in the interest of both types of landowner to instruct their tenants in new methods for improving yields such as the selections of seeds, the application of new farming techniques, and the use of fertilisers. From the middle of the 1760s the nobility and the Church were the moving forces in the establishment of a series of agricultural societies known as the Sociedades Económicas de Amigos del País. Before long these Economic Societies had the backing of the reformist Ministers and bureaucrats of the Spanish Enlightenment who saw them as an effective instrument for fostering economic development.[15]

The early progress of the Economic Societies was slow. After the foundation of the Basque Society of Friends of the Country (the Sociedad Bascongada de Amigos del País) in 1765, it was another nine years before further societies were founded at Beaza and Tudela. In 1774, however, the fiscal of the Council of Castile, the Conde de Campomanes, published his famous Discourse on the development of popular industry of which 30,000 copies were distributed to mayors, intendants and bishops who in turn passed on copies to their clergy.[16] In the wake of the publication of this document the Council of Castile received a number of petitions from towns and villages throughout the region who wished to set up their own Economic Societies. In most cases these petitions originated from the nobility and the clergy; the Economic Societies of Lugo and Medina Sidonia were founded by the local bishop. Although peasants, artisans and manufacturers appear on the membership lists of the societies, only rarely were they included among the founders. Further evidence of the predominant role of the land-owning class in the establishment of the Economic Societies is shown by the absence of these institutions from

Barcelona, Cádiz, Corunna and Bilbao, towns where an active bourgeoisie had grown up.[17]

The Economic Societies developed a variety of interests and pursuits, including the feasibility of substituting mules for oxen as beasts of burden, the establishment of agricultural colleges, and reading the latest treatises of the physiocrats and other reformers. Some of the more conscientious of their members studied political economy and impressed upon their organisation the need to establish Chairs in that discipline. In 1784 the Economic Society of Aragon secured the appointment of a Professor of Economics and Commerce. The Economic Society of Segovia even went so far as to demand that all mayors and intendants be forced to study political economy.[18]

For the first twenty years of their existence the Economic Societies continued to receive the active support of enlightened governments, although in no case did the State play an active role in their foundation. This support disappeared following the revolutionary events in France after 1789. Inevitably the Bourbon government feared that the type of issues debated by the societies could constitute a threat to the continued existence of the *ancien régime* in Spain. After the beginning of the War of Independence in 1808 the Economic Societies started to wane. Yet for a number of years their ideals continued to flourish throughout the Peninsula until their paternalism gave way under the onslaught of liberalism in the 1830s and 1850s.

AGRICULTURAL PRODUCTION AND FOOD CRISES

Although we do not possess a complete set of statistical evidence, there is no doubt that agricultural production in Spain rose during the eighteenth century. It also seems certain that most of the increase in production was due to an extension of the area under cultivation by the breaking of marginal land rather than to more intensive farming. Both the interior and the periphery of the country saw an extension of the land under cultivation, most notably in the second half of the century. However, this process was not an even one. In a small number of provinces agricultural output declined in the course of the century. Memoranda sent to the government in 1763 on the subject of the proposed agrarian law indicated a fall in the area under cultivation in the provinces of Ciudad Rodrigo, Soria, Salamanca and Extremadura. The intendant of Soria informed his masters that land previously under the plough in that province now lay uncultivated. Contemporary accounts and petitions from Extremadura claimed that many areas given over to the migrating flocks of the Mesta had been cultivated in former times. Moreover a work on the political economy of Aragon, published in 1798, advised against extending the area under cultivation in favour of greater intensification. In actual practice, it would appear from regional studies, that, despite the influence of both rising prices and the Economic Societies, neither on large nor small holdings were there any effective or systematic developments. This was particularly the case in central and southern Spain. Large farmers tended to remain entrenched in traditional attitudes, while small farmers persevered with such outmoded implements as the roman plough and to let their lands lie fallow in alternate years.[19]

A clear indication of the limited progress made by Spanish agriculture during the eighteenth century is shown by the failure of the country's farmers to grow enough cereals to meet the needs of the expanding population. Increased production of wheat in the first half of the century brought the virtual eradication of famine except in a number of single years: 1709, 1723, 1734 and 1752. However, the second half of the eighteenth century saw the incidence of a series of lengthy famines in the years 1763–65, 1784–93 and 1800–04, which obliged Spain to import large quantities of wheat. Between 1756 and 1773 net imports of wheat amounted to 17·3 million bushels. By 1793 Cabarrús calculated that Spain needed to import 2·3 million bushels annually, while the *censo de frutos y manufacturas* put the annual deficit in 1799 at a fantastic and unbelievable 33 million bushels.[20]

As we have seen, the type of agricultural development that took place in eighteenth-century Catalonia made that region in particular more prone to shortages of wheat than the centre of the Peninsula. The poorly developed system of internal communications did not permit the Catalan deficits to be made up by the surpluses of Castile. Catalonia avoided the worst excesses of crisis by imports from such wheat-producing areas as Philadelphia, the Baltic, the Black Sea and Tunis. Between 1778 and 1784 three-quarters of the wheat which arrived at Barcelona came from abroad; overland traffic in wheat being far less important. One advantage of Catalonia's reliance on imports was that wheat prices there were stabilised, while they fluctuated violently in Castile according to the size of the harvest. The price of wheat for the month of May in Medina de Rioseco, for instance, was nearly five times as great in 1804 at 155 reales per *fanega* than it had been in 1793, when it stood at 32·5 reales per *fanega*, and nearly two and a half times as great as in 1803, when one *fanega* of wheat fetched 61 reales.[21]

PROPOSALS FOR AGRARIAN REFORM

Shortages of food in the last third of the eighteenth century caused the State to take a keen interest in the problems of Spanish agriculture. The outbreak of bread riots in Castile, Catalonia and Extremadura in 1766 forced Charles III to take a series of initiatives. In May 1766 the government decreed that in the province of Extremadura 'all cultivable land belonging to the towns, as well as the wastelands and those belonging to the municipalities, shall be ploughed and cultivated . . . and distributed by lot to the neediest inhabitants'. Further decrees in 1767 and 1768 extended this system first of all to Andalusia, then to La Mancha and finally to the whole of Spain. Unfortunately for the neediest inhabitants, it was not they who benefited, but rather the landlords who controlled the municipalities.

Another frustrated attempt at reform by the enlightened Ministers of Charles III was the proposed agrarian law. In April 1766 Charles III issued his famous *Expediente de la ley agraria*, which called for the views of the intendants on the problems of the Spanish countryside. The replies of the intendants, who included the visionary intendant of Seville, Pablo de Olavide, formed the basis of what might have been a compassionate and advanced agrarian law if the government had not capitulated in the face of vociferous opposition from the landlords. In consequence, the findings of the *expediente* remained unpublished until 1784.

The main weight of the criticisms of the intendants was directed against the entailment of agricultural property. Their professed belief was that the land belonging to the Church, the municipalities, or held in mortmain was incapable of higher yields. Both Olavide and Gaspar Melchor de Jovellanos of the semi-official Economic Society of Madrid viewed land tied by entail as the most important obstacle to agricultural progress.

The main concern of Olavide was the large areas of wasteland or *baldíos*, which he believed should be broken up into working plots. The aim of Olavide's proposed redistribution of land was not purely economic but social as well. The ploughing up of additional land would increase the output of cereals, thus bringing an improvement in the material conditions of the rural classes. Olavide also attacked the Mesta, which, he was convinced, destroyed arable farming without substantially encouraging livestock farming. Now was the time, he argued, to abandon this disastrous policy, and foster the development of Spanish agriculture. Olavide's solution was a rural utopia composed of 'an immense number of new farmers, an infinite multiplicity of fruits and livestock, an active and industrious commerce and communications system'.[22]

Olavide's ideals were echoed by other paternalists such as Campomanes and the Conde de Floridablanca. They found little support, however, among liberal individualists such as Jovellanos. In his report on the agrarian law of 1795 Jovellanos called for an economic solution alone to remedy Spain's evils. In his opinion, not only wastelands but also commons, entailments and inheritances should be sold off on long leases to the highest bidder. Instead of family plots, Jovellanos and the Economic Society of Madrid argued for the creation of private property by the application of the laws of supply and demand.[23]

In the turbulent years after 1789 neither view prevailed. The Bourbon Ministers took fright at the slightest proposal of reform lest it trigger off violent disturbances. Jovellanos' works were put on the Roman index. The only measure to make headway was the disentailing of 6·4 million reales of revenues in property belonging to the Church.

THE GENESIS OF INDUSTRIAL CAPITALISM

The earliest attempt at intervention in economic matters on the part of the Bourbon monarchy was a scheme to reverse Spain's industrial decline, a product of the final century of Habsburg rule. The aim of the Bourbon governments was a policy of import substitution pioneered in France by Colbert. A number of royal factories were built, each one granted monopoly status and given a State subsidy. Their charge was to manufacture luxury goods previously imported from abroad. The prototype of the royal factories was built at Guadalajara in 1718 to manufacture high-quality woollen goods. In subsequent years the Guadalajara factory established subsidiaries at San Fernando and Brihuega. In addition, royal factories were established throughout the realm for the production of tapestries, swords, paper, pottery, stockings, and other luxury items. At his summer residence of San Ildefonso Philip V built a factory which made high-quality glassware and mirrors. Charles III brought a collection of artisans with him from Naples, who established a royal porcelain factory at El Buen Retiro, outside Madrid.[24]

In the 1780s the town of Guadalajara had nearly 800 modern looms which provided jobs for almost 4,000 weavers. The royal factory was among the largest in Europe and was kept supplied by 40,000 spinners from as far away as Madrid and La Mancha. In its heyday in the 1740s new managers and artisan workers were brought over from England to introduce a series of new lines. The French traveller Bourgoing considered the quality of its products as high as that of *julienne* woollens and also commented on their relative cheapness. However, the seeds of industrial capitalism in Spain were not to be found in the operations of the royal factories, as instanced by the fate of the Guadalajara enterprise. Sheltered from outside competition by its regal patrons, the Guadalajara factory was never a financial success. In 1783 it made losses amounting to 200 million *reales*, a factor which appears to have forced the closure of the factories at San Fernando and Brihuega in the following year.[25]

Despite hand-outs of the State, the previous industrial stagnation of Castile was reinforced in the eighteenth century by poor communications and consequently high transport costs. Bourgoing gives a critical account of their retardative influence on internal trade. 'One scarcely sees', he comments, 'any other traffic than that in wine and olive oil carried on the backs of mules and asses from one province to another, that of grain, which likewise depending on the exclusive aid of beasts of burden, goes to remedy with the surplus of one district the scarcity of a neighbouring district, and above all that of wool, which takes the route to Bilbao, Santander, and the other ports of the northern coast from the sheepfolds and washing places scattered throughout the two Castiles. Materials needed by the factories, merchandise which passes from the frontiers and ports to the interior is almost always transported by the same slow and consequently expensive means.'[26] The only area of central Spain with an adequate system of communications was the region around Madrid, where a comprehensive network of roads had been constructed for the provisioning of the Spanish capital with food. Inter-regional trade scarcely existed.[27]

The deficiencies of internal trade within Spain and the poverty of the markets of the interior made it virtually certain that the industrial developments of the eighteenth century, and of the nineteenth, would be confined to the provinces of the periphery. The Basque provinces, Valencia and Catalonia, apart from possessing more prosperous regional markets than Castile, had already begun to build up a foreign trade in primary products.

The Basque provinces owed their industrial and commercial fortunes to their geographical situation on the main trade route between central Spain and northern Europe. The port of Bilbao built up an export trade in Castilian wool and local iron ore and an import trade in wheat and manufactured goods. Bilbao iron had an international reputation by the sixteenth century. In the eighteenth the Basques exported a whole range of hardware, firearms, swords, and anchors, which were produced throughout the region. Spain's American colonies alone took almost 4,000 tons of Basque iron goods in 1790. However, most of the techniques employed in the Basque iron industry were primitive by comparison with the developments of Abraham Darby of Coalbrookdale, who as early as 1709, had succeeded in producing iron by the use of coke. The exclusive use of charcoal furnaces in the Basque region was leading to the exhaustion of the region's forests by the end of the eighteenth century.[28]

The eighteenth century witnessed spectacular progress in the Valencian silk industry. In 1718 the city of Valencia had 800 silk looms; by 1769 there were 3,196, including 107 stocking frames. When Joseph Townsend visited Valencia in 1787 he estimated the number of looms at 5,000, including 300 stocking frames, but this appears something of an exaggeration.[29] The upsurge of Valencian silk was in marked contrast to the declining fortunes of the industry in Granada, Toledo and Barcelona. Lyons too went into decline after 1770. Yet by the time of the French revolution of 1789 the Lyons silk industry was probably half as big again as the Valencian industry. Moreover Lyons silk was in general of a much higher quality than its main Spanish rival, although the Frenchman Bourgoing conceded that the moiré silk produced by the Valencian manufacturer Joaquín Manuel Fos was equal to anything produced in his native land.[30]

Impressive as they were, the achievements of the Basques and Valencians could not compare with the industrial progress made in eighteenth-century Catalonia. The emergence of a modern capitalist cotton textile industry in the north-eastern corner of Spain so astounded contemporary travellers that they talked of Catalonia as a little England. The initial expansion of the Catalan cotton industry depended on the existence of a prosperous regional market in agricultural products. But in the second half of the century Catalan manufacturers came to rely on Spain's American colonies, which provided a vigorous and expanding market for their products.

The Catalan economic take-off in the eighteenth century has been reconstructed by Pierre Vilar. In the first stage of his model, between 1715 and 1735–38, Catalonia experienced an increase in the amount of wheat produced. As wheat prices fell the consumer profited from the situation and the population rose. The social class which benefited most from these developments was the landlords, who increased seigneurial dues, lowered wages, and charged higher rents. Foreign demand for wines led to the planting of more vines, and viticulture became a profitable occupation. In the second stage of Vilar's model, between the years 1735–38 and 1764–72, the classical Malthusian platform of old economies was almost reached. The cultivation of wheat was extended to poor soils and agricultural income continued to rise. Yet the small farmer was excluded from sharing in the profits. As the large numbers who were born in the 1720s and 1730s arrived on the labour market, wages fell still further. Meanwhile the profitability of viticulture led to a reduction in the area occupied by cereals in favour of vines. Wheat prices therefore increased by 50 per cent as peasant incomes fell. The droughts of 1748–53 threatened the region with disaster. Catastrophe was averted by wheat imports, a measure which also kept down prices. To avoid a fall in wine prices the commercially-minded wine growers began to export their product to Spanish America. This development was to presage the growing importance of foreign trade to the Catalan economy. Taking the years 1760–64 as a base index of 100, the amount of foreign trade carried by sea, measured by an *ad valorem* tax on trade, increased from 62 in 1750 to 519 in 1800. Finally, in the last third of the eighteenth century, Catalonia experienced a spontaneous upsurge of industry. During the foundation years of the cotton industry (1772–92) Catalan landowners faced high wages and lower profits from the soil, the result of the narrowly averted population crisis of the middle of the century. Capital accumulated in agriculture began to be directed towards the manufacture of printed cottons. The promise of higher wages attracted a number of immigrants to Barcelona. However, in other manufacturing towns, and in the mountains, industry came to rely on a less vocal female and child labour force.[31]

The great stimulus to the Catalan textile industry was a royal decree of

1717, supplemented by another in the following year, which prohibited the introduction in Spain of Asian and Chinese silks. In 1737–38 the first bleachfields were laid out for the bleaching of cotton cloths used in the manufacture of *indiennes*. The factory of Esteban Canals, established in Barcelona in 1737, is generally considered the earliest example of a modern industrial enterprise in Spain.[32] Between the years 1745 and 1755 there were still only ten mills in existence in Barcelona which produced cotton cloths. Some firms, such as that of Campins at Mataró, went bankrupt for lack of financial and technical know-how. Nevertheless by the end of the 1750s Catalan mills sold their products throughout the Spanish market and had secured a foothold in the Caribbean market.

The first spinning mills in Spain date from 1765. Using Maltese cotton, the factories of Canals and Magarola produced increasing quantities of yarn by the use of the old-fashioned spinning wheel. The first mechanical innovations were brought into Catalonia from England after 1780; the spinning jenny around 1780, the water frame after 1791, and the mule after 1803. Of all these innovations the most significant for Catalonia was the mule, worked by water or steam power, which according to Jordi Nadal symbolised the transition from domestic industry to factory production.[33]

The number of workers in the Catalan cotton industry rose considerably after the introduction of spinning and the beginnings of mechanisation. The extent of the increase is, however, open to different interpretations. Josep Fontana claims that in 1760 there were 10,000 workers in the cotton industry, rising to five or six times that number by the end of the century.[34] Pierre Vilar cites figures for 1805 which show that Barcelona had ninety-one cotton mills employing 10,000 workers, while outside the Catalan capital the cotton industry gave jobs to another 20,000.[35] Among the other Catalan towns which developed a cotton industry were Reus, Berga, Olot and Mataró.

The crucial factor in the growth of the Catalan cotton industry was American trade. Freedom of trade with the Spanish empire, previously legally restricted to Seville and Cádiz, was conceded to Barcelona in 1765. The subsequent importance of the colonial trade to Catalonia, especially the cotton industry, was shown by the volume of exports. At the beginning of the nineteenth century Laborde calculated that Catalonia exported goods worth 24 million francs, while sending goods worth only 7 million francs to the rest of Spain. Moreover, out of the 9 million francs of cotton textiles produced in Catalonia, 2 million francs went to the Peninsula and 7 million francs were exported. The main destination of these exports was Spanish America. Laborde's evidence is confirmed by the *Almanak Mercantil* of 1801, which indicated that one-third of the textile production of Barcelona was destined for the Spanish market while the remainder went to the colonies.[36]

The colonial market made possible the development of a modest though modern industrial sector in Catalonia, without a parallel development of the national market. By such a process a conflict was averted between the industrial bourgeoisie and the privileged classes of the *ancien régime*. There was a tacit agreement: the Spanish countryside for the landed nobility and the Church, and colonial trade for the bourgeoisie. Since the old order left them alone, the manufacturing classes came to believe that they owed their prosperity to enlightened despotism. Thus when revolutionary ideas swept Europe in the aftermath of the events in France, the industrial bourgeoisie was reluctant to sacrifice peace and prosperity for an uncertain future.[37]

THE ECONOMIC COLLAPSE OF THE ANCIEN RÉGIME

Between 1779 and 1808 Spain fought a series of wars with Great Britain, all of which disrupted Spanish foreign trade, in particular trade with the American colonies. The wars from 1796 to 1801 and 1804 to 1808 profoundly affected all those industries in the colonial trade. Fontana has shown the pronounced decline in Spanish exports to America in the period 1804–07.[38] There is no lack of contemporary accounts which included the Catalan cotton industry in the general crisis. One author commented: 'In the first seven years of the present century the manufacture of cotton in Catalonia experienced the effects of the war with the English. The seizure of cargoes going to the Spanish overseas possessions and the risings in various states of South America . . . caused great losses to both manufacturers and speculators.'[39]

Table 1 Spanish trade with the American colonies, 1803–07

	No. of boats	Tonnage	Value of exports (million reales)
1803	68	11,635	62·6
1804	105	17,302	76·8
1805	20	1,302	2·5
1806	6	359	1·2
1807	1	55	0·2

Pierre Vilar, however, paints a more optimistic picture of these years. Evidence for 1802, 1805, 1807 and 1808 from almanacs, witnesses and fragments of statistical material which survive prove conclusively to Vilar that during the war with the British Catalan industry not only survived but made progress. Many firms, including those of Gónima, Rull, Bosch and Gassó, introduced new techniques of spinning and weaving into their mills. The textile industry moreover spread during this period along the valleys of the Pyrenees, in search of free power from waterfalls and a cheaper labour force.[40]

The ravages of the Napoleonic wars, during which Catalonia was an almost constant battlefield, brought the near ruin of Catalan industry. All accounts are of one accord that, when the French armies withdrew, Catalonia had lost a good deal of the capital built up in the previous half-century. Moreover the struggle of the Spanish colonies for their independence led to the commercial penetration of British and North American manufactures into that part of the world and the closure of a vital market to Spanish exports. Although the more enterprising manufacturers in Catalonia took advantage of the French occupation to smuggle goods into the markets of the Continental System, once Napoleon was defeated and the colonial markets were lost as well the resurrected *ancien régime* had little to offer by way of compensation. The industrial bourgeoisie had to be satisfied with the internal market of Spain, whose economic base was a backward agriculture.

NOTES

1   Jordi Nadal, *La población española (siglos XVI a XX)* (Barcelona, 1971), pp. 82 ff; Antonio Domínguez Ortiz, *La sociedad española en el siglo XVIII* (Madrid, 1955), pp. 69–75.

2   Nadal, *op. cit.*, p. 87; Pierre Vilar, 'La Catalogne industrielle: réflexions sur un démarrage et sur un destin', in Pierre Léon et al. (eds). *L'industrialisation en Europe au XIXᵉ siècle* (Paris, 1972), p. 424; Emili Giralt y Raventós, 'Problemas históricos de la industrialización valenciana', *Estudios Geográficos*, 112–13 (1968), 370.

3   Domínguez Ortiz, *loc. cit.*, p. 74.

4   *Ibid.*, pp. 76–297.

5   *Censo de frutos y manufacturas de España e islas adyacentes* (Madrid, 1803); Josep Fontana, 'El "censo de frutos y manufacturas" de 1799: un análisis crítico', *Moneda y Crédito*, 101 (1967), 54–68.

6   Edward E. Malefakis, *Agrarian Reform and Peasant Revolution in Spain: Origins of the Civil War* (New Haven and London, 1970), pp. 11–34.

7   Angel Marvaud, *La Question sociale en Espagne* (Paris, 1910), pp. 153–62.

8   Gerald Brenan, *The Spanish Labyrinth: an Account of the Social and Political Background of the Spanish Civil War* (Cambridge, 1967), p. 92.

9   Henry Swinburne, *Travels through Spain in the Years 1775 and 1776* (London, 1779).

10   Albert Balcells, *El problema agrarí a Catalunya (1890–1936): la qüestió rabassaire* (Barcelona, 1968), p. 28.

11   Antonio Joseph Cavanilles, *Observaciones sobre la historia natural, geografía, agricultura y frutos del reyno de Valencia*, 2 vols (Madrid, 1795–7).

12   Gonzalo Anes, *Las crisis agrarias en la España moderna* (Madrid, 1970), p. 181.

13   Pablo de Olavide, 'Informe de Olavide sobre la ley agraria', ed. Ramón Carande, *Boletín de la Real Academia de Historia*, cxxxix (1956), 386–7, cited in Richard Herr, *The Enlightenment in Spain* (Princeton, 1958), p. 105.

14   *Ibid.*, p. 374, cited in Herr, *op. cit.*, p. 106.

15   Gonzalo Anes, 'Coyuntura económica e ilustración: las Sociedades Económicas de Amigos del País', in Economía e ilustración en la España del siglo XVIII (Barcelona, 1969), pp. 13–41.
16   Pedro Rodríguez de Campomanes, Discurso sobre el fomento de la industria popular (Madrid, 1774).
17   Anes, Coyuntura económica e ilustración, p. 26.
18   Ibid., pp. 35–7.
19   Anes, Las crisis agrarias, pp. 165–98.
20   Josep Fontana, 'Formación del mercado nacional y toma de conciencia de la burguesía', in Cambio económico y actitudes políticas en la España del siglo XIX (Barcelona, 1973), pp. 21–2.
21   Ibid., p. 25.
22   Olavide, op. cit., passim; Marcelin Deforneux, Pablo de Olavide ou l'afrancesado, 1725–1803 (Paris, 1959), pp. 129–71.
23   Gaspar Melchor de Jovellanos, Informe de la Sociedad Económica de esta Corte al Real y Supremo Consejo de Castilla en el expediente de ley agraria (Madrid, 1795); Gonzalo Anes, 'El informe sobre la ley agraria y la Real Sociedad Económica Matritense de Amigos del País', in Economía e ilustración, pp. 95–138.
24   Joseph Townsend, A Journey through Spain in the Years 1786 and 1787, with Particular Attention to the Agriculture, Manufactures, Commerce, Population, Taxes and Revenue of that Country, II (London, 1791), p. 233
25   Jean François Bourgoing, Nouveau voyage en Espagne, ou tableau de l'état actuel de cette monarchie, I (Paris, 1789) pp. 49–50.
26   Ibid., II, p. 156.
27   David Ringrose, Transport and Economic Stagnation in Spain, 1750–1850 (Durham, N. C., 1970), pp. 120–7.
28   Bourgoing, op. cit., II p. 168; Alfonso de Churruca, Minería, industria y comercio del País Vasco (San Sebastian, 1951), pp. 12–16.
29   Townsend, op. cit., III, pp. 254–5.
30   Bourgoing, op. cit., III, pp. 90–1.
31   Vilar, loc. cit., pp. 424–6.
32   Jaime Vicens Vives, Historia económica de España, 6th edn. (Barcelona, 1969), p. 487.
33   Jordi Nadal, 'The failure of the industrial revolution in Spain, 1830–1914', in Carlo M. Cipolla (ed.) The Fontana Economic History of Europe, vol. 4, No. 2 (London, 1973), p. 607.
34   Fontana, op. cit., p. 39.
35   Vilar, loc. cit., p. 425.
36   A. de Laborde, Itinéraire descriptif de l'Espagne, II (Paris, 1827–30), pp. 169–72; Almanak mercantil o guía de comerciantes para el año 1802 (Madrid, 1801), p. 254, both cited in Fontana, op. cit., p. 40.
37   F. Torrella, El moderno resurgir textil de Barcelona (Barcelona, 1961), pp. 187–91; Pierre Vilar, 'Ocupació y resistència durant la Guerra Gran i en temps de Napoleó', in Assaigs sobre la Catalunya del segle XVIII (Barcelona, 1973), pp. 96–9.
38   Fontana, op. cit., p. 44.
39   B. C. Aribau, cited in Fontana, loc. cit., pp. 43–4.
40   Vilar, La Catalogue industrielle, pp. 429–30.

CHAPTER 2

The failure of the liberal agrarian reforms

THE DEVELOPMENT OF THE SPANISH POPULATION IN THE NINETEENTH CENTURY

From 1797 to 1900 the population of Spain increased from 10,541,000 to 18,594,000, a rise of approximately 75 per cent, almost half as fast again as the demographic increase of the eighteenth century. Unprecedented as this increase was in Spanish terms, the net rise in population was considerably below the European average. In the same period the population of Great Britain expanded three and a half fold, while Germany, Austria–Hungary, Belgium, the Netherlands and the Scandinavian countries more than doubled their inhabitants. The only countries with a worse record of demographic increase were Ireland, whose population fell by nearly a half after the disastrous potato famine of the late 1840s, and France, with a rate of increase of just over 50 per cent.

The regional imbalances of population increase of eighteenth-century Spain were continued into the nineteenth century. Thus in 1877 the central regions of Aragon, León and the two Castiles contained no more than 30·42 per cent of the total population, as compared with 35·68 per cent according to the census of 1797. During the same period Catalonia increased its share of national population from 8·14 per cent to 10·53 per cent, more than doubling its size from 858,818 inhabitants to 1,752,033. The other regions which expanded their population were, in order of significance, Murcia, Extremadura, Andalusia, Valencia, Galicia, the Basque region and Asturias—all but two in the strict sense peripheral. Compared with the eighteenth century, the most notable feature was the slowing down of the rate of demographic increase in Valencia, a region which remained overwhelmingly agricultural during the nineteenth century, and its overtaking by Catalonia, which was to experience the beginnings of an industrial revolution in the 1830s. The reversal of the trend towards 'depopulation' in Extremadura, for two centuries the *cause célèbre* of the pamphleteers, can be partly explained by a small addition of territory. [1]

One clear indication of Spain's demographic backwardness was the sluggishness of urbanisation. The census of 1900 showed that 50·92 per cent of Spaniards lived in communities of fewer than 5,000 inhabitants, 40·06 per cent in centres of between 5,000 and 100,000 and a mere 9·01 per

Table 2   Estimated populations of various European countries, 1800–1910
(millions)

	1800	1850	1900	1910
Denmark	0·9	1·6	2·6	2·9
Finland	1·0	1·6	2·7	3·1
Norway	0·9	1·5^a	2·2	2·4
Sweden	2·3	3·5	5·1	5·5
Belgium	3·0	4·3^b	6·7	7·4
Holland	2·2	3·1	5·1	5·9
Great Britain	10·9	20·9	36·9	40·8
Ireland	5·0	6·6	4·5	4·4
France	26·9	36·5	40·7	41·5
Portugal	3·1	4·2	5·4	6·0
Italy	18·1	23·9	33·9	36·2
Switzerland	1·8	2·4	3·3	3·8
Germany	24·5	31·7	50·6	55·5
Austria–Hungary	23·3	31·3	47·0	51·3
SPAIN	10·5^d	15·5^e	18·6	19·9

(a) 1855, (b) 1845, (c) 1867, (d) 1797, (e) 1857.

Source. André Armengaud, 'Population in Europe, 1700–1914', in Carlo M. Cipolla (ed.), The Fontana Economic History of Europe, vol. 3 (London, 1973), p. 29.

cent of the population in centres of over 100,000 inhabitants. A significant proportion of the final category was concentrated in Madrid and Barcelona, much of whose expansion came only in the last two decades of the century. Madrid, the administrative capital, grew at an ever-expanding rate throughout the nineteenth century, from 160,000 inhabitants in 1800 to 281,000 in 1850, 398,000 in 1880 and 540,000 in 1900. Barcelona, the centre of Spanish capitalism, expanded its population from 115,000 in 1800 to 175,000 in 1850. Thereafter it nearly doubled in size from 1850 to 1880, when it contained 346,000 souls, increasing to 533,000 in 1900. However, the fastest-growing centre in the last quarter of the nineteenth century was Bilbao, home of the expanding metallurgical sector, which more than quadrupled its population from 17,500 in 1875 to 80,000 in 1900.[2]

The large number of censuses carried out in the course of the century, reliable after 1857, allows us to build a dynamic model of Spanish population growth. Between 1797 and 1860 the rate was 0·63 per cent per annum, as compared with an average of 0·42 per cent from 1717 to 1797. From 1860 to 1910 the average rate declined to 0·49 per cent. Thus superficially Spain appears to display similar demographic tendencies to England and Wales, whose population rose by 1·25 per cent per annum between 1795/96 and 1861, falling to 1·18 per cent between 1861 and 1911.

Table 3   The population of Spain, 1797–1910

Year	No. of inhabitants
1797	10,541,221
1822	11,661,865
1834	12,162,172
1857	15,464,340
1860	15,673,481
1877	16,634,345
1887	17,549,600
1897	18,108,610
1900	18,594,000
1910	19,994,600

Source. Jaime Vicens Vives, *Historia Económica de España*, 6th edn (Barcelona, 1969), p. 560, partly corrected by Miguel Artola, *La burgesía revolucionaria, 1808–69* (Madrid, 1973), p. 62.

However, a more detailed analysis reveals the Spanish case to be dissimilar to the more developed area.[3]

In the first third of the nineteenth century the new phase of wars and economic difficulties brought a slower rate of population growth than in preceding decades. The reign of Charles IV, who was deposed in 1808, was marked by a wave of disastrous famines: that of 1803–04 was reminiscent of the seventeenth century. The War of Independence from 1808 to 1814 has been variously estimated to have led to between 500,000 and one million deaths. Disease too was rampant in this period. Yellow fever killed 6,884 of Málaga's 51,745 inhabitants in 1803; in the following year it claimed 31,718 victims in Andalusia, and in 1821 6,244 victims in Barcelona. In the succeeding decade yellow fever gave way to cholera, which crossed into Spain from Portugal in 1833, killing 102,511 people in the next two years.[4] In sharp contrast, the quarter of a century from 1833 to 1860 saw a period of fast population growth. Not only were the population losses due to the War of Independence made up but further stimuli to demographic growth were provided by the entry of new lands into cultivation as a result of the disentailing of lands held in mortmain and the beginnings of the industrial revolution in Catalonia. The subsequent downturn in the demographic increase in the next fifty years was an emphatic illustration of the long-term failure of the mid-century agrarian reforms. As agricultural yields on recently broken marginal lands failed to keep up with the rise in population, Spain suffered a recurrence of famine. The years 1868, 1879, 1887, 1898 and 1904–05 brought the return of food crises. Deprived of alternative employment in industry, the peasant farmers of the Canary Islands, Pontevedra, Corunna, Oviedo, Santander and elsewhere booked their passage to the republics of the former Spanish empire and the colonial outpost of Cuba.

Table 4   Net balance of the movement of passengers by sea, 1882–1913 (exits minus entries)

Year	Balance	Year	Balance
1882	13,286	1898	−77,695
1883	3,901	1899	−62,722
1884	4,839	1900	5,638
1885	596	1901	3,843
1886	4,589	1902	−6,630
1887	14,152	1903	2,572
1888	23,554	1904	30,144
1889	72,404	1905	64,030
1890	11,064	1906	52,863
1891	5,180	1907	51,288
1892	8,258	1908	71,362
1893	19,833	1909	50,675
1894	14,691	1910	91,922
1895	64,472	1911	70,512
1896	98,864	1912	133,994
1897	−9,156	1913	72,653

Source. Jordi Nadal, *La población española: siglos XVI a XX* (Barcelona, 1971), p. 165.

THE ABOLITION OF THE SEIGNEURIAL REGIME

Despite the limited measures adopted by the reformist Ministers of the Enlightenment, the seigneurial regime survived into the nineteenth century, in some ways strengthened. In the first third of the century seigneurial land predominated in Catalonia, Valencia, New Castile, Andalusia and Extremadura, where the nobility continued to be favoured by high food prices and rising rents. In some regions the nobility attempted to increase their income by seeking to exact forgotten rights from the peasantry along with the more vigorous application of traditional rights. This form of aristocratic counter-offensive presented a serious threat to the peasantry, already, in many areas, at the limits of subsistence.[5] However, when the seigneurial regime was finally abolished it was not due to peasant pressure but the result of a deliberate choice by the State.

Citing Lenin, Josep Fontana draws the distinction between two types of agrarian reform in the late eighteenth and early nineteenth centuries; the Prussian model of reform from above, as instanced by the Stein–Hardenberg reform of 1807–11, and the experience of revolutionary France from 1789–93 of reform from below. Without doubt, Spain fits more easily into the former classification. South of the Pyrenees the abolition of the seigneurial regime was effected by an alliance of the liberal bourgeoisie and the latifundist aristocracy, with no parallel process of peasant revolution. Thus agriculture was permitted to adapt to the exigencies of a modern economy without substantially eroding the dominant position of the privileged classes. In short, Spain provides us with an example of the French revolution of 1789 in reverse: agrarian reform was carried out at the expense of the peasantry. This helps to explain the opposition of the Spanish peasantry to bourgeois revolution and the espousal of large sections of its members of the reactionary cause.[6]

It was the insurrection of May 1808 which led to the renewal of interest in agrarian reform in Spain. A decree abolishing the feudal regime was issued by the 'intruder government' of Joseph I in December 1808. This decree was to act as a precedent to a further decree of August 1811 by the liberal Cortes of Cádiz, which suppressed the exclusive or monopolistic rights of the *seigneur*, such as fishing, hunting, flour milling, the pressing of grapes, and the use of waterfalls, woods and meadows. These former preserves of the nobility were handed over to the village or *pueblo* in accordance with common law and the municipal regulations established in each *pueblo*.[7]

By distinguishing between jurisdictional and personal service the law of 1811 had important repercussions for the peasantry with regard to possible indemnification. Discrepancies in its interpretation led to social tensions and riots in a number of areas, above all Galicia and Valencia, where the proportion of seigneurial lands was high. So much confusion surrounded the liquidation of such a complex structure as the seigneurial regime that a commission was appointed in 1813 to resolve any discrepancies in interpretation. The commision was, however, stillborn; the return of absolutism in the shape of Ferdinand VII led to a decree of May 1814 abrogating the liberal legislation of 1811.

The revolution of 1820 allowed a weak liberal regime to take up the legislation of the Cortes of Cádiz. A law of December 1820, the result of a pact with the Church, whose lands were to remain untouched, and the nobility, who sought to profit by it, suppressed all entailed estates, making it possible for the nobility to sell off their lands. Once again the contradictory nature of the reform sharpened social antagonisms in the countryside. Despite the suppression of tithes the Spanish peasantry were unable to pay over their contributions, which were demanded in cash. Moreover the freedoms conceded by the men of 1820 favoured the sheep grazers of the Mesta, provoking the expulsion of peasant farmers from lands they had hitherto cultivated. Hence the rearrival of Ferdinand VII in 1823, to be followed by the suspension of the law of 1820, was a cause for celebration among the majority of the rural population.[8]

After the death of Ferdinand in 1833 Spain was plunged into a violent civil war, known as the First Carlist War, in which the liberal reformers sided with the regency of his widow, María Cristina, while the absolutists and the Church rallied to the reactionary cause of his brother, don Carlos, who aimed to turn Spain into a theocratic corporate State. In order to win over the nobility to the Regency a law of 1837 again allowed the breaking of civil entail, an act not displeasing to the nobility, who realised that as a consequence of their entry into the commercial market the value of their estates was bound to increase.[9] The only serious threat to the traditional form of land ownership during the Regency was the alienation of ecclesiastical property. Latifundism was actually reinvigorated, since the aristocracy bought up the disentailed lands of the Church. Strong proof to this development is provided by the list of fifty-three taxpayers who, in the middle of the nineteenth century, paid over 50,000 reales in territorial contributions. The list contained the names of thirteen dukes, fifteen marquises, fifteen counts, nine plebeians and the canal de Castilla enterprise.[10]

ECCLESIASTICAL DISENTAILING

The sale of Church lands was initiated by the liberal Progressive government of Mendizábal in 1836–7. This legislation capitalised on popular manifestations of anti-clericalism in 1835, when convents were looted and burned down by mobs. In June 1835 the religious orders were dissolved, with the exception of those dedicated to teaching and the care of the sick, and their estates confiscated to be renamed national property. Thus to many the name of Mendizábal has become a symbol both of liberal disentailing and of anti-clerical policies. Others, meanwhile, like the legal historian, Francisco Tomás y Valiente, stress the social and economic policies of Mendizábal as embodied in the alienation of Church lands.[11]

The earliest intentions of Mendizábal were not far removed from the programme of Olavide half a century before: 'to create a large family of proprietors whose tastes and whose very existence depend primarily on the complete triumph of present institutions'. This so-called family of proprietors would be composed not only of 'capitalists and landowners' but also of 'honourable and hard-working citizens'. To this effect his original resolve was to auction off small plots of land which men of modest means could afford.[12]

A law of July 1837 provided for two types of buyer: those who paid in cash and those who did so in public debt. The first group of buyers were allowed sixteen years to pay off the purchase at 5 per cent interest, and the second eight years at 10 per cent. Both groups of buyer had to make a down payment of 20 per cent of the sale price at the moment of purchase. However, the owners of public securities had the distinct advantage of being permitted to make payment in consolidated and non-consolidated debt, which although quoted well below par, was accepted in exchange for land at its nominal value.

In the event, the destination of national property was determined not so much by liberal or any other ideology as by financial expediency. The timing of the sale of Church lands coincided with the exhaustion of the Spanish Treasury, a National Debt of horrifying dimensions, and the need of the Progressives to finance a costly civil war which had thrown the administration into almost total disarray. Without wasting time, therefore, Mendizábal chose to auction off large amounts of national property. Inevitably the sudden unloading of Church lands on to the market favoured those who, unlike the peasantry, had money to spare or the ability to obtain public securities. Such people included members of the royal family, the aristocracy, wealthy merchants, politicians, the provincial bourgeoisie, and industrialists who chose to invest their savings in land for reasons of security and social status. Corruption was rife; official auctions brought about the creation of massive private fortunes. For its part, the rural proletariat demonstrated its disapproval by occupying the newly transferred lands and burning crops.[13]

In spite of the frequently repeated claim that the religious scruples of the Spaniards held back the sales of Church property, the evidence suggests that the demand for land at this time was considerable. Not even the threat of excommunication could deter the greed of the buyers. By 1845 nearly three-quarters of Church real estate had been sold off. In the Balearic Islands the proportion was as high as 99 per cent. There was even a large number of transactions in the ultra-Catholic province of Navarre, while in some areas the clergy themselves were included among the buyers.

The lack of a complete set of local studies makes it impossible to present any overall quantification of the full effects of the alienation of Church lands. A recent investigation of the sale of Church property in the province of Seville by Alfonso Lazo shows that as a result of ecclesiastical disentailing property was concentrated in far fewer hands. Before the sale of national property the lands owned by the Church in that province were farmed by 6,000 families; after the auctions they were exploited by only 460 families. One distinctive feature of the sale of national property in Seville was that estates of 1,000 hectares and above were rare; the main group of purchasers was the bourgeoisie, anxious to ensure its income and consolidate its prestige.[14]

In 1843 the Progressive party, which had supported the sale of Church lands, fell from power. Their successors, the Moderates, restricted the sale of national property by a law of April 1845 but significantly did not annul the 1837 law. Six years later, in March 1851, a concordat was reached with the Vatican by which the Papacy acknowledged the validity of past expropriations while the Spanish State in return agreed to recognise the right of the Church to acquire property by legal means, to return assets not yet alienated and to pay the secular clergy an annual income. However, scarcely had the concordat been published than the Moderates were overthrown by the 1854 revolution.

THE GENERAL DISENTAILING LAW OF 1855

With the victory of the Progressives in 1854 the question of civil and ecclesiastical entailment was once more high on the agenda. During the Moderate decade (1843–54) there had been discussions among exiled Progressives on the sale of the common lands, the standard device of agrarian reformers elsewhere in Europe. Circumstances too had altered since the Mendizábal legislation: the Carlist revolt had been successfully put down in 1839 and the Mon reforms of 1845 had helped to put Spanish finances in some order. Moreover, north of the Pyrenees enormous changes were taking place in the economic conditions of Britain, France, Belgium and Germany. The 1840s and early 1850s witnessed a boom in railway construction in those countries which promised a radical transformation of their economic structures. With an eye to these developments, the Progressives hoped to use the funds obtained by the public auction of national property to encourage the modernisation of the Spanish economy through the construction of railways, canals and other public works. In the event, the efforts were to be frustrated by the overwhelming economic backwardness of Spain, which made the railways in particular highly unprofitable ventures.[15]

The law of May 1855, with a few exceptions, provided for the sale of all lands held in mortmain, including the common lands of the municipalities. As to the destination of the income obtained by the State, the law stipulated that during its first year of operation a fixed amount of the proceeds would be set aside to cover the eventuality of a budgetary deficit but that subsequently half the revenue brought in from the sale of alienated land should be allocated to the amortisation of public debt and half to the construction of public works.

Common land was put up for sale in every Spanish province, apart from the Canary Islands, Navarre and Orense. The auctions began in 1855 but were suspended in the following year. After sales resumed in 1859 millions of hectares of common land were transferred into private hands. Sales remained at a high level until 1868, after which date they fell dramatically. The composition of the lands sold off in the period 1855–68 was as follows: common lands 50 per cent, at auction prices; Church property 30 per cent; and land belonging to the State, religious charities, or sequestrated from such individuals as don Carlos, 20 per cent.[16]

The high proportion of sales in cash probably reflected the growing wealth of the country during two decades of peace, the impetus to

Table 5 Total volume of land sales at auction prices, 1821–67 (million reales)

Period	Church property	Common lands	Other property	Total property	Censos and foros	Total sales
1821–23	99·9			99·9		99·9
1836–49	3,820·1			3,820·1	635·3	4,455·4
1855–56	323·8	159·8	283·1	766·7	174·7	941·4
1859–67	1,275·9	2,028·7	911·9	4,216·5	222·3	4,438·8
Total	5,519·7	2,188·5	1,195·0	8,903·2	1,032·3	9,935·5

Source. Josep Fontana, 'Transformaciones agrarias y crecimiento económico en la España contemporánea', in Cambio económico y actitudes políticas en la España del siglo XIX (Barcelona, 1973), p. 178.

economic growth provided by the Mendizábal reforms and the beginnings of the industrial revolution. It may also have reflected a growing disenchantment among investors with the first experiences of railway construction. There is a marked correlation between rises in land sales and years of crisis; for example, land sales increased steeply in 1866, which witnessed the collapse of the Barcelona stock exchange, an institution which specialised in railway shares.[17]

Table 6   The balance sheet of disentailing (million reales)

1821–23	99·9	1848	106·8
1836	87·8	1849	228·9
1837	304·3	1855–56	941·4
1838	173·4		
1839	349·5	1859	882·7
1840	290·2	1860	707·6
1841	382·9	1861	372·0
1842	555·7	1862	379·2
1843	978·4	1863	305·5
1844	604·9	1864	424·8
1845	178·1	1865	348·8
1846	106·7	1866	575·5
1847	107·8	1867	442·7

Source. Josep Fontana, 'Transformaciones agrarias y crecimiento económico en la España contemporánea', in Cambio económico y actitudes políticas en la España del siglo XIX (Barcelona, 1973), p. 179.

THE DEVELOPMENT OF SPANISH AGRICULTURE DURING THE LIBERAL REFORMS

An analysis of Spanish agriculture in the nineteenth century presents the historian with a series of almost insurmountable obstacles, particularly in the field of quantification. There are no reliable statistics for most of the century on the total area under the plough; hence we do not know how far this was modified by the breaking of entail. Reliable data on the volume of harvests were not obtained until the last decade of the century. To work out changes in Spanish agriculture in the first half of the nineteenth century, the most satisfactory method is to compare the 1799 censo de frutos y manufacturas, with all its acknowledged errors, with figures for the export of agricultural products, which first appeared in 1849. The censo de frutos y manufacturas calculated the total cereal harvest in 1799 as 73·5 million bushels. Taking away the seed corn, it estimated that the amount available for human consumption must have been of the order of 61·5 million bushels. The censo de frutos y manufacturas further calculated that to feed a population of 10·5 million the total amount of grain needed would be

94·5 million bushels. Hence Spain would have needed to import the substantial amount of 33·0 million bushels. From other evidence we know that the harvest was poor throughout the country in 1799. However, there is no evidence to suggest that at any time in the eighteenth century were such large quantities of cereals imported. We are therefore forced to the conclusion that even if the 1799 *censo de frutos y manufacturas* contains substantial errors, as Josep Fontana suggests, there is little doubt that at the beginning of the nineteenth century Spain was incapable of producing enough cereal to feed her own population.[18]

By comparison, the trade figures for the period 1849–81 show that in twenty-six of these thirty-three years exports of grain exceeded imports, and that only in seven years, including the crisis years 1856–58, 1867 and 1879, did imports of cereal exceed exports. Moreover, in the same period, despite the increase in population from 10·5 million in 1799 to 16·6 million in 1877, Spanish agriculture also exported large amounts of wine and to a lesser extent olive oil. On the other hand, all thirty-one years from 1882 to 1913 showed an adverse balance. Thus it would appear at a first glance that up to 1881 the cultivation of new lands following alienation brought about significant developments in agriculture, but that after that date the negative effects of the change were revealed.[19]

In practice, there were probably more nuances of change than the above analysis would suggest. Gonzalo Anes attempts a periodisation of the affects of the various phases of alienation of land on the development of Spanish agriculture. He sees three basic periods. In the first stage, from 1814 to 1836, there was only a limited extension of the area under the plough without a corresponding intensification of production and without the introduction of new techniques. During the second stage, from 1836 to 1855, not only was there a considerable extension of the area under cultivation but more intensive methods of farming were introduced as well. This latter development was the direct consequence of the transfer of ecclesiastical property into private hands. Anes cites evidence that, prior to the disentailing legislation, the Church left uncultivated some of the most fertile lands which it possessed in Catalonia, while the peasantry was obliged to cultivate lands of much poorer quality. Finally, in the third phase of disentailing, from 1855 to 1868, the predominance of civil disentailing led to the extension of the land surface cultivated, but this almost always took place on marginal land. Hence diminishing returns set in for arable farming which in turn triggered off a recession in livestock farming.[20]

The main use to which the disentailed lands were put was the cultivation of cereals. In order to protect the cereal-growing interior of Spain the men of 1820 embarked upon a policy of protectionism which differed somewhat from their other liberal views. A decree of August 1820 banned the import of wheat, barley, rye, maize, millet, oats and all other cereals and flours, so long as the price of one *fanega* of wheat did not exceed 120 reales in the principal markets, apart from the Balearics and the Canary Islands. The effect of this prohibitionist legislation was to prevent the coastal provinces from buying foreign wheat and to secure the Cuban and Puerto Rican markets for the Castilian flour millers who built up an important export trade through the port of Santander. Amended in January 1834, the 1820 law remained on the statute book until the free trade reforms of Figuerola in 1869.[21]

Under the aegis of this monopoly of the home market, the area under cereals in the central provinces of Salamanca, Valladolid, Burgos, Soria, and Cuenca expanded enormously. Nicolás Sánchez Albornoz estimates that between 1803 and 1857 a further 7 million hectares were dedicated to cereal production. Jaime Vicens Vives, citing Larraz, believes that approximately four million hectares were added to the area of cultivation in the first half of the nineteenth century, of which 2·2 million hectares were given over to wheat growing.[22] Whatever the exact figure, it appears likely that Spain fell in with similar developments elsewhere in Europe during the same period. In France the number of hectares under the plough increased from 23 million in 1815 to 26 million in 1852, while Prussia also saw an extension of the area cultivated from 12·5 million hectares in 1816 to 15·7 million in 1870.[23]

In the case of cereals, large amounts of marginal land were given over to their cultivation whose economic return was so low that by the 1860s diminishing returns had set in. Jaime Vicens Vives, using the questionable estimates of Salvador Millet, claims that wheat production per hectare fell from 6·31 metric quintals in 1800 to 5·8 metric quintals in 1860 and that of cereals from 6·47 to 6·20 metric quintals over the same period. In some regions shockingly low yields continued into the twentieth century. The average yield of cereals in the province of Almería was a mere 2·86 metric quintals per hectare as late as 1926–35.[24]

After cereals the crop which benefited most from alienation was wine. Vicens Vives, again citing Millet, claims that the area under the vine trebled in the first sixty years of the nineteenth century from 400,000 hectares to 1·2 million hectares.[25] There is strong literary evidence that in the course of these years the cultivation of the vine spread from the coastal zones of Galicia, the eastern littoral and the south to the central regions of León, La Mancha and La Rioja. A British consular report of 1859 told of a traveller a few years previously who passed through the little town of Aranda del Duero in Old Castile. There he came across a group of brick-layers who were using wine instead of water to mix their cement who assured the inquisitive fellow that such occurrences were not uncommon.[26]

Exports of wine made a significant contribution to the Spanish trade figures. In 1829 it accounted for slightly over one-eighth of Spanish exports and was third in value after wheat and raw wool. By 1851 wine was easily the most important item of Spanish exports, providing well over a quarter of the total. Figures for 1857 showed that wine exports accounted for nearly one-third by value of goods sent abroad.[27]

However, the main stimulus to the Spanish wine trade in the nineteenth century was the invasion of French vineyards by a parasite known as phylloxera, which wiped out the majority of French vines in the decade after 1868. France was, at that time, the world's largest consumer and exporter of wine and the gap left by the outbreak of phylloxera was enormous. Exports of cheap Spanish table wine, particularly to France, increased more than tenfold between the late 1860s and the early 1890s, and were greatly aided by the Franco-Spanish commercial treaty which remained in force from 1882 to 1892. The 1880s brought a period of exceptional prosperity to the wine growers of Catalonia, causing contemporary observers to refer to a 'gold fever'.[28]

THE AGRICULTURAL CRISIS OF THE LATE NINETEENTH CENTURY

The increased levels of wheat production which resulted from the ploughing up of marginal land, together with the boom in the wine trade, aided and encouraged by the outbreak of phylloxera in France, served to disguise important structural weaknesses in Spanish agriculture. In the last quarter of the nineteenth century these weaknesses were visibly exposed by factors external to the Spanish economy, above all by the opening up of the North American prairies by a combination of immigrant labour and the spread of mechanisation. Coinciding with these developments was a transport revolution which between 1870 and 1890 reduced the cost of wheat shipments across the Atlantic by more than three-fifths.[29]

The arrival of North American wheat in the Spanish ports led to a dramatic collapse of the home market in cereals. As the 1887 commission set up to study the agrarian crisis was to show, it was less expensive to transport wheat by steamship from the United States to Spanish ports than to carry Castilian wheat by rail from the interior to the coast. In the case of Barcelona the proportion of wheat which reached the city by rail, and therefore Spanish in origin, slumped from 60 per cent of the total in 1884 to just 11 per cent in 1886.[30]

The slump in wheat prices brought about by the influx of foreign grains meant that many Castilian wheat growers could no longer keep up production on the large tracts of marginal land which they farmed. Thus, in common with their counterparts in Prussia and the Paris basin, they agitated forcefully for the State to intervene in order to defend the interests of the farming community, which to all intents and purposes meant the cereal growers. Just as the Prussian Junkers sought to cement an alliance of rye and iron, and the landowners of the Société des Agriculteurs de France worked through Méline for an agreement between agriculture and big business, so the wheat interests of Valladolid formed a protectionist triangle with the Bilbao ironmasters and the Barcelona mill owners and petitioned the Spanish Cortes for an increase in the tariff on imported grains. By the end of the 1880s their lobbying activities had succeeded in winning over most of the Conservative party and a fair section of the Liberals, converted to free trade by the Figuerola reforms. With the victory of the Conservatives under Antonio Cánovas in the elections of 1890, the recent converts to protectionism lost little time in imposing the first stage of a tariff barrier in 1891, which was to be further raised by the ultra-protectionist measure of 1906.[31]

Table 7   Arrival of cereals in Barcelona, 1884–86 (kg millions)

Year	By rail	By sea
1884	72·5	54·9
1885	54·4	76·5
1886	13·9	111·0

Source. Josep Fontana, 'Transformaciones agrarias y crecimiento económico en la España contemporánea', in Cambio económico y actitudes políticas en la España del siglo XIX (Barcelona, 1973), p. 184.

At the end of the century a blow was dealt to the flour millers of Spain by the loss of the Antilles. In their last years as colonies Cuba, Puerto Rico and the Philippines took 60 million kilos of flour annually from the metropolis. The coastal mills had worked round the clock at harvest time to provide for the traffic, while new mills were built exclusively to serve the colonial market. The loss of this lucrative trade following the Spanish–American war of 1898 brought bankruptcy and ruin to many millers in the central provinces, the Levante, and the north, and opened up a new rivalry between the millers of the coast and those of the interior. The former called for a relaxation of the 1891 legislation, while the latter were more interested in maintaining a monopoly of production for the home market.[32]

Throughout the 1880s the great profits to be made in viticulture went some way to compensate the farming community for the crisis in cereals. In 1892, however, the French, whose vineyards were returning to normal, repudiated the commercial treaty with Spain. By this time phylloxera was beginning to gain a foothold in the Peninsula. After outbreaks in the coastal provinces of Málaga in 1876, Gerona in 1879 and Orense in 1881, the disease gradually encroached on the centre of Spain. In Catalonia, the scene of wild euphoria during the 1880s, the area of land surface planted with the vine fell drastically from 385,000 hectares in 1888 to only 41,325 hectares in 1899. Between 1890 and 1900 2,000 inhabitants from El

Priorato in Tarragona (25 per cent of the population) moved to the city of Barcelona or emigrated to Latin America.[33] In La Rioja the number of plants was reduced by half, while in Valencia and Aragon the growers contemplated devastated fields. The total number of hectares under vines fell from 1,706,501 in 1889 to 1,367,845 in 1907, when planting with American vine stock immune to phylloxera ceased. Production of wine also fell considerably, from 29 million hectolitres in 1892 to an average of 21·2 million hectolitres for the period 1892–1902. With the recovery of French viticulture Spanish exports fell badly. Shipments to France slumped by more than 75 per cent between the peak year of 1891 and 1900. The British consul in Málaga reported in 1907 that shippers complained bitterly of the loss of trade.[34]

Table 8   Spanish wine exports to France, 1877–1900 (million hectolitres)

1877	1·8	1889	7·1
1878	2·3	1890	7·9
1879	3·4	1891	9·7
1880	5·1	1892	5·6
1881	5·7	1893	3·6
1882	6·2	1894	2·2
1883	6·3	1895	3·0
1884	5·2	1896	5·2
1885	5·7	1897	3·3
1886	6·4	1898	4·7
1887	7·3	1899	3·2
1888	7·9	1900	2·2

Source. José Elías de Molins, *Algunos datos y consideraciones sobre los trigos y vinos de España* (Barcelona, 1904), p. 236.

To complete the picture of gloom for Spanish agriculture at the end of the nineteenth century, the crisis in arable farming was matched by a similar crisis in livestock farming. This latter phenomenon almost certainly had its origins in the mid-century reforms. The extension of cultivation which followed the alienation of entailed lands was widely believed to have inhibited the progress of stock raising. The 1887 commission concluded that 'the immense quantities of real estate which civil disentailment thrust into the hand of individuals, the suppression of common and royal lands, and the breaking of new ground have constantly and ever more insistently decreased the area of pasture and cover in which our stock raising found sustenance and life. All the land won by agriculture, all the energy which individual initiative has expended in order to convert into arable land what beforehand had only been dedicated to pasture has been prejudicial to our herds and flocks.'[35]

There were, nevertheless, one or two chinks of light amid the prevailing darkness. In the last two decades of the nineteenth century the production of olives probably more than doubled at a time which saw the emergence of the two great olive-producing regions of Spain, Andalusia and Catalonia. The incentive to step up production was provided by the Latin American market, where there was a strong demand for olive oil among the large numbers of recent emigrants from Spain and Italy. Primitive harvesting techniques and the failure to modernise the refining process, however, served mainly to benefit Spain's Italian competitors.

The 1880s saw the introduction of sugar-beet cultivation into Spain. The first mills for refining beet were constructed in Córdoba and Granada in 1882; yet owing to the desire of the politicians to placate the planters of Cuba and the Philippines it was not until the early 1890s before the next mills were built, at Málaga, Antequera, Aranjuez, Almería, Vich, Gijón and Saragossa. For most of the 1890s demand remained infinitely superior to supply. However, within twelve months of the loss of the last remnants of empire enough refineries had been built to permit the export of refined sugar. The first of a new wave of factories were set up in the provinces of Granada and Málaga in 1899, but before long there were dozens of imitators throughout the rest of Spain. Aragon, Castile and Extremadura produced sugar beet of excellent quality on previously uncultivated land. With encouragement from the Finance Minister, Villaverde, there was very soon a boom in sugar refining. Prices of refined sugar fell from 120 pesetas per 100 kilos in January 1900 to seventy-five pesetas by July 1901. Many refineries were forced to close down while others went bankrupt. By 1903 excess production was so evident that a sugar trust was formed to try and raise prices by limiting output.[36]

The only real manifestation of an alternative to the low-yielding mono-cultures of wheat, wine and olives was the rise of fruit growing, which developed on a large scale in the last quarter of the nineteenth century. Fruit growing, however, required heavy capital investment in both fer-tilisation and irrigation. Emili Giralt has shown that the modernisation of Valencian agriculture, the classic example of this development, deprived the region of the industrial revolution that might have been expected, given the large amount of capital formation in the eighteenth century. The huerta of Valencia was the first region in Spain to use guano as a fertiliser. Imports of guano began in 1847 and rose considerably over the following decades. In the 1870s and 1880s the region's artesian wells and irrigation schemes began to attract the attention of the experts. The main crop to benefit from this expensive transformation of Valencian agriculture was the orange. The number of hectares devoted to its production rose from 2,765 in 1872 to 37,500 in 1910-15. Exports of oranges increased from 111,000 tons in 1882 to 300,000 tons in 1899, and 500,000 tons in 1913.[37] Other export crops in this line included almonds from Tarragona and preserves from Logroño, which were a growing source of income by the turn of the century. In overall terms, however, fruit growing accounted for less than 6 per cent of total agricultural production by value in 1914.

Table 9   The total value of agricultural production in 1914 (million pesetas)

Mountains and scrubland	200
Wheat	860
Other cereals	691
Vegetables	157
Hay and stubble	286
Meadows and grassland	296
Vines	378
Olives	199
Root crops and tubers	264
Fruit trees	261
Horticulture	375
Industrial plants	34
Livestock	585
Poultry	212
Total	4,799

Source. José Cascón, 'Ojeada general a la agricultura española', *Revista de Economía Política*, VIII (1957), 101–02.

The agrarian depression of the last two decades of the nineteenth century underlined many of the fundamental weaknesses of Spanish agriculture. By focusing attention on the maladies of the countryside the crisis also sparked off a variety of diagnoses and suggested remedies. While the monumental seven-volume report of the 1887 Agricultural Commission gathered dust on the shelves a motley collection of landowners, journalists, aspiring politicians and plain cranks outlined their proposals for a solution of the problem. In general the landowners refused to concede that the crisis was in any way related to the overwhelming retardation of Spanish agriculture and called for a series of moral and political reforms. One critic blamed the current evils on the surfeit of university degrees, the Spaniards' love of bullfights and the keeping of pedigree dogs, and, among other proposals, called for the introduction into Spain of the bicycle.[38] The more thoughtful concentrated on those areas ignored or even prejudiced by the liberal reforms: cheap credit, irrigation, the use of fertilisers and farm machinery, and the limited extent of the internal market.[39]

The lack of capital to carry out agricultural improvements was recognised in 1864 in the influential book of Fermín Caballero, *The Development of Rural Population*, which rated it the main economic cause of Spain's agricultural backwardness. Without the means of new investment Spanish farmers were condemned to low yields by traditional methods of

production. Since the Middle Ages they had been able to obtain credit by
selling off their crops to public granaries known as pósitos which in turn
sold them back seed corn for planting. Yet by the middle of the nineteenth
century these archaic institutions were both corrupt and unable to provide
the large amount of credit needed to increase the output of the marginal
land which was coming into production.[40]

Until the beginning of the twentieth century attempts to increase
agricultural productivity by the use of fertilisers and agricultural machinery were restricted geographically. Outside the area of intensive cultivation in Valencia, Murcia and Alicante fertilisers were rarely applied to
the soil; in 1910 total Spanish consumption of fertilisers was only 570,000
metric tons while imports came to 59 million pesetas. Even so, this represented more than twice the tonnage used seven years previously. Also
in 1910 imports of agricultural machinery amounted to 47 million pesetas,
with a further 6 million pesetas of machinery produced in the Peninsula.
At the same time Spain possessed 546,035 horses, 904,735 mules and
836,741 donkeys with a combined value of 1,215 million pesetas, not to
mention the large numbers of oxen used to pull the ploughs.[41]

As the nineteenth century drew to a close the main concern of a new
breed of reformers was for State intervention in the provision of irrigation.
The spiritual leader of a mounting campaign was Joaquín Costa, one of the
greatest visionaries of modern Spain, whose call was for a política hidráulica or hydraulic policy. Costa's solution, and what he termed the
fundamental basis for the social and agricultural development of Spain,
was a programme of irrigation based on a network of dams, reservoirs and
irrigation canals which would harness the water supplies of the Iberian
Peninsula.[42] His opportunity was to come in 1898, when Spain's humiliat-
ing defeat at the hands of the United States brought the disappearance of
her last vestiges of empire in the New World. Costa found himself in the
forefront of a movement for economic regeneration whose basic platform
included plans for public works projects, irrigation and reforestation. In
February 1899 Costa was made president of a National Producers' League
(Liga Nacional de Productores), formed from the Chambers of Agriculture.
Under the full glare of publicity the Liga Nacional issued a manifesto
calling for the immediate and simultaneous construction by the State of
canals and reservoirs and the rapid improvement of secondary roads and
highways.[43] While Costa toyed with political opposition and was eventually to join the Republican party, his most influential supporter, Rafael
Gasset, was invited to join the Conservative Government of National
Regeneration of Francisco Silvela in April 1900 as Minister of Agriculture,
Industry and Public Works. With the aid of a group of highway engineers,
it was Gasset who in 1902 introduced a Plan of Hydraulic Works, a badly
thought out scheme which nevertheless formed the basis of future irrigation developments. Despite the fact that the regime was threatened with

anarchist revolts in the south in 1902 and that tens of thousands were thrown out of work or left half starving by a famine which lasted from the early spring of 1904 to the high summer of 1906, the Gasset plan foundered on the financial orthodoxy of the Spanish Treasury.[44]

Costa and Gasset were two of the many victims of the new oligarchy of landowners and financiers who acquired their wealth in the middle of the nineteenth century and consolidated their political power with the restoration of the Bourbon monarchy in 1875 after the collapse of the First Spanish Republic. This narrow-minded class of absentee landowners, who spent the summer season in Biarritz or San Sebastian and for the rest of the year determined the political future of Spain from Madrid, rarely visited their estates except for such pastimes as hunting, shooting and the rigging of elections. They had little if any interest in the modernisation of Spanish agriculture, preferring to protect the existing system by the imposition of higher tariffs.

NOTES

1   Miguel Artola, *La burguesía revolucionaria, 1808–69* (Madrid, 1973), pp. 68–70.

2   José Felix de Lequerica, *La actividad económica de Vizcaya en la vida nacional* (Madrid, 1956), p. 56.

3   Nadal, *The Failure of the Industrial Revolution in Spain*, p. 535.

4   Nadal, *La población española*, pp. 100–34.

5   Gonzalo Anes, 'La agricultura española desde comienzos del siglo XIX hasta 1868: algunos problemas', in Servicio de Estudios del Banco de España, *Ensayos sobre la economía española a mediados del siglo XIX* (Madrid, 1970), pp. 236–8.

6   Josep Fontana, 'Transformaciones agrarias y crecimiento económico en la España contemporánea', in *Cambio económico y actitudes políticas en la España del siglo XIX*, pp. 149–96.

7   Salvador de Moxó, *La disolución del régimen señorial en España* (Madrid, 1965), p. 52.

8   Anes, *La agricultura española*, pp. 242–3.

9   Moxó, *op. cit.*, p. 156.

10   Ramón de Santillán, *Memoria histórica de las reformas hechas en el sistema general de impuestos de España* . . . (Madrid, 1888), pp. 122–3, cited in Anes, *La agricultura española*, p. 247.

11   Francisco Tomás y Valiente, *El marco político de la desamortización en España* (Barcelona, 1971), pp. 73–4.

12   *Ibid.*, p. 79.

13   Antonio Miguel Bernal, 'Burguesía agraria y proletariado campesino en Andalucía durante la crisis de 1868', in *La propiedad de la tierra y las luchas agrarias andaluzas* (Barcelona, 1974), p. 115.

14   Alfonso Lazo, *La desamortización de las tierras de la Iglesia en la provincia de Sevilla 1835–45* (Seville, 1970), pp. 110–11.

15   See below, chapter three.

16   Francisco Simón Segura, 'La desamortizacion de 1855', *Económia Financiera Española*, 19–20 (1967), 120–5.

17   Fontana, *Transformaciones agrarias y crecimiento económico*, pp. 180–1.
18   *Censo de frutos y manufacturas de España e islas adyacentes* (Madrid, 1803).
19   Nadal, *The Failure of the Industrial Revolution in Spain*, pp. 557–8.
20   Anes, *La agricultura española*, pp. 260–1.
21   Nicolás Sánchez Albornoz, 'La legislación prohibicionista en materia de importación de granos, 1820–68', in *Las crisis de subsistencias de España en el siglo XIX* (Rosario, 1963), pp. 15–45.
22   Nicolás Sánchez Albornoz, 'La crisis de subsistencias de 1857', in *España hace un siglo: una economía dual* (Barcelona, 1968), p. 117; Vicens Vives, *op. cit.*, p. 587.
23   Alan S. Milward and S. B. Saul, *The Economic Development of Continental Europe, 1780–1870* (London, 1973), pp. 353 and 393.
24   Salvador Millet y Bel, '*Historia de l'agricultura espanyola durant els segles XIX i XX*' (unpublished, 1941), cited in Vicens Vives, *loc. cit.*, p. 585.
25   Vicens Vives, *op. cit.*, p. 589.
26   Cited in Angel Marvaud, 'Les vins espagnols et le commerce d'exportation', *Revue Economique Internationale* (1906), pp. 364–76.
27   Juan Plaza Prieto, 'El desarrollo del comercio exterior español desde principios del siglo XIX a la actualidad', *Revista de Economía Política*, vi (1955), 26–55.
28   Jaime Vicens Vives, *Cataluña en el siglo XIX* (Barcelona, 1961), pp. 65–7.
29   Wilfrid Mandelbaum, *The World Wheat Economy, 1885–1939* (Cambridge, Mass., 1953).
30   *La crisis agrícola y pecuaria*, 7 vols (Madrid, 1887–89); Josep Fontana, 'La gran crisi bladera del segle XIX', *Serra d'Or*, 2nd series, ii (November 1960), 21–2.
31   Antonio Cánovas del Castillo, 'La producción de cereales en España y los actuales derechos arancelarios', *Problemas Contemporáneos*, iii (Madrid, 1890), 335–49; Manuel Pugés, *Como truinfó el proteccionismo en España: la formación de la política arancelaria española* (Barcelona, 1931), pp. 274–306.
32   Luis Ribera, 'Las admisiones temporales del trigo', *Revista de Economía y Hacienda*, ix (25 August 1906), 809–10; Asociación de Fabricantes de Harina, *Admisiones temporales de los trigos* (Barcelona, 1906).
33   Balcells, *op. cit.*, p. 37; Vicens Vives, *Cataluña en el siglo XIX*, p. 67.
34   El comercio de vinos, *Revista de Economía y Hacienda*, ix (26 May 1906), 497–8; José Elías de Molins, *Algunos datos y consideraciones sobre los vinos y trigos en España* (Barcelona, 1904); *Diplomatic and Consular Reports on Trade and Finance*, Parliamentary Papers, 1907, cxvi (Málaga) p.205, henceforth referred to as P.P.
35   *La crisis agrícola y pecuaria*, i, 361, cited in Nadal, *The Failure of the Industrial Revolution in Spain*, p. 563.
36   Gaston Routier, 'L'industrie sucrière en Espagne', *Revue Politique et Parlementaire* (1900), pp. 132–42.
37   Giralt, *op. cit.*, pp. 389–93.
38   Santiago Maroto, *La crisis agrícola y pecuaria en España y sus verdaderos remedios* (Valladolid, 1896), pp. 466–95.
39   Joaquín Sánchez de Toca, *La crisis agraria y sus remedios en España* (Madrid, 1887); Santiago Martínez y González, *La crisis de la agricultura, sus causas y remedios* (Salamanaca, 1893).
40   Fermín Caballero, *Fomento de la población rural* (Madrid, 1864), pp. 130–1.
41   Angel Marvaud, *L'Espagne au XXe siecle* (Paris, 1914), pp. 300–1.
42   Joaquín Costa Martínez, *Política hidráulica: misión social de los riegos en España* (Madrid, 1911), p. 3.

43   Luis Morote, *La moral de la derrota* (Madrid, 1900); *Revista Nacional*, 10 April 1899.

44   Joseph Harrison 'The Spanish famine of 1904–06', *Agricultural History*, XLVII (1973), 300–7, and 'The regenerationist movement in Spain after the disaster of 1898', *European Studies Review*, 9 (1979), forthcoming.

CHAPTER 3

An industrial revolution manqué, 1830–75

After the promising signs of the late eighteenth century, particularly in the Catalan textile sector, the poor performance of national industry in the nineteenth century bears witness to a marked discontinuity in Spanish economic development. Although industry did not stagnate in the course of the last century, it made painfully slow progress and in so doing fell a considerale distance behind its main European rivals. At a time when Britain, Belgium, France and Germany were laying the foundations of modern capitalist economies, the failure of the industrialisation process south of the Pyrenees confirmed Spain as a prime example of economic backwardness. Moreover, if we consider that unlike other Mediterranean countries of the standing of Greece and Italy she was neither politically dismembered nor subjected to foreign rule, the relative retardation of her economy is all the more emphatic.[1]

A great part of the responsibility for Spain's inability to build a sound industrial base must be placed with successive governments, who pursued a variety of mistaken and counter-productive policies which proved highly detrimental to the private sector in the long term. The liberal agrarian reforms of the 1830s and 1850s were not the least harmful of these measures, diverting large amounts of capital away from employment in Spanish industry.[2] Another significant obstacle to industrial progress was the close interdependence between the State and the nation's finanical institutions, which caused the public and private sectors to compete for the limited funds available. The *raison d'être* of this unhealthy competition was the declining fortunes of the Spanish Treasury, whose revenue fell by nearly a quarter in the first three decades of the nineteenth century, following the collapse of the American trade. The proportion of ordinary revenue represented by customs duty dropped by 60 per cent in the period 1791–1800 to 1831–40. Over the same period the receipts of the British Exchequer almost trebled.

In spite of increased receipts from the sale of disentailed lands from the mid-1830s onwards, Spain continued to suffer from a series of budgetary deficits for which there was no other solution for the State but to raise loans. The volume of public debt rose steadily, nearly trebling in the third quarter of the century. In order to attract funds the State offered high rates of interest without regard to the needs of industry, thus driving the capital market into purely speculative ventures.

Table 10   Index of ordinary revenues, Spain and Great Britain, 1791–1880 (1791–1800 = 100)

Year	Spain	Great Britain
1791–1800	100·0	100·0
1801–07	93·7	210·4
1814–20	79·0	336·6
1821–30	77·2	286·6
1831–40	102·2	254·0
1841–50	136·4	275·2
1851–60	211·2	296·6
1861–70	303·8	342·1
1871–80	323·8	371·3

Source. Josep Fontana, *La quiebra de la monarquía absoluta 1814–20: la crisis del Antiguo régimen en España* (Barcelona, 1971), p. 61.

When it came to obtaining loans the State had a number of advantages over the industrial sector. The Bank of Spain, whose assets accounted for approximately one-half of all the issuing banks, specialising over-whelmingly in short-and long-term loans to the government. In the period 1852 to 1873 the average annual amount which the bank lent to private interests was a mere 20 million pesetas, whereas an average of 82·1 million pesetas was immobilised in government loans. The State Deposit Fund (Caja de Depósitos), which was in operation from 1852 to September 1868, concentrated its activities entirely on supplying the Treasury with funds. Similarly, from 1858 to 1866 the Bank of Barcelona, the second largest issuing bank in the country, loaned on average 378,000 pesetas on indus-trial equity and 2·3 million pesetas, i.e. six times as much, on public debt securities. Only the Bank of Bilbao, founded in 1857, played an active role in the financing of industrial development.[3]

BANKING AND INDUSTRIALISATION

The first modern Spanish bank was the Bank of Saint Ferdinand (Banco Español de San Fernando), the precursor of the Bank of Spain, which was founded in 1829 as a successor to the ruined Bank of Saint Charles (Banco de San Carlos). The new institution was as unenterprising as its pre-decessor and inherited much of its conservatism. Its managers, all of whom were royal appointees, chose to limit the function of the bank to

Table 11   Spanish public debt in circulation, 1849–76 (million pesetas)

1849	3,857	1864	3,958
1850	3,611	1865	4,344
1851	3,566	1866	4,566
1852	3,738	1867	5,577
1853	3,805	1868	5,541
1854	3,435	1869	6,666
1855	3,500	1870	6,799
1856	3,370	1871	6,773
1857	3,434	1872	7,929
1858	3,452	1873	8,780
1859	3,448	1874	10,184
1860	3,506	1875	10,307
1861	4,038	1876	12,139
1862	3,848		

Source. Gabriel Solé Villalonga, *La deuda pública española y el mercado de capitales* (Madrid, 1964), p. 27.

discounting bills with three reliable signatures and the transfer of funds between the ports and provincial capitals on behalf of merchants and landowners. With the outbreak of the First Carlist War, four years after its establishment, the Bank of Saint Ferdinand came to specialise in advances to the hard-pressed Spanish Treasury backed by receipts from taxation and, commencing in the financial year 1836–37, also undertook the collection of taxes for its most important customer. Some idea of the extent of the interdependence of the bank and the State can be ascertained by looking at the bank's published profits. According to its own calculations, between 1830 and 1848 48·1 per cent of the gross profits of the bank—probably an underestimate—consisted in interest on direct loans and other services to the government.[4]

The main source of investment to industry and commerce was a collection of merchant banks, the most distinguished of which was the Catalan house Girona Hermanos, Clavé y Cía, a partnership controlled by the Girona family, which was granted the charter for the Bank of Barcelona in 1844. Nevertheless, the resurgence of the Catalan textile industry during the 1830s and 1840s was financed not by the banks but by the repatriated savings of émigrés returning from Spain's former colonies in Latin America, and by personal fortunes acquired in Cuba.[5]

The ending of the civil war in 1839 heralded a lengthy phase of prosperity which encouraged the foundation of a number of financial institutions. The Bank of Barcelona was one of three joint-stock banks established in the 1840s with the right of issue, the other two being the Madrid-based Bank of Isabel II (Banco de Isabella II), founded in 1844, and the Bank of Cádiz, established in 1846 as a branch of Isabel II. In addition, a small

number of joint-stock banks were founded in this period without the right
to issue banknotes, among them two Madrid banks, the Union Bank (Banco
de la Unión) and the Development and Overseas Bank (Banco de Fomento
y Ultramar), and the Valenciana de Fomento of Valencia.

The Bank of Isabel II introduced a new style of banking, far removed
from the ultra-cautious approach of the Bank of Saint Ferdinand. The
newcomer was an offspring of that same mood of heady speculation which
produced the frenzied purchases of national property. Among its directors
was the notorious financier and politician José de Salamanca. From the
day it first opened its doors the Bank of Isabel II became involved in a bitter
rivalry with the Bank of Saint Ferdinand which led to a massive increase in
banknote circulation from 6 million pesetas in January 1844 to 28 millions
in September 1845. In its brief but hectic life of only three years the Bank of
Isabel II knocked a good deal of the complacency out of its rival—a
complacency which had resulted from the Saint Ferdinand's previous
monopoly of note issue—and forced it to look increasingly to the private
sector. Among its many innovations were the printing of banknotes of
small denominations (200 reales compared with the 500 reale notes of the
Bank of Saint Ferdinand), branch banking, current accounts, and loans to
industrial and railway companies, with the companies' own shares acting
as collateral. During the first two years of its existence, which coincided
with an upturn in the trade cycle, the Bank of Isabel II made fabulous
profits for its shareholders. Thereafter its highly speculative undertakings
led to its rapid demise. In order to avoid suspending payments and declaring itself bankrupt it was obliged to merge with the Bank of Saint
Ferdinand in February 1847.

The crisis of 1847–48 sparked off the collapse of many of the new breed
of banks, including the Union Bank, which did little more than finance the
speculative ventures of its board of directors, and the Development and
Overseas Bank, which had been set up to finance a shipping company
which never commenced operations. No less dramatically, the New Spanish Bank of Saint Ferdinand (Nuevo Banco Español de San Fernando), the
hybrid formed by the amalgamation of the two giants, was forced to
suspend convertibility owing to the stock exchange crash of 1848, and it
was 1851 before it was able to resume normal operations. More successful
in riding out the crisis were the provincial banks: the Bank of Barcelona,
for example, survived this early test of its financial skills by calling in all
unpaid capital.[6]

The effect of the 1848 crisis was to put a brake on company formation for
a while. In an atmosphere which closely resembled the aftermath of the
South Sea Bubble, the Moderate government enacted a new corporation
law in 1848 which banned all joint-stock companies except issuing banks,
public transport companies, companies enjoying legal privileges and
those concerned with 'the general welfare' of the community. With these

exceptions, all other concerns were prevented from organising as either joint-stock companies (sociedades anónimas) or as partnerships (comanditarias par acciones). It was not until the triumph of the Progressives in the revolution of 1854 that this restrictive piece of legislation was modified, and a further fifteen years before it was abolished.[7]

The banking laws of 1856 were among the flurry of liberal economic legislation of the Progressive Biennium (1854–56),which also included the Disentailing Law of 1855 and the General Railway Law of the same year. The Banks of Issue Law established what was termed a system of 'the plurality of issuing banks' which extended the right of issue to one bank in each town, either a local bank or a branch of the New Spanish Bank of Saint Ferdinand (now rechristened the Bank of Spain). By this law the issue of banknotes was not permitted to exceed three times the paid-in capital or the bank's gold reserve, whichever was smaller. The Credit Companies Law of 1856, which was modelled on the charter of the French investment bank, the Crédit Mobilier, allowed merchant banks to take part in a wide range of activities, including loans to government, tax collection, industrial promotion and commercial banking.[8]

From 1856 to 1864 the Spanish banking system experienced a phase of extraordinary expansion. The number of issuing banks rose during this period from 3 to 21, bringing a doubling of the amount of banknotes in circulation from 227·9 to 499·1 million reales. At the same time the number of credit companies rose from nil to thirty-four, with a total employed capital of 1,135 million reales, nearly four times that of the banks of issue (306·4 million reales).

The first three successful applications to form a credit company were all French. These were the Crédito Mobiliario Español, the Sociedad Española Mercantil e Industrial and the Compañía General de Crédito en España. The Crédito Mobiliario Español had a nominal capital of 114 million pesetas which was not fully paid in until 1864. This was almost four times the capital of the Bank of Spain, which remained at 30 million pesetas until 1865, and one-fifth the size of Spanish government receipts for the financial year 1863–64, which stood at 577 million pesetas. Among it original board of directors were many men of noble blood, among them the Dukes of Alba, Galliera, Glücksberg and Rivas; the Marquis of Ferrari, and Count de Morny; various members of the Haute banque parisienne (Mallet, André, Des Arts, D'Eichtal); other European Bankers, Fould, Seillière and Galliera included; and the founders of the Crédit Mobilier, Emile and Isaac Pereire.[9]

The Sociedad Española Mercantil e Industrial had a total authorised capital of 76 million pesetas, although its paid-in capital never exceeded 22·8 million pesetas, which it achieved in the year 1857: thereafter the figure fell to 15·2 million pesetas until the company was dissolved in 1868. Gathered together on its board were names as prestigious as those of the

Table 12 Joint-stock companies in existence, 1829–74 (December of each year; saving banks excluded)

Year	Banks of issue	Credit companies	Others	Total
1829–43	1	0	0	1
1844	3	0	0	3
1845	3	0	1	4
1846	4	0	3	7
1847	3	0	3	6
1848–54	3	0	1	4
1855	3	0	2	5
1856	4	6	3	13
1857	10	6	3	19
1858	10	7	3	20
1859	10	7	3	20
1860	11	8	3	22
1861	11	12	3	26
1862	12	17	3	32
1863	14	20	3	37
1864	21	34	2	57
1865	21	35	2	57
1866	21	32	1	54
1867	21	26	0	47
1868	20	21	0	41
1869	19	14	0	33
1870	16	14	0	30
1871	16	14	2	32
1872	16	14	4	34
1873	16	13	4	33
1874	1	13	8	22

Note. After 1864 (and especially after 1867) the number of banks of issue and credit societies may be inflated, since some of them went out of business without officially being dissolved.
Source. Gabriel Tortella, 'La evolución del sistema financiero español de 1856 a 1868', in Ensayos sobre la economía española a mediados del siglo XIX (Madrid, 1970), pp. 18–19.

Crédito Mobiliario; Alejandro Mon, a perennial Finance Minister in Moderate governments; Ramón de Santillán, the Governor of the Bank of Spain; the Duke of Sevillano; the bank's organiser, James de Rothschild, of the Rothschild bank in Paris; and his two representatives in Spain, Daniel Weisweiller and Ignacio Bauer.

The third of the large French credit companies, the Compañía General de Crédito en España, had an authorised capital of 99·75 million pesetas, of which no more than a third was ever fully paid in. Its founders were a group of financiers led by Adolphe Prost of the Compagnie Générale des

Caisses d'Escompte, and its board too included a distinguished assortment of bankers, politicians and aristocrats. When Prost went bankrupt in 1868 control of the bank passed to the brothers Louis and Numa Guilhou.

The first credit companies based entirely on domestic capital were founded in the provinces, the earliest of which was the Sociedad Catalana General de Crédito, with a capital of 30 million pesetas. Other important Spanish companies included the Crédito Mobiliario Barcelonés (unrelated to the Pereires), which had a capital of 12 million pesetas, and the Crédito Castellano of Valladolid, with a capital of 11·7 million pesetas. The greater part of the resources mobilised, however, came from outside the Peninsula: in 1864 at least 85 per cent, and possibly as high as 95 per cent, of the capital of the Crédito Mobiliario was foreign.[10] Indeed, the failure of the Rothschild bank in Spain to subscribe its capital fully was largely due to its stated aim to mobilise the savings of Spaniards rather than to invest French funds.

RAILWAYS AND INVESTMENT

The area which benefited most from the foundation of credit companies in Spain was railway promotion. Prior to the General Railway Law of 1855 only 456 km of track had been laid since the opening of the first line from Barcelona to Mataró in October 1848, an average of 67·84 km a year. About half this total was taken up by the main line from Madrid to Albacete, with the remainder consisting of small stretches of line which ran inland from a number of ports: Barcelona–Granollers, Barcelona–Molins de Rey, Játiva–Valencia–El Grao, Jerez–Puerto Santa María, Gijón–Langreo and Sabadell–Moncada.[11]

The General Railway Law of 1855 offered a series of concessions to companies proposing to construct new lines, such as free entry into the country of all capital goods, rolling stock and fuel for a period of ten years. With these incentives Spain experienced a real railway boom financed by massive imports of foreign capital. By the end of 1864 1,553·2 million pesetas had been invested in railway companies, almost sixteen times as much as had been invested in the whole of Spanish manufacturing industry (98·4 million pesetas).[12] In the thirteen years from 1856 to 1868 4,898 km of railway were built, an average of 377 km per annum.

Leading the field in railway construction were the Crédito Mobiliario which founded the Compañía de los Ferrocarriles del Norte de España (known as the Norte), and the Sociedad Española, founders of the Compañía de los Ferrocarriles de Madrid a Zaragoza y Alicante (the MZA). A strong sense of competitiveness had already developed between the Pereires and Rothschild during the construction of the French railway system: after 1856 it spilled over the Pyrenees.[13]

In 1855 the Chemin de Fer du Midi, belonging to the Crédit Mobilier,

Table 13   The extension of the railway network, 1848–68

Year	Km constructed	Year	Km constructed
1848	28·25	1859	297·82
1849	–	1860	764·36
1850	–	1861	456·43
1851	48·34	1862	360·40
1852	25·45	1863	837·75
1853	115·93	1864	494·48
1854	114·45	1865	766·51
1855	142·50	1866	317·00
1856	47·58	1867	41·29
1857	147·73	1868	188·17
1858	180·64		

Source. *Memoria sobre las obras públicas en 1867, 1868, y 1869, comprendiendo lo relativo a ferrocarriles* (Madrid, 1870), cited in Jordi Nadal, 'Los comienzos de la industrialización española (1832–68): la industria siderúrgica', *Ensayos sobre la economía española a mediados del siglo XIX* (Madrid, 1970), p. 210.

which linked Paris with Bordeaux, was about to reach Bayonne. The Pereires envisaged extending this line via Madrid to Cádiz, the southernmost port in Spain. However, a direct line south from Irún, on the Franco–Spanish border, would run across mountainous and sparsely populated territory. The Pereires therefore decided to adopt a more roundabout route which wound its way to Madrid through the established commercial centres of Old Castile. Unfortunately for their plans, the southern section of the proposed concession was acquired by José Salamanca, who agreed to turn over his stretch of line from Madrid to Almansa, upon completion, to Rothschild and four directors of the French Grand Central Railway. Nevertheless the Pereires persevered with their proposals for the northern half of the line, and in 1856 obtained a concession for a railway between Valladolid and Burgos. Soon afterwards they acquired a further charter for a branch line from Venta de Baños on the main line to Alar de Rey which linked up with another line then under construction from Santander.

These concessions formed the basis of the Norte, which was constituted in December 1858 with a capital of 100 million francs in common stock, with the possibility of raising an additional 50 million francs in bonds. The company also received a cash subsidy of 56 million francs, raised in France by the Crédito Mobiliario Español on the credit of the Spanish government. The Crédito Mobiliario Español took 26 per cent of the stock, the French Crédit Mobilier 15 per cent, the French directors of these institutions 35 per cent, two Belgian banks, the Société Générale and the Banque de Belgique took 15 per cent, with the Spanish directors of the Crédito Mobiliario Español coming in too for nominal amounts.[14]

The southern half of their proposed system offered far less favourable prospects for the Pereires. Apart from losing the concession of the Madrid–Almansa line to their rivals, they saw another stretch of line from Jerez to Puerto Real (near Cádiz) conceded to a Spanish company, and the charter for the line from Córdoba to Seville granted to a group led by Charles Laffitte. Although the Pereires joined forced with Laffitte to obtain confirmation of the Córdoba–Seville line in 1857, the concession for the line from Seville to Jerez went to the Prost–Guilhou group, which later also obtained the concession for the line from Cádiz to Puerto Real. In 1860 this group paid an exorbitant price for the Jerez–Puerto Real line, thus gaining overall control of the line from Cádiz to Seville and bringing the company's capital to 34 million francs.[15]

Over the same period, Rothschild and Morny (president of the Grand Central) built up a railway system of even greater extent than the Norte. Their plans closely resembled those of the Pereires, their aim being to extend the Grand Central to Saragossa and Madrid, thereafter continuing in two directions, south-eastwards to the Mediterranean and south-westwards to Portugal. With Salamanca's concessions safely in his pocket, Rothschild obtained a further concession extending the southern main line from Almansa to Alicante. Early in 1856 he obtained a charter for a line from Madrid to Sargossa, and was thus in a position in December of that year to organise the Madrid–Saragossa–Alicante company, the famous MZA. The MZA had a capital of 120 million francs in 240,000 shares, of which Rothschild personally took 66,000 shares, the Sociedad Española Mercantil e Industrial 64,000, and another group which included Morny 110,000. A further 56,000 shares were reserved for subscription by the shareholders of the Grand Central at par.[16]

The rationale of the Progressives in encouraging railway building was to 'promote public wealth'. Their plan was the construction of a network of lines ahead of demand in the hope that the availability of cheap transport services would stimulate investment in manufacturing industry. This process is known as development by excess capacity of social overhead capital. However, in actual practice these plans were to be frustrated. As we have seen, instead of stimulating investment in industry, during the railway mania of 1856–64 the railways took over nine-tenths of the funds available for investment. Moreover, after the main lines had been built the railway companies found that traffic was so limited that receipts scarcely covered variable costs. The companies thus found themselves unable to pay interest or dividends, let alone pay off the capital invested in the construction of the network.[17] All and sundry should have been fore-warned by the advice of the master of English railway building, George Stephenson, who was sent to Spain in 1845 to investigate the prospects of

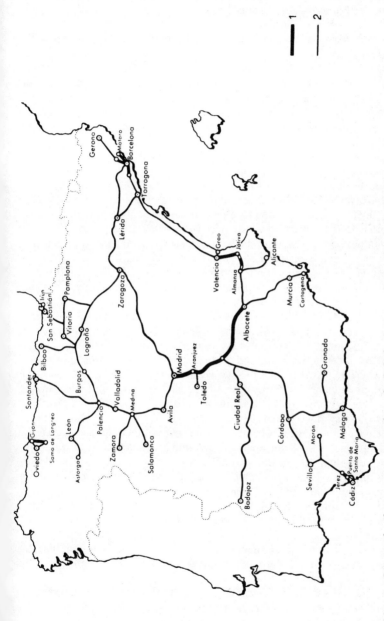

Map 3 Stages of railway construction: lines built before 1868: 1 lines constructed before the 1855 Act, 2 lines constructed between 1855 and 1868. (After J. Vicens Vives, *Historia social de España y América*, 5 vols (Barcelona, 1959), 4 (ii), 270.)

railway construction there for a consortium of British capitalists. 'I have been a whole month in the country,' he wrote, 'but have not seen during the whole of that time enough people of the right sort to fill a single train.'[18]

In some of the more advanced industrial countries, it has been argued, a positive shift in aggregate demand sparked off a chain reaction among closely linked interdependent sectors—the so-called multiplier effect. Yet, in a quasi-subsistence or dual economy like Spain, the wide dispersal of markets and the absence of many branches of industry meant that the multiplier effect could not be expected to act as a stimulus to economic growth. Nevertheless, what was theoretically possible in the Spanish case was backward linkage effects from the railways to those industries which in general provided them with materials. However, the decision to allow foreign railway companies to bring in all the materials they required had the result of nullifying this potential effect also.[19]

There can be few better illustrations of the misguided policy of the State with regard to railways than its effect on the iron industry. After 1830 the Spanish iron industry received important stimuli for growth from the demands of agriculture and the textile industry. The demand for farming implements made of iron lasted for thirty years, the duration of the dis-entailing process, and did much to prolong the life of outmoded furnaces and foundries specialising in the production of high-quality malleable iron. The demand from the textile industry followed the adoption of mechanical looms between 1840 and 1860. Lack of domestic capital, however, held up the construction of modern plant. Thus by the middle of the 1850s Spain needed to import modest amounts of steel ingots, wire, tinplate, sheet, strip, hoop and plate iron. In this situation the General Railway Law of 1855 could have acted as a positive incentive to the development and modernisation of the metallurgical industry. In the event a great opportunity was missed. The provision of free entry for railway material led to a massive increase in imports of every kind of iron and steel product. After 1857 imports of iron products began to exceed the entire production of the Spanish iron and steel industry. In the quin-quennium 1861–65 (the first period for which statistical evidence is avail-able) imports of iron goods stood at 482,171 tons, more than double the Spanish production (228,277 tons).[20]

Spanish ironmasters might have benefited from the removal of the railway companies' exemption from duties in 1864, but by that time the meagre returns to the companies acted as a deterent to further expansion. As the official enquiry of 1866 was to show, at the very moment that the ironmasters of Spain were able to meet the new demand presented by railway construction, the latter began to contract drastically.[21]

The most deleterious effect of the railway building programme was that by entrusting the construction of the Spanish network to foreign com-panies, each with its own conception of what was most beneficial to them,

Table 14   Imports and production of iron in Spain, 1849–68 (metric tons)

Year	Imports	Production
1849	9,956	–
1850	11,932	–
1851	12,268	–
1852	11,795	–
1853	11,305	–
1854	16,479	–
1855	16,392	–
1856	16,253	15,227
1857	46,675	–
1858	69,503	–
1859	49,199	–
1860	30,696	–
1861	106,330	34,532
1862	91,865	48,106
1863	122,460	45,331
1864	107,038	50,775
1865	54,478	49,433
1866	28,551	39,259
1867	32,044	41,933
1868	30,687	43,161

Source. Jordi Nadal, Los comienzos de la industrialización española (1832–68): la industria siderúrgica, pp. 212–13.

the Progressives and their successors ensured the economic colonisation of Spain by European capitalism. Instead of connecting the industrial producers with the consuming public in the formation of a national market, the lines built by the Pereires, Rothschild and Prost–Guilhou for the most part radiated from Madrid to the ports and the French frontier. Areas with little to offer to the great foreign enterprises in terms of foodstuffs or raw materials, such as Galicia, had very poor connections with the rest of Spain, while Almería in the south-east had none at all.

The Crédito Mobiliario was reinforced in its decision to build up its rail network in northern Spain by the strong belief that the area served by its lines contained abundant supplies of coal. From the very beginning the Pereires had a vision of a vertically integrated industrial empire in the north, with coal mines, gasworks, briquette factories and ironworks built alongside the railway. The Norte line was envisaged as an artery upon which every other enterprise was dependent.[22]

There is an interesting parallel after 1860 between the type of economic development (or underdevelopment) which was experienced in both Spain and Latin America. Although Spain is part of the continent of Europe and underwent its own independent process of industrialisation in the textile sector in the late eighteenth and nineteenth century along the lines of the general European model, Castile and the Basque region in particular present us at this time with a partial example of the type of capitalist underdevelopment outlined by Andre Gunder Frank for nineteenth-century Latin America.[23]

As the outward-orientated exporting lobby of landlords, mine owners and merchants gained strength and found an expression for their interests in the liberalising of trade, so Spain (like Latin America) was converted into a satellite of the industrial metropolis of north-west Europe, which extracted often irreplaceable supplies of raw materials for its own use, sending back large quantities of manufactured goods and surplus capital.

MINING AND METALLURGY

One indicator of Spain's underdevelopment in the course of the nineteenth century was its growing role as a leading supplier of industrial raw materials to the advanced capitalist nations of western Europe. Three metals provided the basis of Spanish mineral exports; lead, copper and iron. The rise of the lead industry took place after the Napoleonic war in response to a decree of November 1817 which allowed for the free working and exploitation of Spanish mines. Mining was centred on the mountain chain formed by the Sierras of Gador, Almagrera and Cartagena in the south-east of the Peninsula. The first sign of the new activity was in 1822, when the Málaga firm of Reín y Cía erected a factory for smelting ore at Adra, in the province of Almería, the nearest port to the Gador mines. Later in 1838 the centre of lead production switched to the Sierra de Almagrera with the discovery of the rich Jaroso vein.[24]

Lead soon came to play a vital role in the country's balance of trade. In 1827 it accounted for 8·40 per cent of exports. Official statistics for the period 1849–68 (which omit the years 1860–65) show the value of lead exports as fluctuating from a minimum of 5·84 per cent of total exports in 1855 to a maximum of 10·18 per cent in 1861, with an average of 8·41 per cent for the twenty years, exactly equal to the 1827 figure. Apart for such abnormal circumstances as the Crimean War, when Spanish flour and grain were in high demand, exports of lead bars regularly ranked second in importance after wine. Moreover, with the decline of lead mining in Britain and Germany at this time, Spain began to export to Italy, France, Holland, Prussia, Russia and as far afield as China. From 1820 to 1868 the nation struggled for hegemony of lead exports with Britain. After 1868 Spain assumed a position of unrivalled world leadership until she was eventually overtaken by the United States in 1898.[25]

By the end of the 1830s the south-east, formerly renowned for its poverty, had become one of the wealthiest regions in Spain. Returns from lead mining and smelting reached extraordinary proportions, due largely to low running costs. In one mine in Jaroso, the Observacíon, exploitation and administration accounted for little more than 8 per cent of total costs in 1845. As early as 1836 high wages had attracted 20,000 workers to the region. Yet, in the end, the wider consequences of all this activity were disappointing: lead mining and smelting failed to provide the basis for the general economic take-off of the south-east, largely because of the essentially pre-capitalist and speculative nature of the lead industry. Mines were by and large not extensive in size, and investment in them was small. The practice of letting and sub-letting mines for brief periods, moreover, caused the majority of firms to be more interested in making quick profits than rational exploitation.[26]

With the exhaustion of the Gador deposits in the 1860s the lead industry of Adra went into sharp decline. Its eclipse emphasised the uncompetitiveness of native enterprise. Henceforth the overriding factors in the progress of the lead industry were the construction of railways and the new mining laws of 1868, which allowed the provincial governors to make concessions in perpetuity, both of which coincided with a sharp increase in demand from abroad and the availability of foreign capital. To counteract the exhaustion of indigenous supplies, the British prospected in Jaén, where they set up Linares Lead, the first foreign company to be founded in Spain, in 1862; the Alamillos, Thomas Sopwith, and the most renowned of all, the Fortuna company. Among the companies founded by French capital were the La Cruz of Jaén and the only real competitor of the Fortuna, the Cie Minière et Metallurgique des Asturies. After 1858 Stolberg and Westphalia of Aachen opened up a number of mines at Aquisgrán. In the opinion of Jordi Nadal, it was not long before Spain witnessed the almost complete colonisation of her lead industry.[27]

Copper too was exploited to meet foreign demand. Its expansion dates from the visit to Spain in 1853 of the French engineer Deligny, a representative of the great Décazeville metallurgical complex in Aveyron. Deligny's optimistic reports led to the foundation in that year of the first foreign company set up to mine copper, later to be merged into the Paris-based Mines de Cuivre de Huelva. The main stimulus for the exploitation of Spain's copper resources was the demand of the British chemical industry for sulphuric acid. This was because the pyrites deposits of Huelva contained not only copper and iron but also a high sulphur content. It was two British firms which were to dominate the industry, the Tharsis Sulphur and Copper Mines Ltd, of Glasgow, established in 1866 with a capital of £300,000, which was raised to £1 million two years later, and the Rio Tinto Company Ltd, which by the middle of the 1880s had become the world's leading producer of pyrites.[28]

South-east Spain also led the way in the production of iron in the first half of the nineteenth century. The pioneer of regional exploitations was the Málaga businessman Manuel Heredia, who had previously built up a considerable fortune through the export of local wines and olives and had opened up the Serranía de Ronda to the mining of graphite. In 1828 Heredia set up a company known as La Concepción to exploit the magnetic ores of the Sierra Blanca at Ojén near Marbella. Four years later in 1832 the Heredia company constructed the first charcoal-fired blast furnace for non-military purposes in Spain. Initially its output was restricted to the manufacture of iron hoops for the company's wine and olive oil casks. In 1836 Heredia built a new works at Málaga called La Constancia which had seven puddling furnaces and three reverbatory furnaces. The disruption caused to the iron industry of the north between 1833 and 1839 by the First Carlist War brought great prosperity to these two plants as well as to a third concern, the El Pedroso company, which was established in Seville in 1832. Heredia, who acquired the reputation of leading ironmaster in Spain, employed 1,911 workers in 1840, 1,084 at Marbella and 827 at Málaga.[29]

Such was the upheaval in the north caused by the civil war that the old-fashioned Andalusian iron industry retained its national domination for another thirty years. From the middle of the 1860s, however, the mounting costs of its antiquated technology led the region to be replaced as the leading iron producer of Spain by Asturias. Jordi Nadal shows that in 1865 the Heredia company had to spend 120·4 pesetas on charcoal to obtain one ton of cast iron, while the Asturian firm of Duro y Cía of La Felguera was faced with an outlay of only 2·67 pesetas on coke and 5·1 pesetas on coal to obtain the same amount of iron. Despite the fact that labour was marginally more expensive in Asturias, one ton of pig iron in Oviedo cost 103·8 pesetas, compared with 158·2 pesetas in Málaga. Not until 1879, when Vizcaya began to import Welsh coke, which returned as ballast in the iron ore carriers, was Asturias's ascendency ended.[30]

The Basque iron industry, traditionally in the forefront of Spanish developments, experienced a pronounced decline for the greater part of the nineteenth century. The First Carlist War was but one of a series of obstacles to its growth, the others being the disappearance of colonial markets, the running down of the Spanish navy and competition from Andalusia. Vizcaya's technological backwardness in this period is shown by the fact that it was not until 1849 that the first charcoal-fired blast furnace commenced operations at the firm of Santa Ana de Bolueta, and not until 1865 that the Nuestra Señora del Carmen factory at Baracaldo first produced pig iron, using coke as a fuel. In both cases Vizcaya was nearly two decades behind its rivals in Málaga and Asturias.[31]

The big factor in the emergence of the Vizcayan industry was the discovery of the Bessemer process in 1856 for the conversion of non-phosphoric ore into iron. From the middle of the 1860s the opening up of narrow-gauge railways and the completion of the first loading bays in the Ría of Bilbao were evidence of a growing interest of foreign capitalists in extracting the high-grade ores of the province. British steelmakers in particular sought to supplement Cumberland haematite with the local red haematite known as *vena* which was between 58 and 61 per cent pure. During the next decade British, French, German and Belgian concerns financed the establishment of a number of subsidiary companies around Bilbao. In 1871 the leading Basque ironmasters, the Ibarras, set up two large mining enterprises in which they held one-quarter of the shares; the Orconera Iron Ore Company Ltd and the Société Franco-Belge de Mines de Somorrostro. Also linked with these concerns were the Dowlais Iron Company, the Consett Iron Company, Krupp of Essen, the French Société Denain and the Société Cockerill of Belgium.[32] Yet the early prosperity of the Bilbao iron trade was cut short by the Third Carlist War, which paralysed the commerce of the port for over a year. It was not until the return of peaceful conditions with the restoration of the Bourbon monarchy in 1874 that the accumulated profits of the mine owners and exporters were to contribute to the take-off of the Vizcayan metallurgical industry.[33]

The slow progress of the Spanish coal industry during the eighteenth and early nineteenth century was almost entirely the result of insufficient demand. There was no lack of initiatives: a mining law of May 1780 was the first of a series which granted a host of privileges in order to encourage the exploitation of mines. At the prompting of Jovellanos, legislation of September 1790 and August 1792 proclaimed the absolute freedom to exploit for coal. As a measure of the Enlightment's concern to develop the coal industry, both Jovellanos and the engineer Casado de Torres were commissioned to study the Asturian coal trade. Most of the interest centred on ways of reducing transport costs, which, it was believed, constituted the main obstacle to the industry's advancement. Jovellanos proposed the construction of a coal highway from the mines of Langreo to the port of Gijón, while Casado de Torres favoured canalisation of the river Nalón. Half a century later, thanks to the efforts of the banker and mining concessionaire Aguado, Jovellanos's road was finally completed. Yet by this late date his scheme was already outmoded, nor did it bring about any substantial reductions in the costs of coal at the ports. In 1844 the Duke of Riánsares, husband of Queen María Cristina, made a proposal to construct a railway line from Langreo to the port of Gijón and was eventually granted a government subsidy in 1849.

These early initiatives, however, tackled the problem of coal supply from the wrong angle. Far more crucial to the early failure of the coal industry was the inability of Asturian ironmasters to make iron using locally produced coke as a fuel. The naval arsenal at Trubia in the province of Oviedo repeatedly failed during the twelve years of its existence from 1796 to 1808 to utilise Langreo coal. The problem of the industry's stagnation was not overcome until 1847 or 1848, when the factory at Mieres finally managed to produce pig iron using local coal, though the process was not regularised until 1852.[34] At about the same time the Cía Asturiana de Minas de Carbón, one of the two mining enterprises of any consequence, began to use coal for smelting zinc ore from its mines in Guipúzcoa.

During the 1860s and 1870s the bulk of the coal mined in Asturias was consumed by the leading iron and steel works at Mieres and La Felguera, which were sited on the banks of the rivers Cuadal and Nalón. Their troubled expansion restricted the progress of the coal industry, whose prosperity had become tied to that of the metallurgical sector. In 1865 19·5 per cent of the 339,328 tons of coal mined in Oviedo were shipped out of the province to other regions of Spain, while the corresponding percentage for 1881 was still only 24·7, out of a total production of 482,634 tons.[35]

THE CATALAN TEXTILE INDUSTRY

The termination of the Napoleonic war was the prelude to a lengthy period of economic stagnation in the Catalan cotton industry, until that moment the only industry to have displayed signs of modern development. The political insecurity of the times, the spread of smuggling and the dearth of capital all contributed to a situation of near chaos in the Principality. Added to this, the ban on the export of textile machinery from Britain severely handicapped the re-equipment of the industry after the destruction wreaked upon Catalan mills by the French armies of occupation. Yet the main problem faced by the Catalan manufacturers was the shrinking of the market for their products following the independence of most of the former Spanish empire in the New World.

With the possibility of exports practically eliminated owing to British competition, the mill owners of Catalonia were forced to look to Spain. Their solution was the integration of the national market with the cereal-growing regions of the interior, satisfying the wants of the periphery—at that time chronically deficient in wheat—and in return being supplied with manufactured goods. In order to obtain the political backing of the Catalan manufacturing classes, the absolutist monarchy gave support to their economic aspirations by raising the tariff on foreign textile imports thus securing for them a larger slice of the domestic market. Finally, in 1832, it banned altogether the introduction of cotton textile manufactures.[36]

The 1832 tariff was both cause and effect of an event which has been seen as the most significant development in the history of the Catalan textile industry: the construction of the Bonaplata mill in Barcelona. José Bonaplata, the founder of the mill, had recently returned to Catalonia after a spell of exile in Great Britain, where he had studied the latest mechanical innovations in the cotton industry. The Barcelona mill was the first in the

Peninsula to incorporate a number of these innovations. It was the first factory in Spain to contain a Watt steam engine, which drove the mechanical looms, and the first cotton mill in Spain to install a calico printing machine. In addition, the firm of Bonaplata Rull, Vilaregut y Cía provides us with the earliest instance in the Peninsula of the use of cast iron in the construction of machinery. Within a year of coming into operation it employed between 600 and 700 workers and was generally considered to have already had an incalculable influence on the industry of Catalonia, serving as a model for new ideas. The Factories Commission, an agency of the Catalan mill owners, claimed that, owing to its innovations, cotton spinning in the region had undergone a complete revolution and that finished goods were both of higher quality and cheaper in price.[37] Jordi Nadal cites a reference to the Bonaplata mill, which was burned down by rioters in 1835, as the starting point of a 'true industrial revolution'.[38]

Between 1836 and 1840 Spain imported 1,229 machines, including twenty-three steam engines, ninety-two spinning machines, and 966 jacquards. After 1841, when Britain at last lifted its ban on the export of machinery, imports of machinery into Spain rose considerably. In 1841 only 231 out of the country's 25,111 looms were mechanically operated; by 1850 the number had risen to 5,580 out of 29,588, while in 1861 nearly half Spain's looms (9,695 out of 21,721) were mechanically operated. In line with developments elsewhere, the mechanisation of cotton spinning in Catalonia was even more rapid that that of cotton weaving. The number of mechanised spindles rose steeply from 27,220 in 1835 to 763,051 in 1861, while the total number of spindles increased only marginally, from 719,169 to 770,417, in the same period. Thus within a quarter of a century there was an almost complete mechanisation of the spinning section, although it was not until the 1860s that the less efficient mule jenny gave way to the self-acting machine.[39]

The reduction in the price of Catalan textiles, which was noted by the Factories Commission, went a great deal of the way to securing the extension of the national market sought after by the previous generation of manufacturers. It was undoubtedly helped by the disentailing process, the effect of which was to increase the spending power of the rural population. In response to the growing demand for cotton textiles, imports of raw cotton into Barcelona, the main port of entry, increased sixfold from the time of the construction of the Bonaplata mill to the eve of the cotton famine caused by the American civil war.

Two of the most significant effects on the mid-century expansion of the Catalan cotton industry were the changing pattern of its geographical location and the sharp contraction in the number of firms. The first of these effects was a product of the growing importance of imports of raw cotton and of the coal which was used to fuel the steam engines. The cotton industry was particularly strengthened in the ports of entry, above all

Table 15   Machines in use in the Catalan cotton industry, 1835–61

	1835	1841	1850	1861
Spinning				
Manually operated spindles (Berga-danas or jennies)	691,949	315,162	183,778	7,366
Mule jennies	27,220	323,937	475,490	?
Continuous	–	22,744	51,040	?
Self-acting	–	–	96,328	?
Total	27,220	346,681	622,858	763,051
Total spindles	719,169	661,843	806,636	770,417
Weaving				
Manually operated looms	?	24,880	24,008	12,026
Mechanically operated looms	?	231	5,580	9,695
Total looms	?	25,111	29,588	21,721

Source. Jordi Nadal and Enric Ribas, 'Una empresa algodonera catalana: la fábrica "De La Rambla" de Vilanova, 1841–61', Annales Cisalpines d'Histoire Sociale, 1 (1970), 75.

Barcelona, and along the more accessible valleys of the rivers Ter, Llob-regat, Fluviá and Cardoner. The locality of Igualada in the interior of the region, which rose to prominence because of its water supplies, presents a classic example of a declining mill town in this period and contrasts sharply with the locality of Vilanova on the Costa de Garraf, which was best placed to take advantage of coal imports from Britain. In 1850 Igualada occupied second place in Catalonia in terms of the number of spindles, of which it possessed 63,500, divided among fifty-four enter-prises, out of a regional total of 806,636. Eleven years later Igualada had only 15,516 spindles, shared between thirteen enterprises out of a total of 770,417. The main victims of this rapid decline were the small factories and workshops using the bergadanas, which were hit by the onset of mechanisation. In contrast the number of machines in Vilanova trebled between 1850 and 1861: the quantity of mechanised spindles increased from 17,436 to 47,792 while the total of mechanised looms also rose from 359 to 1,107.[40]

The concentration of the industry into fewer hands was the result of the increasing cost of machinery. In 1841 there were 4,470 establishments in Catalonia, employing 81,169 workers, an average of 18·6 per factory. Nine years later, with the spread of the mechanical loom and the self-acting spinning machine, the number of enterprises had fallen by over two-thirds

Table 16   Imports of raw cotton into the port of Barcelona, 1792–1861 (metric tons)

Year	Imports	Year	Imports
1792	1,144	1842	4,933
1793	750	1843	2,672
		1844	7,088
1816	867	1845	15,419
1817	1,109	1846	6,898
1818	1,137	1847	7,426
1819	1,996	1848	10,753
1820	2,013	1849	12,351
		1850	15,271
1824	1,971	1851	14,768
		1852	15,958
1827	2,782	1853	14,968
		1854	14,647
1834	3,416	1855	17,131
1835	2,912	1856	25,808
1836	3,682	1857	14,217
1837	4,342	1858	18,767
1838	5,178	1859	21,773
1839	3,740	1860	21,203
1840	8,387	1861	20,053
1841	8,449		

Source. Jordi Nadal and Enric Ribas, 'Una empresa algodonera catalana: la fábrica "De La Rambla" de Vilanova, 1841–61', p. 74.

to 1,471, while the labour force fell slightly to 75,436. The statistics for 1861 indicated that the number of enterprises had more or less stabilised at 1,455, while the labour force rose by over a third to 104,000, an average of 71·5 workers per factory.[41]

Although most factories employed between ten and twenty workers, it was in these years that the great textile enterprises of Catalonia were founded, including the firms of José Coma and Saury, Baurel y Cía in 1838, the Vapor Vell, founded in 1840 by Juan Güell with the fortunes he had made in Cuba, the spinning concern of Fernando Puig (later Sert Hermanos y Solá) in 1846, and the largest enterprise in Spain, España Industrial, founded in 1847 by the seven Muntada brothers.

Together with leading financiers in the region, such as Girona and Arnús, these great family firms, whose fortunes were often enlarged by intermarriage, formed a powerful and vociferous political lobby christened the grupo catalán in Madrid.[42] In Spanish politics, Catalan businessmen tended to support the Moderate party, which imposed the French system of political centralism on the country. Their quid pro quo for this support was the maintenance of the system of tariff protection in defence of regional industry, with which they were rewarded until the revolution of 1868 brought to power a new political alliance which favoured free trade.

In spite of the great progress of the Catalan textile industry, which took it to fourth place in the world behind Britain, France and the United States and ahead of Belgium and Italy by the middle of the century, the new industrial elite of Catalonia was well aware that the great weakness of the region's industrial structure was it lack of diversification. Even as late as the first decade of the present century the amount of capital invested in the cotton industry was four times as great as that invested in the woollen industry and six times as large as that of the metallurgical sector.[43]

The woollen industry installed its first mechanical loom in Sabadell in 1832 and its first steam engine in 1838. However, the impact of the cotton boom in the succeeding decade meant that as late as 1851 this emerging centre of the Spanish woollen industry, along with Tarrasa, still contained more cotton mills (sixty-three) than woollen mills (fifty-eight). However, as the process of mechanisation in the cotton industry spread into the valleys of the Llobregat and Cardoner, the outmoded cotton enterprises of these two towns were killed off, leading to a subsequent specialisation in woollens. In 1862, the year of the cotton famine, there were 142 woollen mills in Sabadell and only eight cotton mills; four years later, in 1866, there were 193 of the former and fourteen of the latter. Sabadell alone employed 8,000 workers in its woollen industry in 1871 and contained 50,000 spindles and 1,070 looms.[44]

The attempt to diversify its industrial structure led to an enthusiastic search for raw materials, especially coal and iron, within the Principality in the period from 1830 to 1850. Over sixty companies were formed for this purpose in the 1830s. Yet, apart from small deposits of lignite discovered at Fígols and La Pobla de Lillet, anthracite at Desaigües in Tarragona, and poor-quality coal at San Juan de las Abadesas, the results were disappointing. At the end of the century Catalonia produced 60,000 tons of lignite a year, whereas she annually imported one million tons of British coal.[45]

The coming of the railways provided a further incentive for diversification. Undaunted by the meagre success of the prospectors, the region gave birth to the first great Spanish metallurgical concern, La Maquinista Terrestre y Marítima of Barcelona, which was established in 1855 with a capital of 20 million reales. The boom of 1855–57 also encouraged the launching of other metallurgical companies, among them the Fundición Barcelona de Bronces and the Herrería Barcelonesa, which grew up in competition with La Maquinista. It was hoped that the new industry would serve a dual purpose, to supply the textile industry and to develop its own momentum. However, in common with the Basque metallurgical industry, it soon became the victim of the liberalising legislation which allowed the free entry of railway materials into Spain. In its initial years of expansion, even the ambitious Maquinista was forced to restrict its production to textile machinery (in competition with Britain, which paid 2 per cent duty), small boats and marine engines. During the railway boom of 1856–66 it did not construct a single locomotive, nor did it produce a single length of track.[46]

THE CASE OF VALENCIA

If Catalonia failed to build on the base of the textile industry to achieve all-round growth in the mid-nineteenth century, Valencia presents us with the even more surprising case of an economy which failed to take off at all. By the middle of the nineteenth century the region of Valencia had all the necessary pre-conditions to embark upon an industrial revolution. It had an expanding population which had increased from 934,724 in 1794 to 1,246,270 in 1857. There existed a qualified labour force trained over the previous century in artisan skills. In 1837, five years after the construction of the Bonaplata mill in Barcelona, the first steam engine was installed in the region, at Patraix, in a factory capable of providing jobs for 400 silk spinners. The first railway was built from Valencia to El Grao in 1852, four years after a similar stretch of line was opened from Barcelona to Mataró, and three years before the line from Gijón to Langreo. In 1868 the city of Valencia was linked by rail to Barcelona and thence to the French border. Moreover, there existed a powerful group of financial institutions in the País Valenciano, including the Sociedad de Crédito Valenciano, founded in 1858 with a capital of 24 million reales; the Caja Mercantil de Valencia, established in 1864 with 7·5 million pesetas; and the Crédito Mercantil de Valencia, founded in the same year with a capital of 6 million pesetas. Despite all these factors, the Valencian economy failed to develop. There were only exceptions, such as the flourishing ceramics industry of the capital, the traditional industries of Alcoy, and the transformation of rope-sandal making in Elche into a modern footwear industry.

The traditional explanation of the decline of the Valencian silk industry, which might have formed the basis for an economic take-off, blames the attack of *pébrine*, a parasite of the silk worm, which struck in 1854 and had its maximum impact in 1865. The lack of raw silk which resulted from the disease of the silk worm was widely accredited with having caused the disappearance of the silk industry. Emili Giralt, however, argues that the real reason for its decline must be sought in the under-capitalisation of firms, the lack of modern equipment (which would have allowed home production to compete with imports), and the lack of tariff protection. Consumer demand within Spain for silk goods rose considerably in this period: yet, unlike France and Italy, this demand was not met by raw material imports.[47]

It would also appear that a good deal of the capital previously accumulated in the region was invested not in industry but in the purchase of land,
whose agricultural potential offered far greater security to the investor.
Between 1837 and 1845 252 million reales were spent on the acquisition of
disentailed ecclesiastical property in the País Valenciano. After 1855 all
we know is that 122 million reales were given over to the purchase of the
remaining ecclesiastical land. To this we must add whatever was spent on
the acquisition of common lands, while, in addition, subsequent agricultural improvements were to take large amounts of middle-class savings.[48]

THE ECONOMIC CRISIS OF 1866 AND THE 1868 REVOLUTION

The period from the end of the First Carlist War to the crisis of 1866 has
been widely considered as one of general prosperity, interupted only by
the intermittent crises of 1847–49 and 1856–58. Behind this wave of
prosperity, it is argued, was the disentailing legislation, which increased
both agricultural production and internal spending power on consumer
goods, and the mobilisation of credit. However, it is clear that the 1866
crisis, which had a profound effect on the Spanish economy and society,
soon put a brake on this development.

The prime mover of industrial progress in the 1840s and early '50s was
the cotton textile industry, where mechanisation produced a growing
amount of cloth at falling prices which was consumed by an expanding
home market. In the following decade large foreign investments caused
the cotton euphoria to be replaced by the railway boom. Nevertheless, by
the early and mid-'60s both these innovatory (or potentially innovatory)
sectors were threatened; the textile industry after 1862 by the cotton
famine caused by the American civil war, and railway construction after
1864 by declining expectations of profit. The railway companies
announced that prosperity could disappear at any moment.

When the inevitable financial crash came in May 1866 it was felt most
severely in Barcelona, whose stock market had become over-committed to
railway promotion.[49] The Overend Gurney collapse of 1866 had no direct
repercussions in Spain, although the crisis on the London money market
underlined the dangers of allowing foreign exploitation, as raw material
prices fell, seriously affecting Spain's balance of payments. In the following year the harvest failed, giving rise to a famine in 1868, in this case
exposing the weakness of the liberal agrarian reforms. This first crisis of
Spanish capitalism seriously threatened all those who opposed the Moderate party. In the forefront of those willing to overthrow the established
political system were the railway companies, the breeding ground of many
of the leading figures of the Restoration, men like Sagasta, Cánovas, Mon-
tero Ríos, and the father of the future Liberal leader Canalejas.[50] On 12
January 1867 the noted writer and influential Progressive, Pascual Madoz,

wrote to his friend the conspirator General Prim, 'The situation in the country is bad, very bad. Credit collapsed. Rural and urban wealth severely diminished. Businesses have gone bankrupt, and I do not know what can save us from this conflict . . . No one pays because no one can pay. If you sell no one buys, not even it you give the thing away at fifty per cent of its cost.'[51] Thus the industrial revolution manqué of the mid-nineteenth century contributed to the political revolution of 1868.

NOTES

1 Gabriel Tortella Casares, Los orígenes del capitalismo en España (Madrid, 1973), p. 3.
2 See above, chapter two.
3 Gabriel Torella Casares, 'Spain 1829–74', in Rondo Cameron (ed.), Banking and Economic Development: Some Lessons of History (New York, 1972), p. 95.
4 Ramón Santillán, Memoria histórica sobre los bancos de San Carlos, Español de San Fernando, Isabel II, y de España, 2 vols (Madrid, 1865), I, pp. 234–5.
5 Nadal, The Failure of the Industrial Revolution in Spain, p. 608.
6 José María Tallada Paulí, Historia de las finanzas españolas en el siglo XIX (Madrid, 1946), pp. 229–31.
7 Gabriel Tortella Casares, 'El principio de responsibilidad limitada y el desarrollo industrial de España, 1829–69', Moneda y Crédito, 104 (1968), 69–84.
8 Gabriel Tortella Casares, 'La evolución del sistema financiero español de 1856 a 1868', Ensayos sobre la economía española a mediados del siglo XIX, pp. 26–39.
9 Nicolás Sánchez Albornoz, 'De los orígenes del capital financiero: La Sociedad General de Crédito Mobiliario Español, 1856–1902', España hace un siglo: una economía dual, pp. 179–218.
10 Tortella, La evolución del sistema financiero español de 1856 a 1868, p. 102.
11 Rafael Anes Álvarez, 'Las inversiones extranjeras en España de 1855 a 1880', in Ensayos sobre la economía española a mediados del siglo XIX, p. 189; Francisco Waís San Martín, Historia general de los ferrocarriles españoles, 1830–1941 (Madrid, 1967), pp. 63–80.
12 Tortella, Orígenes del capitalismo en España, p. 177.
13 Rondo Cameron, France and the Economic Development of Europe, 1800–1914: Conquest of Peace and Seeds of War (Princeton, 1961), p. 249.
14 Ibid., p. 251.
15 Ibid., pp. 252–3.
16 Ibid., pp. 254–5.
17 Tortella, Orígenes del capitalismo en España, pp. 11–12.
18 Cameron, France and the Economic Development of Europe, p. 212.
19 Tortella, Orígenes del capitalismo en España, p. 12.
20 Jordi Nadal, 'Los comienzos de la industrialización española (1832–1868): la industria siderúgica', Ensayos sobre la economía española a mediados del siglo XIX, pp. 211–15.
21 Información sobre el derecho diferencial de bandera y sobre los de Aduanas exigible a los hierros . . ., vol. II, Hierros (Madrid, 1867), pp. 136 and 307, cited in Nadal, Los comienzos de la industrialización española, p. 216.
22 Tortella, La evolución del sistema financiero español, pp. 95–101.

23   Andre Gunder Frank, *Capitalism and Underdevelopment in Latin America* (Harmondsworth, 1971).

24   Jordi Nadal, 'Industrialización y desindustrialización del sureste español, 1817–1913', *Moneda y Crédito*, 120 (1972), 4–6.

25   *Ibid.*, pp. 6–9; Josep Fontana, 'Colapso y transformación del comercio exterior español entre 1792 y 1827: un aspecto de la crisis del antiguo régimen en España', *Moneda y Crédito*, 115 (1970), 13.

26   Nadal, *Industrialización y desindustrialización del sureste español*, pp. 11–14 and 60–2.

27   *Ibid.*, pp. 60–5.

28   W. G. Lawson, *The Rio Tinto Mine* (London, 1904); S. G. Checkland, *The Mines of Tharsis: Roman, French, and British Enterprise in Spain* (London, 1967).

29   Nadal, *Industrialización y desindustrialización del sureste español*, pp. 22–37.

30   Nadal, *The Failure of the Industrial Revolution in Spain*, pp. 601–2.

31   *Ibid.*, p. 602: Francisco Sánchez Ramos, *La economía siderúrgica española*, vol. I. *Estudio crítico de la historia industrial de España hasta 1900* (Madrid, 1945), pp. 141–66.

32   Lequerica, *op. cit.*, p. 47; Pablo de Alzola y Minondo, *Monografía de los caminos y ferrocarriles de Vizcaya* (Bilbao, 1898), pp. 119–20; and, by the same author, *Memoria relativa al estado de la industria siderúrgica en España* (Bilbao, 1896) pp. 10 ff.

33   Pablo de Alzola y Minondo, *Progreso industrial de Vizcaya* (Bilbao, 1902), p. 77.

34   José Alcalá Zamora y Quiepo de Llano, 'Producción de hierro y altos hornos en la España anterior a 1850', *Moneda y Crédito*, 128 (1974), 194.

35   Luis García San Miguel, *De la sociedad aristocrática a la sociedad industrial en la España del siglo XIX* (Madrid, 1973); Nadal, *The Failure of the Industrial Revolution in Spain*, pp. 585–90.

36   Fontana, *Colapso y transformación del comercio exterior español*, pp. 20–4; Miguel Izard, *Industrialización y obrerismo: Las Tres Clases de Vapor, 1869–1913* (Barcelona, 1973), pp. 36–7.

37   Graell, *op. cit.*, pp. 38–44.

38   J. Yllas y Vidal, *Memoria sobre los perjuicios que ocasionaría en España . . . la adopción del sistema de libre cambio* (Barcelona, 1849) p. 50; cited in Jordi Nadal and Enric Ribas, 'Una empresa algodonera catalana: 'la fábrica "De la rambla" de Vilanova, 1841–61', *Annales Cisalpines d'Histoire Sociale*, I (1970), 77.

39   Nadal and Ribas, *Una empresa algodonera catalana*, pp. 75–6.

40   *Ibid.*, pp. 77–8.

41   Izard, *op. cit.*, p. 43.

42   Vicens Vives, *Cataluña en el siglo XIX*, pp. 83 and 194–7.

43   J. Vilá Valentí, 'El origen de la industria catalana moderna', *Estudios Geográficos*, 78 (1960), 31.

44   Vicens Vives, *Cataluña en el siglo XIX*, p. 94.

45   *Ibid.*, p. 100.

46   Alberto del Castillo, *La Maquinista Terrestre y Marítima, 1855–1955* (Barcelona, 1956).

47   Giralt, *op. cit.*, pp. 381–2.

48   *Ibid.*, pp. 385–8.

49   Nicolás Sánchez Albornoz, 'La crisis financiera de 1866 en Barcelona', in *España hace un siglo: una economía dual*, pp. 153–5.

50   Josep Fontana, 'Cambio económico y crisis política: reflexiones sobre las causas de la revolución de 1868', in *Cambio económico y actitudes políticas en la España del siglo XIX*, pp. 116–18.
51   V. Álvarez Villamill and R. Llopis, *Cartas de conspiradores: la revolución de setiembre* (Madrid, 1929), pp. 274–5, quoted in Nicolás Sánchez Albornoz, 'El trasfondo económico de la Revolución', *Revista de Occidente*, xxiii (1968), 59.

CHAPTER 4

The emergence of a modern economy, 1875–1914

THE RESTORATION

The bourgeois revolution of 1868 created a political vacuum which was to remain unfilled for a period of seven years in spite of two heroic but abortive attempts to introduce new forms of government into the country: the constitutional monarchy of Amadeo I, who reigned only briefly, from November 1870 to February 1873, and the ill fated First Federal Republic of 1873, which had four presidents in the eleven months of its existence. Inevitably this spell of political instability proved an obstacle to material progress. This was certainly the case in the north, where the Carlists took advantage of the lack of firm government to declare a state of siege. Thus the restoration of the Bourbon monarchy in December 1874 was widely acclaimed by the economic community. A generation of Basque entrepreneurs, in particular, paid homage to Antonio Cánovas, architect of the Restoration settlement, for re-establishing a climate of peace and order which prepared the way for prosperity.[1] In the case of Catalonia the *febre d'or* caused by the massive increase in the wine exports brought great benefits to all sections of the economic life of the region and went some way to overcome the inelastic demands of the Spanish peasantry for Catalan manufactures. The achievement is all the more remarkable when we remember that this small measure of progress took place at a time when the major economies of western Europe languished under the so-called Great Depression, which was to drag on for more than twenty years.

As we have seen from the precarious situation of the wheatlands of Castile, whose very livelihood was threatened by the arrival of cheap and plentiful supplies of grain from North America and Russia, not everywhere in the Peninsula joined in the Restoration boom.[2] The south-east, after its halcyon days of the middle of the nineteenth century, was dwarfed by developments in the north and entered what Jordi Nadal terms a phase of 'disindustrialisation'.[3] Moreover the limitations of Spanish economic development in the early and middle years of the Restoration are demonstrated by an analysis of census data. From 1877 to 1910 the country's active population remained remarkably stagnant. The only pattern that can be discerned is a slight trend away from agriculture to industry, with the service sector remaining basically unaltered.

Table 17 Occupation of the active labour force according to census data, 1877–1910 (%)

Year	Agriculture	Industry	Services
1877	70	11	19
1887	66·5	14·6	18·7
1900	66·34	15·99	17·67
1910	66·00	15·82	18·18

In addition, Catalonia continued to dominate Spanish industry in terms of employment, although it is impossible to give exact figures. According to local surveys of 1905 the working population of Barcelona stood at 144,788 and that of Madrid at 97,140. Escarra put the active population of Catalonia at that time at 300,000. By comparison, the province of Vizcaya, which made the most noteable advances in terms of technology and organisation, had only 20,000 workers at the beginning of the century, the same total as was accredited to Asturias in 1909.[4]

The early Restoration brought a consolidation in the fortunes of the Catalan textile industry. Imports of raw cotton rose from 33,000 tons in 1875 to 54,000 tons in 1883, an annual increase of almost 8 per cent. Soon however, the restricted purchasing power of the rural community led to a sharp decline in the rate of expansion of the cotton industry. Between 1883 and 1889 raw cotton imports rose from 54,000 tons to 63,000 tons, an increase of less than 3 per cent a year.[5]

Behind this new crisis were two important developments; the end of the wine exporting euphoria following the appearance of phylloxera in the Principality in 1885, and the growing tendency on the part of Restoration governments towards a policy of free trade. Eighteen eighty-two saw the drawing up of the Franco–Spanish commercial treaty, which was largely inspired by the landowners of the south, who sought to increase their own exports of wine as a quid pro quo for the easy entry of French manufactures. This provoked a hostile reaction from the protectionist industrial bourgeoisie of Catalonia, who were moved in 1885 to court the support of religious and cultural groups in the region in writing a memorandum to Alfonso XII in defence of the moral and material interests of Catalonia.[6] Four years later, heartened by the initial support for such an initiative, the leading employers' associations of the region joined together to form what was to become the most influential pressure group in Spain, the Fomento del Trabajo Nacional.

After 1880 the textile manufacturers of Catalonia turned increasingly to the remaining colonial markets of Cuba, Puerto Rico and the Philippines in order to maintain their existing growth rates. In alliance with the flour exporters of Santander, they lobbied central government, from whom they obtained two major concessions, the Law on Commercial Relations with the Antilles of July 1882, which for customs purposes considered the overseas provinces as part of the Spanish mainland, and the Cuban and Puerto Rican tariffs of 1891 and 1892 respectively, which raised substantial barriers against import into the colonies from outside Spain. Both of these measures were directed against the United States, which was in a far better position geographically and for other reasons to supply her near neighbours, and thus earn back some of the expenditure that went on the purchase of sugar and cigars.

Table 18   Spanish exports to Cuba, Puerto Rico and the Philippines, 1891–99 (million pesetas)

Year	Cuba	Puerto Rico	Philippines
1891	114·9	17·1	14·1
1892	145·3	20·4	18·9
1893	127·9	24·1	22·7
1894	117·1	28·7	28·6
1895	136·3	44·4	25·8
1896	255·9	43·1	41·3
1897	252·9	33·1	79·4
1898	67·4	14·0	27·9
1899	73·8	17·6	11·7

Source. El Trabajo Nacional, 1908, pp. 424–6.

From 1891 until their loss in 1898, exports of Spanish products to the colonies more than doubled. The part played by Catalonia in this short-lived spree was considerable. Figures for 1895 show that the port of Barcelona exported 124 million pesetas of goods to the overseas possessions. Exports of manufactured goods were valued at 108 million pesetas, of which 39 million were yarn and textiles and 24 million footwear.[7]

The scale of operations in the Catalan cotton industry was small by European standards. At the beginning of the present century the largest cotton mill in Catalonia contained only 25,000 spindles, 900 looms and 20 printing machines. Other leading mills had from 5,000 to 15,000 spindles and between 100 and 400 looms. In both Britain and France, by comparison, the average spinning establishment at the turn of the century contained 50,000 spindles. Moreover, measured by the total number of spindles in use, the Spanish industry was almost insignificant internationally. In 1907 Spain possessed 1·85 million spindles (over half of which did not produce for the market), whereas the British spinning section was over twenty times as big, with 43·16 million spindles. Elsewhere Germany had 9·19 million spindles, France 6·61 million, while even Italy, a comparative newcomer to the cotton industry, had 2·87 million spindles. If we take as our yardstick the number of bales of cotton imported from the United States, Britain in 1906, with 3,996,119 bales, took over fifteen times as much raw material as Spain, which took 275,868 bales.[8]

Two of the most striking aspects of the relative backwardness of Catalan industry were the almost complete absence of joint-stock companies and the limited recourse to borrowing of industrial enterprises. At the turn of the century the Barcelona stock exchange had only fifteen registered joint-stock companies, compared with a total of 1,000 for Spain as a whole (mainly assurance, public utility and mining companies). Moreover, although there were a number of banks represented in Catalonia, including the Banks of Barcelona, Sabadell, Tarrasa, the Hispano Americano and the Hispano Colonial, not to mention branches of foreign banks, the role they played in industrial development was very restricted. It is difficult to know whether to blame the banks for their antiquated procedures, or Catalan businessmen for their lack of financial acumen. Most of the family firms of the Principality financed their own developments out of profits. According to the chairman of the spinning section of the Fomento del Trabajo Nacional, their owners were far too honourable, dignified and obstinate to append their signatures to commercial contracts.[9]

Although secondary to the cotton textile industry, Catalan woollens firmly established themselves in the home market during the Restoration. By 1900 there were approximately 200,000 spindles and between 3,500 and 4,000 looms in Catalonia which gave employment to some 25,000 workers, one-third of the number of workers in Catalan cotton mills. In addition the woollen manufacturers of Tarrasa and Sabadell also began to seek outlets abroad. Thus in 1891 the Bank of Sabadell opened a branch in Buenos Aires which was to serve as a bridgehead for the town's woollen exports. These efforts, however, met with little success, and only small quantities of woollens were exported.[10]

Measured in terms of export earnings, one of the most successful industries of late nineteenth-century Catalonia was the cork industry, which enjoyed something of a golden age in the 1890s. This was in response to a rising demand for cork stoppers from the vintners and brewers of France, Germany, Britain and a number of other European countries. Exports of cork stoppers increased from 1,416 millions in 1889 to 3,300 millions in 1900. However, this praiseworthy achievement was due to traditional unmechanised modes of production. The cork industry of Catalonia at this time was overwhelmingly an artisan industry, with over 800 separate establishments centred around San Feliú de Guixols, Palamós and Port Bou. Although cork-cutting machinery was introduced into San Feliú as early as 1880, the process of mechanisation did not become widespread until the early twentieth century.[11]

Table 19   Principal industries of Catalonia at the beginning of the twentieth
century (value in millions of pesetas)

Industry	Capital employed	Total value of production	Exports	Numbers employed
Cotton	460	424	49·7	83,900
Woollens	100	82	3·0	25,000
Chemicals	17	13	–	1,400
Linen	35	28	2·5	2,400
Silk	28	30	3·0	3,000
Paper	14	17	6·5	2,500
Metallurgy and electrical	80	72	0·5	11,000
Cork stoppers	35	55	30·0	12,000
Footwear and leather	20	22	2·3	1,500
Flour milling	26	40	–	2,000
Cement	20	11	–	3,200
Mosaics	5·5	4·5	2·0	2,000
Alcohol	9	11	–	700
Total	849·5	809·5	99·5	151,000

Source. Frederico Rahola y Trémols, 'Del comerç i de la industria de Catalunya',
in F. Carreras y Candi, Geografia general de Catalunya (Barcelona, 1913),
pp. 460–1.

The Catalan metallurgical industry made steady progress at this time.
The 1880s saw the establishment of a number of modern, well equipped
concerns, including the Material para Ferrocarriles y Construcciones in
1881 and the Arsenal Civil in 1887, both of which derived considerable
benefit from the protectionist legislation of 1891. After 1882 the
Maquinista Terreste y Marítima began to produce its first locomotives.
Thus, despite the cyclical crisis of 1886–96, the industry succeeded in
building up its capital stock. However, the continuing backwardness of
the Catalan metallurgial sector was highlighted by the absence of even the
smallest blast furnace in the Principality by the turn of the century.[12]
   In the long term probably the most significant development in the
energy-deprived region of Catalonia was the formation of a number of
companies for the generation of electricity. The high cost and level of
technological expertise required in this field led to the introduction of
management skills and finance from outside into a region which had
previously clung rigidly to its independence from foreign capitalist penetration. The first major electricity-producing enterprise founded in the
Principality was the Sociedad Española de Electricidad, established in
Barcelona in 1881. This was later joined by a number of foreign concerns,
including the Cía Anglo Española de Electricidad, founded in 1882; a

branch of Siemens & Halske of Berlin, in 1890; and the Barcelona de Electricidad, which was formed by the German company AEG in 1894 by absorbing the original Sociedad Española. At first the potential of electricity was not fully realised in Catalonia. By the late '80s it was used only in street lighting in Barcelona, along with the illumination of some of the more fashionable theatres and cafés. Later it was used as the motive power for the city's trams.[13]

Nevertheless, on the eve of the loss of Cuba the Catalan business community was generally defective in entrepreneural initiative. Instead of pressing ahead with the transformation of the Catalan countryside, whose surplus labour was employed in their factories, the industrialists of the Principality by and large perferred to settle for the easy benefits of tariff protection in the home and colonial markets.[14]

In February 1876 the Carlists abandoned the left bank of the Nervión, thus permitting the reopening of the port of Bilbao. This was the prelude to a massive upsurge of exports of iron ore and formed a solid base for Vizcayan prosperity in the late nineteenth century. Between 1876 and 1901 98·6 million tons of ore were extracted in the province, 90 per cent of which was exported, three-fifths of it to Great Britain. Estimates of the value of the ore exports vary greatly. The impressionable young regenerationist Ramiro de Maeztu claimed that earnings from mineral exports from Vizcaya before 1901 amounted to 1,000 million pesetas; but a recent calculation by Manuel González Portilla puts the total at the seemingly more realistic figure of 574 million pesetas between 1876 and 1900. In the peak year of ore exports of 1899, 5·41 million tons of mineral were shipped through the port of Bilbao, compared with a national output of only 8·61 million tons.[15]

The profits of the iron trade were partly utilised by the business community of Vizcaya in the creation of what was by Spanish standards an advanced industrial structure of joint-stock and limited liability companies. In this process of the emergence of modern Basque industrialism, the banks played an active role in the mobilisation of capital, with the Bank of Bilbao, the leading financial institution in the north, quadrupling its own capital in the years from its foundation in 1857 to the turn of the century. From the 1880s onwards the enterprising capitalist class of Bilbao were to put to shame many of the conservative family businessmen of Barcelona.

The first of the new concerns, the San Francisco ironworks, was opened in 1879 at El Desierto, ten miles from Bilbao in the marshes at Sestao. Within five years of its inception its four coke-fired blast furnaces yielded 56,454 tons of cast iron, nearly half the total Spanish output. The excellent results which it obtained led to the foundation of even larger metallurgical concerns which together totally eclipsed the previously dominant Asturian iron industry.

During the second half of 1882 two major limited liability companies were set up in Vizcaya. September 1882 saw the foundation of the metal-lurgical and construction company La Vizcaya with a capital of 12·5 million pesetas and a set of ambitious proposals for the construction of large-scale furnaces to make steel by the Siemens process. This steel was to be destined for the construction of railway lines and of steel hulls for the developing shipbuilding industry. Three months later, in December 1882, the firm of Ibarra y Cía which already owned a number of mines at Guriezo and Saltacaballo, transformed itself into a joint-stock company under the name of Altos Hornos y Fábricas de Hierro y Acero de Bilbao. The new company had a capital of 25 million pesetas, of which half was in shares and half in bonds. Among its grandiose plans Altos Hornos proposed the construction of a new factory at Baracaldo, eight kilometres from Bilbao, at the confluence of the rivers Nervión and Galindo. The new plant, Nuestra Señora del Carmen, was to contain two blast furnaces of 'colossal' dimen-sions by contemporary Spanish standards which would produce enough iron to make one thousand tons of steel ingots a week by the Bessemer process, and three Siemens–Martin furnaces of twelve tons capacity which would produce enough iron to make 18,000 tons of steel a year.[16] Moreover, such was the progress of these two 'giants' that when they merged with La Iberia in 1902 to form Altos Hornos de Vizcaya, the resulting complex covered 150 acres of land, with fifty kilometres of railway track and two kilometres of dock frontage on the Bilbao Ría. Altos Hornos de Vizcaya also contained seven blast furnaces with a daily pro-duction of 600 tons of pig iron, four Bessemer converters and seven Siemens–Martin furnaces with a total annual production of 150,000 tons of steel, a number of rolling mills (seventeen in 1909) which produced 180,000 tons of sheet steel, and a variety of forges, foundaries and boiler-making shops which together employed some 6,000 workers.[17]

The expansion of these two great firms, Altos Hornos and La Vizcaya, and their eventual amalgamation was probably the most significant indus-trial development of the first half of the Restoration, comparable with the emergence of the Catalan textile industry half a century before. Yet we must not be carried away by this single achievement. At the height of the iron trade in 1899 less than a tenth of the mineral produced in Vizcaya was consumed locally. Apart from these two firms there were a number of smaller concerns which sprang up in the 1880s specialising in the manu-facture of a wide range of products, including iron and steel tubes, nuts and bolts, railway rolling stock and engines for steamships. However, their contribution to total output was negligible. As late as 1897 six of the fourteen principal blast furnaces in the three Basque provinces of Vizcaya, Alava and Guipúzcoa were still fired by charcoal.[18]

In acknowledgement of their newly acquired wealth, the leaders of Basque industry were welcomed into the ruling oligarchy of Restoration

Table 20   Iron ore production in Vizcaya, 1876–1901 ('000 tons)

Year	Exports via Bilbao	Coastal trade	Local consumption	Total production
1876	350	10	40	400
1877	750	10	40	800
1878	1,225	29	50	1,303
1879	1,119	30	50	1,198
1880	2,346	39	60	2,445
1881	2,501	50	60	2,612
1882	3,693	47	60	3,800
1883	3,379	47	100	3,526
1884	3,153	38	300	3,491
1885	3,296	41	500	3,837
1886	3,160	44	500	3,704
1887	4,164	27	500	4,692
1888	3,592	41	500	4,133
1889	3,886	18	500	4,403
1890	4,273	23	500	4,796
1891	3,357	24	500	3,881
1892	3,998	27	550	4,575
1893	4,182	31	550	4,763
1894	3,790	56	550	4,396
1895	4,037	34	550	4,621
1896	4,827	46	550	5,423
1897	4,577	52	550	5,179
1898	4,348	62	550	4,960
1899	5,413	32	560	6,004
1900	4,633	47	550	5,230
1901	4,030	43	550	4,623

Source. Julio de Lazúrtegui, *Ensayo sobre la cuestión de los minerales de hierro* (Bilbao, 1910), p. 95.

Spain. Among those who were particularly prominent in national politics were the ironmasters. The founder of La Vizcaya, Víctor Chávarri, became the Liberal party boss (*cacique*) for the district of Valmaseda, while the Ibarra family, founders of Altos Hornos, retained political control of the Baracaldo constituency on behalf of the Conservatives. Moreover the new industrial elite of Vizcaya were lavishly honoured by the Restoration regime; witness the bestowing of such titles as the Marqués de Triano, the *condes* de Cadagua and the Marqueses de Arriluce de Ibarra.

State patronage was not limited to the granting of titles to the active elements or *fuerzas vivas* of Vizcaya; the central government was also in a position to award contracts and make a number of concessions to Basque heavy industry. In 1888 the Spanish navy awarded a contract for the construction of three cruisers to the Anglo-Basque consortium Astilleros del Nervión, which comprised the San Franciso company and the Jarrow firm of Palmer's. The co-founder of the new group was none other than the Liberal deputy for Valmaseda, Martínez de Rivas. As to the vessels, the *Vizcaya*, *Almirante Oquendo* and *Infante María Teresa*, these were to be disastrously sunk with the rest of the Spanish squadron at Santiago de Cuba in the Spanish–American war of 1898.

Upon the announcement of the naval contract the Bilbao chamber of commerce proclaimed that the provincial capital was in the midst of an era of 'splendid prosperity', citing as evidence the inauguration of works for the outport of Bilbao and the whole series of companies which had recently been launched in the town.[19] All these developments did much to counter the growing rumours that in the not too distant future the iron ore mines, the very foundation of regional prosperity, would cease to be productive. These fears, first expressed in the mid-1880s with the exhaustion of the *vena* ores, echoed ever more loudly over the next two decades. In 1901 they were repeated by the British consul in Bilbao, who advised the Foreign Office that 'the iron ore mines in the immediate neighbourhood of Bilbao have seen their palmy days'.[20] Fortunately by that time new moves were afoot which would lessen Vizcaya's dependence on the iron trade.

THE LOSS OF THE LAST COLONIES

For diametrically opposite reasons the two leading industrial regions of Spain, Catalonia and Vizcaya, were dramatically affected by a tragic and painful event which took place in the fateful year of 1898. That event was the fiasco of the Spanish–American war, as a result of which a defeated Spain was deprived of her last remnants of empire. To the manufacturers of Catalonia, whose imperialism was most pronounced during the three-year Cuban campaign of 1895–98, the markets of Cuba, Puerto Rico and the Philippines appeared a necessary alternative to the deficiencies of the home market. Now they were finally forced to pay serious attention to the weaknesses of the Spanish economy. To the business community of Vizcaya, by comparison, the tragedy of 1898 brought nothing but benefits, short of a stock-market crisis of 1901 due to a wave of speculation in the prosperity of the province. In the past Vizcaya, with its emphasis on mineral exports to the developed world, had little commercial contact with the colonies and was thus in no way as hard hit as Catalonia; while the repatriation of the savings of Spanish *emigrés* recently returned from Cuba sparked off a massive increase in company promotion in Bilbao which led to the strengthening and diversification of Basque industry.

The extent of Catalonia's involvement in the markets of the remaining colonies was revealed by the disruptive effects on the Principality's trade of the Cuban revolt which began in 1895. In that year the British consul in

Barcelona wrote to the Foreign Office: 'Every branch of industry is suffering severely, and a financial crisis must soon come if an early change for the better does not take place. Both export and imports have decreased during the past year. The export of linen and cotton goods is practically stopped; the manufacturers have been obliged to discharge a large number of their workmen and pay lower wages to those they still employ. Several spinning and weaving establishments are completely closed, and many others will soon be in a state of forced idleness if the present state of things continues.'[21]

The report for 1896 was equally pessimistic: 'The rebellions in Cuba and Manila which have continued throughout the year, have to a great extent paralysed the commerce of Catalonia, as it is a manufacturing rather than an agricultural district, and the larger part of manufactured goods found a market in the Spanish colonies now completely closed to them. Everywhere in Catalonia mills have been closed, or worked short time with a diminished number of hands. As an example, take the town of Mataró, one of the principal manufacturing places of the district. Here we find out of eight factories making cotton goods, five only are working, and these with only one-third of their complement of workmen, and on average only four days a week, throwing 850 hands out of employment, and forty other factories which normally employ 8,000 hands are now working with half the number.'[22]

There were, nevertheless, some manufacturers who prospered from the wartime situation, including twenty-five companies that produced a cotton cloth called *rayadillo* which was worn by the troops in Cuba and the Philippines.[23] Moreover, even after the politicians had signed away the former colonies, the anticipated decline in the export of manufactured goods did not follow immediately. By a clause in the Paris peace treaty Spain obtained equal treatment with the United States, Cuba's new protector, in her trading relations with the island for a period of ten years. However, the Spanish system of tariff protection was dismantled forever: the Cuban market was now open to all comers.

In the immediate aftermath of the colonial *débâcle* a number of factors worked to the advantage of the manufacturers of Catalonia. It has been claimed that, in the markets of Spain's former colonies, commercial relations between Spanish manufacturers, export houses and their clientele were of sufficiently long standing to stave off a breakdown overnight, and the Catalan industrialists knew the tastes of those markets better than anyone else, whilst new competitors took a long time to adapt to them.[24] The British vice consul in Mahón, Minorca, noted that 'The manufacture of boots and shoes, the principal industry in the island, which so severely suffered in the war with the United States, recovered in 1899 its former importance, preserving the considerable market of Cuba, notwithstanding the exertions of the manufacturers of the United States to obtain it. This is due to the circumstances that the shape of the boots and shoes of America does not suit the tastes of the Cubans.'[25]

Table 21   Exports of cotton thread and textiles to Cuba, Puerto Rico and the Philippines, 1895–1902

| | Total | | To Cuba, Puerto Rico and Philippines | |
Year	Million pesetas	kg million	Million pesetas	kg million
1895	46·6	8·5	44·3	8·1
1896	60·4	10·6	56·6	9·9
1897	70·3	11·7	66·0	11·1
1898	44·9	6·9	34·5	5·4
1899	41·2	6·2	30·3	4·6
1900	37·6	6·1	27·9	4·2
1901	30·0	4·4	15·6	2·4
1902	28·9	4·2	15·7	2·3

Source. El Trabajo Nacional, 1 April 1904, p. 92.

Secondly, a fairly drastic fall in the exchange rate of the peseta, provoked by a drop in business confidence after the disastrous war with the United States, had the effect of encouraging Spanish exports while at the same time keeping out foreign competition. This unexpected side effect of the Cuban tragedy was noted by the British consul in Barcelona in his report to the Foreign Office for the year 1899: 'Owing to the fortunes of war Spain has lost to some extent the valuable markets of Cuba, Puerto Rico and Manila, but on the other hand thanks to her customs tariff and high rate of exchange, she has during the last twelve months enjoyed a complete monopoly of home markets.'[26]

Thirdly, the textile manufacturers of Catalonia were presented with an extraordinary increase in demand by the need to clothe the repatriated troops. The same consul noted that: 'About 200,000 soldiers returned to Spain from Cuba and Manila during the year [1899]; these men on arrival here were clothed in the usual drill suits used whilst campaigning in the tropics, but as they received on returning home the arrears of pay due to them, considerable sums were spent in new outfits, to the manifest advantage of the Barcelona shopkeepers.'[27]

Finally, a fourth short-term advantage in favour of manufacturing industry was the exceptional harvest of 1898 and the above-average yields of 1899, which significantly increased the purchasing power of rural consumers.

These favourable conditions could not continue indefinitely. By the year 1900 the strenuous efforts of Finance Minister Villaverde had stabilised the peseta at a little above its old parity, the defeated army had spent its back pay, the run of good harvests came to a sudden end and in Barcelona the threat of disruptive general strikes loomed large. By September 1900 the Fomento del Trabajo Nacional was already talking of factory closures throughout the province of Barcelona, of lay-offs and what it referred to as el short-time inglés.[28] The bad harvest in Castile in 1902 was judged partly responsible by the Fomento for the poor showing of Catalan industry in that year, while the agricultural depression of 1904–06, which was particularly pronounced in Andalusia, led to a further drop in domestic demand for Catalan manufacturers.[29]

The impact of labour unrest at this time is more difficult to assess. It is true that the general strike of 1902 begun by the metalworkers of Barcelona brought trade and industry to a standstill for a while; however, despite the activities of an increasingly militant and revolutionary proletariat, the industrial bourgeoisie of the region does not appear to have been seriously threatened by its labour force until the massive wave of working-class militancy after the first world war.[30] The Catholic investigator Miguel Sastre, writing of the city of Barcelona, showed that after the eventful year of 1903, when 52 million working days were lost in strikes, over the next decade the impact of strikes was far less dramatic.

Table 22   Number of days lost in strikes in Barcelona, 1903–14

1903	51,806,940	1909	28,045
1904	358,510	1910	854,692
1905	36,042	1911	451,118
1906	25,508	1912	266,490
1907	54,590	1913	1,886,265
1908	23,073	1914	411,116

Source. Miguel Sastre y Sanna, Las huelgas en Barcelona y sus resultados duante los años 1903–14 (Barcelona, 1904–15).

In his study of the period 1903–05 Sastre demonstrated the apparent ease with which the Barcelona employers put down labour unrest in the city. Of 123 strikes over the three years, two-thirds (eighty-one) ended in victory for the employers, one-sixth (twenty-one) in victory for the labour force while the same amount (twenty-one) ended in some form of compromise settlement.

One factor which encouraged the Catalan cotton manufacturers to be firm in their dealings with labour at this time was the mounting cost of raw cotton. In 1906 the president of the spinners' and weavers' section of the Fomento de Trabajo Nacional complained to an international conference in Bremen that American speculators were threatening the livelihood of Catalan mill owners by holding out for higher prices.[31]

Table 23   Conclusion of strikes in Barcelona, 1903–05

Year	Victory to employers	Victory to workers	Compromise	No. of sackings	No. of black-legs taken on
1903	45	12	17	2,040	469
1904	17	5	3	706	616
1905	19	4	1	127	133
Total	81	21	21	2,873	1,218

Source. Miguel Sastre y Sanna, *Las huelgas en Barcelona . . . durante el año 1905* (Barcelona, 1906), p. 98.

Thanks largely to the repatriation of savings from Cuba, the Spanish–American war had a strong positive influence on the economic life of Vizcaya. From 1886 to 1899 636 new companies had been launched in Bilbao; an average of forty-five companies a year, each with a capital of 680,000 pesetas. The aftermath of the loss of Cuba, however, saw the creation of more and larger companies. Thus in 1900 108 new companies were quoted on the Bilbao stock exchange, with a total capital of 161 million pesetas, an average of 1·49 million pesetas per company. The following year brought even giddier heights to the provincial capital when 146 companies were launched with a total capital of 482 million pesetas; an average of 3·30 million per company.[32]

Many of the new companies founded in Bilbao at this time, and much of the new investment, were in established industries. One hundred million pesetas was spent on the purchase of ships from abroad in 1899 and 1900 to facilitate the transport of local ore. In the boom year of 1901 more than two-fifths of the new companies that were formed, and one-quarter of all new investment was connected with the mining sector. Yet the new investment also allowed for a greater diversification of Basque industry. Among the main recipients of the returned savings were banking, insurance, paper, chemicals, sugar refining and hydro-electricity. Of these, banking and insurance in particular attracted large amounts of funds. In 1901, for example, 100 million pesetas was invested in a single insurance company and 98 million pesetas in seven banking institutions.

The substantial investment in banks and credit companies based on Bilbao was without doubt the most significant development of these years. In particular, the Bank of Vizcaya, which was founded in 1901 with a modest capital of 15 million pesetas, soon became a strong rival of the well established Bank of Bilbao, and together they joined the 'big five' of the Spanish banks at a time when the Catalan banks were experiencing a phase of marked decline culminating in the collapse of the Bank of Barcelona in 1920. The Bank of Vizcaya soon began to display an agressive attitude to its competitors, taking over the banking house La Bilbaína in 1902 and the

Banco Vascongado in the following year. In 1915 it was also to acquire the Banco Jacquet e Hijos. Within a brief spell of time the newly founded banks assumed a pioneering role in regional and later national industry, founding and financing a large number of concerns in the fields of sugar refining, cement, tramways, shipping, railways and above all hydro-electricity. Among the hydro-electrical enterprises with which it was connected were the Electra de Viesgo (1906), the Hidroeléctrica Española (1907) and the Compañía Hispano Americano de Electricidad, founded by the Catalan financier Francisco Cambó in 1919.[33]

Table 24   New companies founded in Bilbao in 1901

Number	Type	Normal capital (million pesetas)
7	Banking	98·0
1	Insurance	100·0
12	Hydro-electricity	73·5
2	Railways	10·5
1	Corn milling	2·25
1	Sawmills	0·5
3	Cement	0·375
2	Paper	20·5
3	Chemical industry	6·5
3	Wine	6·0
7	Shipping	17·375
47	Mining	122·25
13	Ironworks	21·5
44	Various	3·5
146	Total	482·75

Source. Parliamentary Papers, Diplomatic and Consular Reports on Trade and Finance, 1903, LXXVIII (Bilbao), p. 867.

By the early months of 1901 the Bilbao market was the centre of a massive wave of speculation. Companies appeared 'as if by magic' and the value of their shares rocketed overnight. Some share prices rose by 350 pesetas on the day after their issue. At first the financial press believed Vizcaya to be on the verge of an industrial renaissance. However, their illusions were soon shattered.[34] In his report to the Foreign Office for 1902, the British consul in Bilbao wrote: 'Depression trod all too quickly upon the heels of the rash and excessive speculation indulged in during the years 1900 and 1901, when one or two brilliant financial successes led to a fever for investments and as much as £19 millions were nominally subscribed in industrial and other enterprises, of which many were overcapitalised and others either altogether unsound or weakened by want of business knowledge on the part of their promoters. The consequent financial strain, coming as it did at a time when little or no return was being received for the large sums invested in shipping, dealt a heavy blow to public confidence, and led to an immediate check on new undertakings.

'In the case of sound and hopeful concerns previously launched, extreme tenderness had to be shown in making calls upon shares already subscribed. Although in some cases these calls were delayed to the fullest possible extent, their eventual pressure forced holders to sacrifice a considerable proportion of their shares at great loss, the markets thus being kept down and a further element of uncertainty added to the financial situation.'[35]

After 1901 nominal capital investment in new companies based on Bilbao fell drastically. However, after 1904 the general situation of the province of Vizcaya began to show signs of recovery. From 1902 to 1909 share prices on the Bilbao exchange began to rise again, before falling slightly in 1911–12.[36]

Table 25   New companies founded in Bilbao, 1900–14

Year	No. of companies	Nominal capital (million pesetas)
1900	108	160·69
1901	147	482·28
1902	91	51·94
1903	98	54·94
1904	71	19·03
1905	57	19·98
1906	88	50·43
1907	30	18·08
1908	86	15·04
1909	72	12·39
1910	66	16·55
1911	64	9·17
1912	64	18·33
1913	71	14·42
1914	58	5·82

Source. Cámara Oficial de Industria y Navegación de Bilbao, Memoria comercial de 1923 (Bilbao, n.d.), p. 337.

THE INDUSTRIALISTS' ATTEMPT TO SEIZE THE INITIATIVE

The profound sense of loss and dishonour occasioned by Spain's humiliation at the hands of the United States caused economic interest groups from all corners of the Peninsula to put forward a series of proposals aimed at the economic regeneration of the nation. In November 1898 representatives of the country's chambers of commerce assembled in Saragossa, where they embarked upon a campaign to rid Spain of the old Restoration clique of corrupt politicians, sterile bureaucrats and underemployed generals whom they judged responsible for the recent catastrophe.[37] At the same time the Fomento del Trabajo Nacional and its sister organisations in Barcelona sought and were granted an audience with the Queen Regent, to whom they outlined the hopes and grievances of the Catalan business community. Their widely publicised claims were essentially fourfold: a free port or neutral zone for Barcelona, State encouragement and assistance for technical education, support for the opening up of substitute markets, and a new taxation system which would encourage national industry.[38]

On the question of how to achieve these goals, rather than act alone the main economic organisations of Catalonia sought out a spokesman within the political oligarchy who would represent their interests in Madrid. Their choice was the former Captain General of the Philippines, Polavieja.[39] In return for their support Polavieja promised his Catalan backers administrative reforms and political decentralisation. In March 1899, unable to form an administration of his own, Polavieja was appointed to the Ministry of War in the self-styled 'Government of National Regeneration' headed by the Conservative Francisco Silvela. Among other matters Polavieja was briefed to put forward the demand of Catalan business for a so-called *concierto económico* or economic agreement along the lines of that obtained by the Basque provinces in 1876, under which the Catalans would be permitted to collect their own taxes and allocate expenditure as they saw fit, apart from such national items as defence and foreign policy.[40]

The rejection of these proposals out of hand by Silvela's Finance Minister Villaverde, together with the latter's proposed cuts in defence spending, out of deference to the vociferous clamourings of the chambers of commerce, left the politically inexperienced general no alternative but to resign. Villaverde, meanwhile, annoyed the Catalans further by a proposal to introduce a form of income tax to be levied on industrial contributions. As a reprisal the middle classes of Catalonia and elsewhere declared a taxpayers' strike and the closing of all shops, known in Catalan as the *Tancament de Caixes*. It was the heavy-handed treatment by the Madrid authorities of this ill prepared revolt, with the imposition of martial law throughout the region and the imprisonment of its leaders, which finally convinced the business community of the desirability of pursing a specifically Catalanist form of political activity.[41]

In the elections to the Spanish Cortes of 1901 the same business groups which had previously supported Polavieja now put up their own candidates, four of whom were elected on a purely regionalist ticket. Three of the successful candidates were, or had been, presidents of leading Catalan economic organisations: Albert Rusiñol, former president of the Fomento del Trabajo Nacional; Sebastià Torres, current president of the Liga de Defensa Industrial y Mercantil; and Bartholomeu Robert, former president of the Sociedad Económica de Amigos del País. Shortly after their electoral triumph the groups responsible for this political breakthrough formed a new party, the Lliga Regionalista. Throughout its history the Lliga was to remain tightly controlled by a closely knit group of politicians, lawyers, businessmen and financiers, the most outstanding of whom was Francisco Cambó, and was referred to, especially by the left, as 'the industrialists' party'.[42]

Before long, however, the Lliga found that its stated political ideology of Catalan nationalism was at variance with the economic aspirations of its leadership.[43] Given the pronounced inability of Catalan industry to compete in world markets, the Lliga had constantly to bear in mind that many of its threats of regionalist politics were merely empty ones, since Catalan manufacturers were dependent on the rest of Spain as an outlet for their products. The official policy of the Fomento also sounded a cautious note. While recognising that Catalan business opinion had been neglected by the politicians in Madrid, dominated by the landed and financial oligarchy of the south and centre, it firmly stated that the industrial future of Catalonia lay within the Spanish nation. The secretary of the Fomento, Guillermo Graell, wrote in 1902 that 'the market of Catalonia is the rest of Spain . . . to such a point that if they separate both will be ruined, commercially, economically and financially. . . .Every Catalan, therefore, who inclines towards separatism is attacking the interests of his country and is a bad Catalan.'[44]

In the period from the loss of Cuba to the outbreak of the first world war this ambiguous stance adopted by the Catalan business community met with fixed fortunes. A mixture of indifference, hostility and suspicion provoked the politicians in Madrid to reject most of the proposals first raised by the Catalans in 1898. Despite two government enquiries, the Bill for a free port for Barcelona, which entailed the construction of a vast modern dockland complex, was thrown out because of opposition from the wheat growers of Castile, who claimed that it would be a haven for all manner of contraband.[45] Attempts to cement commercial relations with the hitherto neglected republics of Latin America was greeted by an empty Cortes, while plans for an industrial school in Barcelona fell through for lack of finance.[46] Their schemes for modernisation defeated, the Fomento de Trabajo Nacional and the other business groups were reduced to the traditional ploy of courting the support of the wheat growers and ironmasters in order to secure greater tariff protection in defence of their interests. The resultant ultra-protectionist tariff of 1906, nevertheless, owed more to the untiring energies of a Basque, Pablo de Alzola, president of the Bilbao steel firm Altos Hornos de Vizcaya, who was appointed president of the commission of enquiry set up in 1904 to report on the most effective ways of revising 1891 tariff.[47]

Undoubtedly the greatest single achievement of the Lliga politicians in these pre-war years was the securing of limited autonomy for Catalonia in 1914 in the shape of the Mancomunitat. Apart from offering the Catalans a certain amount of cultural and political independence from Madrid, it also permitted the business community to put into practice ideas for the extension of the Catalan market through such schemes as the construction of local roads, secondary railways and hydraulic works and the improvement of the telephone network.[48]

The mounting initiatives of the Catalan economic community found a faint echo among the *fuerzas vivas* of Vizcaya. In imitation of their counterparts in Barcelona, Bilbao business groups petitioned, albeit with a similar lack of success, for a free port in 1903, while institutions such as the Unión Ibero Americana strove to develop trading links with Latin America.[49] However, although the Bilbao chamber of commerce sent its representative, Pablo de Alzola, to the Saragossa assembly in November 1898, the disintegration of this movement left the Basques far more muted in their criticisms of Madrid than the politically active Catalans. Alzola was himself 'bought-off' by the offer of the post of Director General of Public Works by the Silvela government in April 1900.[50] With the exception of a few wayward spirits like the millionaire president of the shipowners' association, Ramón de la Sota, the industrial leaders of Vizcaya were far less inclined to adopt a regionalist stance than their Catalan counterparts.

This loyalty to a regime which many had attacked in the heady days of 1898 was partly conditioned by a growing dependence of Basque heavy industry and the banks on government favour and contracts. The destruction of the Spanish fleet in the Spanish–American war, for instance, prompted the shipbuilders, steel makers and armourers of Bilbao to campaign together with the Conservative politician Antonia Maura for its replacement. Their efforts were to be rewarded in November 1908 when the Maura government awarded a 200 million peseta contract to a consortium headed by Vickers and the Marqués de Comillas in which a whole host of Vizcaya firms were represented, including the Banks of Bilbao and Vizcaya, Altos Hornos, Chávarri y Compañía and many others.[51] Clive Trebilcock has argued that the 1908 naval programme, which entailed the construction of three dreadnoughts and a fleet of smaller vessels, probably exerted a strong influence on indigenous shipbuilding techiniques by the provision of patent information, designs and technical supervision as well as a slightly less direct influence on engineering and metallurgical capabilities due to the demands and specifications of the shipyards.[52]

Lobbying by the *fuerzas vivas* of Bilbao, sometimes in alliance with the Catalans, on other occasions with Santander, brought a number of important concessions from the Restoration regime. If the behind-the-scenes manoeuvrings of Alzola, which preceded the 1906 tariff, were the most notable example of State patronage, pressure from Basque interest groups was also instrumental in two other notable pieces of legislation: the law of secondary and strategic railways of 1907–08, which approved the construction of over 12,000 km of narrow-gauge lines, although most of these were never built, and the law for the protection of maritime industries and communications of 1909.

Under the pressure of demands from both the Catalan and Basque business communities the early year of the present century saw a gradual change in the attitude of the State to economic matters. The official conception of Spain as a free-trade economy, exploited by foreign mining, railway and finance companies, destined to supply the tables and furnaces of the advanced world with foodstuffs and raw materials, gradually gave way to the vision of an autarkic capitalist economy. The outbreak of the first world war brought matters to a head.

NOTES

1   Alzola, *Progreso industrial de Vizcaya*, p. 77.
2   See above, chapter two.
3   Nadal, *Industrialización y desindustrialización del sureste español, 1817–1913*, pp. 60 ff.
4   Manuel Tuñón de Lara, *El movimiento obrero en la historia de España* (Madrid, 1972), pp. 372–3.
5   Vicens Vives, *Cataluña en el siglo XIX*, p. 97.
6   *Memoria en defensa dels interessos morals y materials de Catalunya* (Barcelona, 1885).
7   Pedro Corominas, 'Actividad económica de Cataluña', in Pedro Estasén *Cataluña: estudio acerca las condiciones de su engrandecimiento y su riqueza* (Barcelona, 1900), p. 868.
8   Edouard Escarra, *Le développement industrielle de la Catalogne* (Paris, 1908), pp. 25 and 55–8; Frederico Rahola y Trémols, 'Del comerç i de la industria de Catalunya', in Francesc Carreras y Candi, *Geografia general de Catalunya* (Barcelona, 1913), p. 397.
9   Escarra, *op. cit.*, pp. 60 and 194–5.
10   Miguel Carreras, *Elements d'historia de Sabadell* (Sabadell, 1932), p. 399; Escarra, *op. cit.*, pp. 30–2; Rahola, *op. cit.*, pp. 460–1.
11   R. Medir Jofra, *Historia del gremio corchero* (Madrid, 1953), pp. 111–28 and 489–91.
12   Vicens Vives, *Cataluña en el siglo XIX*, pp. 103–5.
13   José Luis Martín Rodriguez and José María Ollé Romeu, Ayuntamiento de Barcelona, Documentos y Estudios, vol. ix, *Orígenes de la industria eléctrica barcelonesa* (Barcelona, 1961), 23–35.
14   Jordi Solé Tura, *Catalanismo y revolución burguesa* (Madrid, 1970), p. 59.
15   Manuel González Portilla, 'Aspectos del crecimiento económico que conducen al desarrollo industrial de Vizcaya', unpublished paper of the I *Coloquio de*

Historia Económica de España, cited in Juan Pablo Fusi, Política obrera en el País Vasco, 1880–1923 (Madrid, 1975), p. 21.

16   Benito de Alzola, Estudio relativo a los recursos que la industria nacional dispone para las construcciones y armamentos navales (Madrid, 1886), pp. 25–32.

17   Fusi, op. cit., pp. 27–8.

18   Sánchez Ramos, op. cit., pp. 227–39.

19   Boletín de la Cámara de Comercio de Bilbao, I (September, 1888), 266–7.

20   P.P. 1903, LXXVIII (Bilbao), p. 347.

21   P.P. 1896, LXXXVIII (Barcelona), pp. 526–7.

22   P.P. 1897, XCIII, (Barcelona), p. 438.

23   Ibid., p. 442.

24   E. Bertrand y Serra, 'Un estudio sobre la industria textil algodonera', Boletín del Comité Regulador de la Industria Algodonera (March, 1931), quoted in Lucas Beltrán Flores, La industria algodonera española (Barcelona, 1943), p. 46.

25   P.P. 1900, XCVI (Barcelona), p. 297.

26   Ibid., p. 265.

27   Ibid., loc. cit.

28   El Trabajo Nacional, 20 September 1900, p. 85, and 30 September 1900, p. 93.

29   Memoria leída en la junta general de socios celebrada el día 25 de enero de 1903 (Barcelona, 1903), p. 4; P.P. 1906, CXXVII (Barcelona), p. 591.

30   P.P. 1902, LXXVIII (Barcelona), p. 1043; P.P. 1903, CIII (Barcelona), p. 475.

31   E. Calvet, Agrupación de hiladores y tejedores del Fomento de Trabajo Nacional . . . memoria del congreso celebrado en Bremen 25–29 junio 1906 (Barcelona, 1906), p. 47.

32   Cámara Oficial de Industria y Navegación de Bilbao, Memoria comercial de 1923 (Bilbao, n.d.), p. 337.

33   Lequerica, La actividad económica de Vizcaya, p. 79.

34   Revista de Economía y Hacienda, 27 April 1903; El Economista, 9 April 1900.

35   P.P. 1903, LXXVIII, (Bilbao), p. 881.

36   P.P. 1905, XCII (Bilbao), p. 439; Información: Órgano Oficial de la Cámara de Comercio de Bilbao, 15 January 1914.

37   Asamblea de las cámaras de comercio de Zaragoza, 20–27 noviembre de 1898 (Saragossa, 1899).

38   Joseph Harrison, 'Catalan business and the loss of Cuba, 1898–1914', Economic History Review, 2nd series, 27 (1974), 431–41.

39   For an expression of the Catalans' support for Polavieja see El Imparcial, 9 November 1898.

40   Fomento del Trabajo Nacional, Exposición elevada al presidente del Congreso de los Diputados con motivo del proyecto de ley de presupuestos para el ejercicio, 1899–1900 (Barcelona, 1899).

41   J. de Camps i Arboix, El Tancament de Caixes (Barcelona, 1961).

42   Joaquín Maurín, Los hombres de la dictadura: Sánchez Guerra, Cambó, Iglesias, Largo Caballero, Lerroux, Melquíades Álvarez (Madrid, 1930), esp. pp. 101–50.

43   Juan Linz, 'The party system of Spain: past and future', in M. Lipset and S. Rokkan (eds), Party Systems and Voter Alignments (New York, 1967), p. 219.

44   Guillermo Graell, La cuestión catalana (Barcelona, 1902), p. 107.

45   El Imparcial, 26 and 27 January 1903.

46   *Ibid.*, 19 March 1904; Graell, *Historia del Fomento del Trabajo Nacional*, p. 387.

47   Angel Marvaud, 'La politique douanière de l'Espagne, 1816–1906', *Annales des Sciences Politiques*, May 1907, 319–21.

48   Mancomunitat de Catalunya, *L'obra realitzada: anys 1914–23*, 3 vols (Barcelona, 1923).

49   C. Béguin, 'Les relations de l'Espagne avec l'Amerique Latine', *Economiste Français*, 14 January 1905; P.P. 1905, xciii (Bilbao), p. 439.

50   *El Imparcial*, 19 April 1900, Tuñón de Lara, *Estudios sobre el siglo XIX español* (Madrid, 1972), pp. 215–18.

51   *La España Nueva*, 29 April 1909.

52   Clive Trebilcock, 'British armaments and European industrialisation, 1890–1914', *Economic History Review*, 2nd series, 26 (1973), 254–72; cf. Joseph Harrison, 'El coste de oportunidad del Programa Naval de 1907: ¿pantanos o acorazados?', *Hacienda Pública Española*, 38 (1976), 111–22.

CHAPTER 5

The formation of a capitalist society

Upon the outbreak of the first world war public opinion was sharply divided into two opposing camps. Most liberals were pro-Ally, while the majority of Spaniards, among them supporters of parties excluded from office such as the Carlists and the Radicals, tended to back the Germans. The distinction, however, was largely academic, since successive governments recognised that Spain was no longer a leading European power and that military intervention was inadvisable.[1] Furthermore a policy of neutrality was not unattractive to large sections of the economic community.

The sector of the economy most favoured by the European conflict was industry. After initial setbacks, from which no nation on the continent was exempt, industry soon entered an era of splendid prosperity which brought fabulous profits to numerous entrepreneurs. The war benefited industry in three main ways. Firstly, in the early days Spanish factories were able to sell large quantities of clothing and war *matériel* to the armies of the belligerents. Secondly, as the war dragged on, and the belligerent nations directed their industrial capacity to the war effort, their traditional markets in Latin America, Asia and Africa were obliged to look to the neutrals to satisfy their demands. Thirdly, with the virtual eradication of British, German and French competition in the home market, Basque and Catalan manufacturers were encouraged to produce import substitutes.

Neutrality also brought some respite to the problems of Spanish agriculture, though the gains were by no means evenly distributed. The prices of some crops such as sugar beet and olive oil rose considerably. Yet while the landowners reaped the benefits, exports of foodstuffs had an inflationary effect on the home market, sending up the cost of living of the already impoverished agricultural labour force. In the Levante the German submarine blockade of 1917 had a doubly damaging effect, severely disrupting the export trade in oranges, almonds and rice, and obstructing the import of fertilisers.[2] Hence the war heightened social tensions in the countryside, leading to a wave of agricultural strikes and an increase in emigration.

The extent of Spain's wartime boom may be gauged from an analysis of her commercial statistics. Throughout the early years of the present century these showed a perennial deficit in foreign trade. Between 1901 and 1914 imports exceeded exports by 1,031 million pesetas. However, the trend was startlingly reversed in the quinquennium 1915–19, when Spain built up a trading surplus of 2,131 million pesetas. By far the most significant contributory factor to the total increase was exports of manufactured goods, which rose, from a base of 100 in 1913 to 241 in 1915, thereafter falling to 215 in 1917. Exports of foodstuffs rose less steeply, from 100 in 1913 to 112 in 1917. The scale of the achievement was exceeded only by an even larger series of deficits in the immediate postwar years, when national industry compensated for the non-availability of certain products during the war by huge imports of machinery, coal, metal goods, chemicals and other items.

Although the wartime boom was cut short by the economic depression of 1920–23, prosperity returned in the middle and late '20s—*los felices veinte*. Thus it came about that the final decade and a half of the Restor-

Table 26   Spain's balance of trade, 1901–22 (million pesetas)

Year	Imports	Exports	Balance
1901	908·3	756·8	−151·4
1902	884·9	813·4	−71·5
1903	933·7	901·2	−32·4
1904	920·8	917·3	−3·4
1905	1,058·4	954·8	−103·6
1906	1,015·1	897·7	−117·3
1907	947·1	943·4	−3·7
1908	980·9	892·9	−87·9
1909	956·9	925·4	−31·4
1910	999·3	970·1	−29·1
1911	994·5	976·0	−18·5
1912	1,051·1	1,045·4	−5·6
1913	1,308·8	1,078·5	−230·3
1914	1,025·5	880·7	−144·8
1915	976·7	1,257·9	281·1
1916	945·9	1,377·6	431·6
1917	735·5	1,324·5	589·0
1918	590·0	1,009·0	418·9
1919	900·2	1,310·6	410·4
1920	1,423·3	1,020·0	−403·3
1921	2,835·9	1,579·6	−1,256·2
1922	2,716·1	1,319·3	−1,396·8

Source. Instituto Nacional de Estadística, *Comercio exterior de España: números índices* (1901–56) (Madrid, 1958), p. 29; cited in Santiago Roldán et al., *La formación de la sociedad capitalista en España, 1914–1920* (2 vols, Madrid, 1973) 1, 25.

ation saw the foundations in Spain of a capitalist society. The proportion of the active labour force engaged in industry rose steadily throughout the period, from 15·82 per cent in 1910 to 21·90 per cent in 1920 and 26·51 per cent in 1930, while the agricultural labour force at last began to assume smaller proportions, falling from 66·0 per cent of the working population in 1910 to 57·30 per cent in 1920 and 45·51 per cent in 1930.[3]

Table 27   Categories of Spanish exports: indices, 1913–17

Year	Live animals	Raw materials	Manufactures	Foodstuffs
1913	100	100	100	100
1914	32	77	99	78
1915	12	70	241	88
1916	57	78	222	117
1917	18	72	215	112

Source. Juan Antonio Lacomba, 'La primera guerra europea y la economía española', in *Ensayos sobre el siglo xx español* (Madrid, 1972), p. 99.

SPANISH INDUSTRY AND THE EUROPEAN WAR

The immediate consequences of the opening of hostilities in 1914 were far from favourable for the Spanish economy. During the first months of the conflict manufacturing industry in Catalonia was almost completely paralysed because of the near impossibility of acquiring raw materials. In September 1914 representatives of all the economic organisations of the Principality met the leaders of the main political groups under the auspices of the Mancomunitat, the regional government, and agreed to approach the government on ways of obtaining supplies of raw cotton. Catalonia also suffered an initial setback because of the closure of traditional European markets for its staple exports of wine and cork. Over 20,000 workers had to be laid off in the province of Lérida in October 1914. Moreover, as foreign banks began to suspend operations, the Barcelona stock exchange was gripped with panic and a number of customers withdrew their current accounts from the Catalan banks.[4] This crisis of bank liquidity was also felt in Vizcaya, where, because of their close connection with the leading industrial companies, some of which were experiencing short-term difficulties, many of the newly formed finance institutions were shown to be vulnerable. In August 1914 the Crédito de la Unión Minera, which had been founded in 1901 with a capital of 16 million pesetas, was forced to suspend payments owing to a panic withdrawal of deposits by the public.[5]

By early 1915, however, the problems of readjustment to the wartime situation had been overcome. In Catalonia business entered a period of feverish activity. A veritable swarm of agents and speculators descended upon the Principality, their wallets stuffed with banknotes, intent upon buying up all sorts of saleable merchandise. Stimulated by this new and heavy demand, Catalan employers re-engaged workers previously laid off and took on large numbers of additional workers, many of whom migrated to Barcelona from the surrounding provinces. Factories worked day and night in an attempt to fulfil their orders, and new installations were built or taken over. Profits rose to undreamt-of heights, leading to the emergence of that much commented upon phenomenon of Catalan society, the *nouveau riche* manufacturer or *magnífico*, who ostentatiously displayed his newly acquired wealth in the cabarets of Barcelona.[6]

The earliest industry to draw comfort from the new situation was the woollen industry of Sabadell and Tarrasa, since high on the list of acquisitions of the foreign buyers were woollen blankets and cloth for military uniforms, both of which were much sought after by the French army. Hitherto blankets were an insignificant item in Spanish exports, totalling a mere ten tons in 1913. Yet in 1915 Spain exported 4,500 tons of them, rising to 6,300 tons in 1916. Thereafter blanket exports fell to 4,700 tons in 1917. Subsequently the Catalan woollen industry captured new outlets for its products in Latin America, particularly the markets of Argentina and Chile.[7] Altogether, total exports of woollen goods from Catalonia rose from 13·5 million pesetas in 1913 to 185 million in 1915, dropping to 129 million in 1916 and 108 million pesetas in 1917.[8]

Table 28   Exports of woollen goods to Argentina and Chile, 1913–17 (kg)

	Destination	
Year	Argentina	Chile
1913	69,866	33,260
1914	28,028	42,565
1915	64,796	9,844
1916	226,474	23,395
1917	305,655	124,482

Source. Economia i Finances, 25 October, 1918.

Not only the traditional sectors of Catalan industry profited from the changed circumstances. In response to demands for alternative supplies by the textile industry, important developments took place in the emerging chemical and pharmaceutical industries, not least in the production of dyestuffs, previously imported from Germany. Import substitution also benefited the nascent metallurgical and engineering industries of Catalonia. By the end of the war the province of Barcelona was giving employment to 10,000 workers in the fields of mechanical engineering, vehicle building and allied trades, the manufacture of sheet steel and repair work.[9]

A less impressive feature was the scale and organisation of many of the new enterprises. Of the 546 new companies founded in Barcelona in 1916, only 181 were limited liability companies, while the combined capital of all new concerns did not exceed 53 million pesetas. With the reappearance of peacetime competition many small and unprofitable firms went bankrupt.[10]

Outside Catalonia, the resurgence of the Spanish economy gathered pace in other industrialising regions, most notably in the Basque country and Asturias. The wartime boom in shipping led to the greatest expansion

Table 29   New companies founded in Barcelona in 1916

Industry	Number	Capital (pesetas)
Foodstuffs	46	5,488,990
Heating and lighting	5	1,351,898
Construction	18	539,844
Hygiene and perfume	7	278,000
Textiles		
Cotton	31	4,098,088
Wool	23	627,800
Others	14	643,508
Handicraft	31	1,392,300
Chemicals	27	1,357,000
Leather and leather goods	21	1,587,837
Wooden goods	9	199,800
Paper	5	70,000
Graphics	26	1,898,483
Iron and steel and metallurgy	47	8,990,222
Vehicles	10	1,366,500
Glass	5	93,500
Agencies	71	1,718,500
Banking stock exchange	3	1,280,000
Transport	17	2,004,200
Electrical material	17	599,750
Jewellery	5	364,678
Furniture	8	101,208
Livestock	3	60,880
Coal	3	5,025,000
Silver work	6	112,537
Diverse	88	11,711,354
Total	546	53,001,877

Source. Roldán et el., La formación de la sociedad capitalista en España, 1; pp. 46–7.

of all time of the Spanish merchant marine, a factor which played a decisive role in the consolidation of Basque capitalism. During the first years of the war leading Basque shipping companies announced spectacular profits. The profits of the top six lines, Cía Naviera Vascongada, Naviera Sota y Aznar, Naviera Bachi, Cía Vasco Cantábrica de Navegacíon, Cía Marítima Unión and Cía Marítima del Nervión, soared from 4,431,300 pesetas in 1913 to 24,141,700 pesetas in 1914 and 52,693,000 pesetas in 1915. Among individual companies, Sota y Aznar increased its profits from 2,550,800 pesetas in 1914 to 16,240,400 pesetas in 1916.[11]

Difficulties in obtaining coal, which before the war accounted for 40 per cent of all consumption, caused a great expansion in the number of mining companies established at this time. The main location of the new mines was in Asturias and León, but shafts were also sunk in other regions of Spain previously unproductive. The number of coal miners in Asturias increased from 17,796 in 1913 to 23,927 in 1916, doubling the original figure by the end of the war. The mine owners too made substantial profits; leading mining companies, Duro–Felguera, Fábrica de Mieres, Hulleras de Turón and others, more than trebled their profits from 2,271,000 pesetas in 1914 to 7,876,000 pesetas in 1916. Less fortunate were those industries which were forced to pay increasingly higher prices for coal. From a base of 100 in 1913, coal prices rose to 138 in 1915, thence to 277 in 1916.[12]

Despite increases in the price of coal, there was a considerable wartime expansion in the metallurgical sectors of the Basque region, Asturias and Santander. From 1914 to 1916 total national production of iron ingots rose in value from 45 million pesetas to 117 million, while over the same period production of steel ingots increased from 63 million pesetas to 172 million. Between 1913 and 1916 the profits of the leading iron and steel companies more than doubled.[13]

The wave of expansion continued throughout 1917 and reached a peak in the Basque region in 1918, when 219 new companies were launched on the Bilbao stock exchange with a total nominal capital of 407 million pesetas, a figure which compares favourably with the previous peak year of 1901. At the centre of this expansion was the banking sector. In 1918 a number of banks were founded in Bilbao, including a branch of the Banco Hispano Americano, with a capital of 100 million pesetas; the Banco Urquijo Vascongado, with a capital of 20 million pesetas; the Banco Agrícola Comercial, with 40 millions; and the Banco Industrial de España, with a capital of 5 million pesetas. Between 1915 and 1918 the portfolio of the Basque banks doubled; between 1915 and 1919 it trebled. Throughout the war the profits of the Basque banks increased annually, more than quadrupling from 4·92 million pesetas in 1914 to 20·32 millions in 1918.[14]

New investment fostered the development of other Basque industries. Companies set up to exploit the Peninsula's potential for hydro-electric power made rapid progress, encouraged by the increase in coal prices. The

Table 30   New companies founded in Bilbao, 1914–23

Year	Number	Nominal capital (million pesetas)
1914	58	5·82
1915	54	8·06
1916	94	34·92
1917	134	164·02
1918	219	407·40
1919	164	96·48
1920	156	70·80
1921	186	63·16
1922	126	50·68
1923	87	25·65

Source. Cámara Oficial de Industria y Navegación de Bilbao, Memoria comercial de 1923, p. 337.

largest individual sum invested in a single company in 1918 was 150 million pesetas, which went to found the Compañía Hispano Portuguesa de Transportes Eléctricos, established by a group of Bilbao capitalists to harness the falls of the Duero. Other industries which benefited from the Bilbao stock-market boom were shipping and metallurgy. In December 1918 Altos Hornos de Vizcaya increased its capital of 32·8 million pesetas, which dated from the foundation of the new company in 1902, to 100 millions. Moreover Basque capitalism began to spread from Vizcaya into the adjacent province of Guipúzcoa, where the paper industry gained prominence after 1918. The upshot of these developments was that by the end of the European war industrial hegemony within Spain had shifted to the Basque region from Catalonia.[15]

THE WAR AND BIG BUSINESS

As the war progressed, employers' organisations from throughout the Peninsula, urged on and championed by the Catalans, stressed the advantages for the country's long-term future of a fully fledged capitalist system. However, as their advice went unheeded and opportunities for consolidating upon the wartime situation slipped past, a rift opened up between the business community and the land-based political oligarchy in Madrid. In the first two years of the war criticism of government indifference and hostility originated mainly from business groups in Barcelona anxious to capitalise of the marked increase in foreign trade, especially with Latin America. Yet from the middle of 1916 a spirit of national solidarity began to develop among businessmen when the Liberal government of Romanones announced its intention of taxing excess war profits. The conflict came more into the open in the summer of 1917 when spokesmen of business interests in the Spanish parliament set up an illegal assembly of parliamentarians in opposition to the Cortes, which they considered an insurmountable obstacle to their vision of a new capitalist society. Though the Assembly was not successful in obtaining its objectives and the industrial bourgeoisie was soon to repent of its revolutionary stance, the events of 1917 illustrate the profound influence of the European war on Spanish society.

Accounts of high living among the newly enriched manufacturing classes of Catalonia have created the overall impression that throughout the war the sole ambition of this group was to get rich quick and spend all its profits on conspicious consumption, irrespective of what the future might have in store. Their failure to invest in new plant and equipment—witness the tiny, undercapitalised firms founded in Barcelona in 1916—has been taken to prove conclusively that Catalan business as a whole was largely responsible for the inevitable slump in the regional economy after the war.[16] This sort of caricature, which contains elements of truth, nevertheless tells only half the story. While the *magníficos* frittered away their fortunes, the main economic organisations of the Principality and their political representatives in the Lliga Regionalista steadily built up a powerful big-business lobby which forcefully articulated the short- and long-term demands of Spanish capitalism. Their aim was a Spain created in the likeness of Catalonia, a so-called Espanya Gran or Espanya Catalana. Throughout the war Catalan deputies such as Rahola, Ventosa, Sedó and Cambó intervened in Cortes debates on industrial policy, finance and the cost of living.[17]

The first major wartime initiative of Catalan business was taken in October 1914, when the Fomento del Trabajo Nacional and other economic organisations again petitioned Madrid for a free port or neutral zone for Barcelona. This item had remained on the agenda of the Fomento since the first claim was put in at the beginning of the century, but it received added impetus when a royal decree of September 1914 granted free port status to the southern port of Cádiz. Not surprisingly, the Catalans felt aggrieved, since it was at their request that two parliamentary enquiries had earlier been set up. Moreover the business community of Barcelona strongly objected to the choice of Cádiz as Spain's first free port. Barcelona was the leading industrial centre, through which passed one-fifth of the nation's foreign trade. Cádiz, by comparison, possessed little industry and a predominantly agricultural hinterland. Of the two, Barcelona was in a far better position to derive long-term benefits from the construction of a vast dockland and factory complex which a free port or neutral zone would bring. The government's decision smacked of political vindictiveness as far as the Catalans were concerned.[18]

The action of the belligerents in abandoning their export markets was viewed by the economic organisations of Catalonia as an opportune moment to increase their own share of world trade. This was particularly the case with Latin America, whose markets had attracted the attention of Catalan manufacturers since the loss of Cuba in 1898. Accordingly in July 1915 representatives of the Fomento and other business groups visited Madrid, where they made known their demands for export subsidies to enable them to capture and retain new markets for their products. The direct consequence of their visit was a special commission set up by the Finance Minister, Bugallal, charged with ' the study of national industry and means of facilitating exports'. In Barcelona, however, the decision was seen as a *prima facie* case of evasion, when the situation appeared to necessitate prompt action before the war was over and such opportunities had disappeared for ever.[19]

Nevertheless the government's delaying tactics on both projects reflected profound disquiet in the rest of Spain towards the intentions of the Catalans. In Saragossa agrarian and business organisations campaigned vigorously against the establishment of a free port in Barcelona, which they considered would lead to the destruction of local industry and rural depopulation.[20] More violent opposition to the Catalans' proposals came from the Castilian wheat lobby. Early in 1915 the Dato government felt obliged to ban a planned meeting in Valladolid summoned to attack the proposals of the Fomento del Trabajo Nacional.[21]

Within Catalonia the effect of government inaction was to create an overwhelming resentment against the political oligarchy in Madrid. Throughout the second half of 1915 all sections of political opinion in the Principality spoke in terms of an 'economic blockade' of the region by entrenched interests represented in the Spanish capital.[22]

When governments did act, in the opinion of the Catalans they conceded too little too late. It was not until October 1916 that a royal decree granted Barcelona a commercial depository, a concession which fell far short of the original demand for a free port. Moreover it was another year before the decree received final approval, and not until 1921 that work was begun on the site. As for the special commission set up by Bugallal to study government incentives to exports, this took eighteen months to report. The resulting 'law for the protection of new industries and the extension of existing ones' of March 1917 allocated 10 million pesetas for use by Spanish industry. It allowed for tax exemptions, tariff protection and guaranteed interest, and promised compensation to exporters in the event of losses incurred. In the first four years of its application 278 claims were made upon it. Yet the Lliga considered this belated measure woefully inadequate. They had demanded a foreign exchange bank and a commission house which would finance exports and provide a complete service of commercial information, but were refused both.[23]

At first the activities of the Catalans were met with stony silence in the

other great industrial region, Vizcaya. In September 1915 Alfonso XIII
visited Bilbao, where he was greeted with expressions of loyalty by a
Vizcayan business community which was busy amassing considerable
fortunes as a result of Spain's neutrality. Bilbao, moreover, had good
reason to be grateful for government patronage, having only recently been
selected as the site for a new naval dockyard, La Constructora Naval.[24]
However, in November 1915 the president of the Bilbao chamber of commerce, Horacio de Echevarrieta, made a widely reported speech in which
he declared, 'I have to state, frankly and without ambiguity, that the
conduct of the Catalans is worthy of the applause, consideration and
sympathy of all those Spaniards who concern themselves with the
development of the nation's wealth and the increase of its industrial
capacity.'[25] Three months later the chamber of commerce made its own
'discreet protest' at the failure of successive administrations to grant Bilbao a free port. This latter statement followed the issuing of the decree
offering a commercial depository to Barcelona.[26]

Yet the measure which eventually brought the two leading industrial
regions together was an attempt in June 1916 by the Liberal Finance
Minister Santiago Alba to tax excess war profits. On 28 June 1916 representatives of economic organisations from all over Spain attended a
protest meeting in the Palace Hotel in Madrid called to attack Alba's Bill.
The next six months witnessed a succession of empassioned debates in the
Cortes on Alba's proposals, which businessmen everywhere violently
opposed. Although many leading politicians spoke against the Bill, the
floor of the Cortes was dominated by Cambó, the parliamentary leader of
the Lliga Regionalista, who eventually forced Alba to withdraw his Bill
from the budget. Very soon Cambó was to emerge not only as the spokesman of Catalan capitalism but also as the champion of the Spanish middle
classes. His whistle-stop tours of Spain in a special train did much to build
up opposition to the Bill, not least in Bilbao, where his visit in January
1917 was a tremendous success.[27]

The Alba–Cambó confrontation was undoubtedly a clash of personalities. Apart from Antonio Maura, these men were possibly the two
most gifted politicians of the moment. At the same time, both Alba and
Cambó embodied rival ideologies, not entirely dissimilar, whose common
purpose was the economic regeneration of the country. Cambó, the greatest living exponent of Spanish capitalism, favoured government intervention to encourage the development of a modern capitalist economy.
Alba, meanwhile, was a disciple of Joaquín Costa, whose gospel was the
regeneration of agriculture by the implementation of a programme of
public works. To Alba, agricultural regeneration could best be achieved by
taxing the wartime profits of big business. This was the source of the
conflict.[28]

The Assembly movement and after

In the summer of 1917 German submarines blockaded the Mediterranean coast, causing havoc to Valencian agriculture. Rebel army officers held the country to ransom over improved pay and conditions, and the Socialists threatened a general strike. In response, Prime Minister Dato, who could no longer command a parliamentary majority, closed the Cortes. Defiantly the Lliga Regionalista summoned an alternative 'seditious' National Assembly to meet in Barcelona on 19 July.

The Assembly movement which lasted until 1 November 1917 was an attempt by the Catalan industrial bourgeoisie represented by the Lliga to cement an alliance with Basque and Asturian industrial interests, whose spokesman was the reformist Republican Melquíades Álvarez, and the petit-bourgeois radicals of Lerroux. Also wooed were the military *juntas*, the Conservative politician Antonio Maura, who considered himself a 'reformer from above', and the essentially reformist Socialist party. The aim of this impossible coalition was to remove from power the wheat and finance oligarchy. However, when Maura and the *juntas* refused to sanction the movement and the Socialists declared a general strike in its support in August, Cambó took fright. A profoundly conservative politician, he had no intention of assuming the role of Spain's Kerensky. At this turn in events, therefore, Spanish capitalism decided that it might be expedient to throw in its lot with the oligarchy. After all, the politicians were themselves under threat from the army and the working class, and in urgent need of new allies.

As a reward for his U turn Cambó was appointed Development Minister in March 1918 in a National Government headed by Maura. Once in office he embarked with enthusiasm on a monumental and all-embracing programme for the development and modernisation of the economy. The object of Cambó's plan was to marry the economic ambitions of Catalonia and Castile. He was careful to indicate that the main beneficiaries of his programme would be the agricultural community, which was offered a comprehensive scheme of public works, agricultural credit and improved communications.[29] In the long run, of course, industry would also gain by securing an extended and more prosperous consumer market. In his planned mining code Cambó made an appeal to patriotism by advocating the nationalisation of the subsoil, hitherto largely exploited by foreign companies. However, the most radical of his schemes was for the nationalisation of the foreign-owned railway companies. The Spanish railway system, already dilapidated in 1914, began to break down during the war because the companies were both unwilling and unable to make new investments in track and rolling stock. Poor communications inconvenienced all sections of Spanish industry; in particular those industries using coal were faced with delays in transporting it from Asturias, while textile factories located in the interior of Catalonia, away from the port of

Barcelona, frequently found it difficult to obtain sufficient supplies of raw cotton to keep the labour force employed.[30] Cambó also hoped that the railway network would be able to take advantage of cheap electric motive power, to be generated by proposed new hydro-electric stations.

Behind his proposals was the vision of a new post-war political economy. Yet, despite his much admired hard work, few of his proposals became law. The Maura coalition proved a shaky affair, and the unfortunate Cambó was permitted only eight months in office.

THE POST-WAR CRISIS

The failure of the industrial classes of Spain to carry through their modernising proposals coincided with the beginnings of a post-war crisis of two dimensions, social and economic. The earliest manifestations of social *malaise* took place in the countryside, especially in the south, where the rising cost of living, coupled with the example of the Russian revolution, gave rise to three years of rural unrest from 1918 to 1921, known as the *trienio bolchevista*. Unconnected, although not unrelated to the events in the Spanish countryside, from the beginning of 1919 the leading industrial centres of the country were rocked by a series of damaging strikes whose frequency and severity reflected the effects of inflation on the industrial proletariat and the rapid growth of militant trade unionism. Events took their most violent turn in Catalonia, where from 1919 to 1923 employers' groups and the anarcho-syndicalist trade union movement the Confederación Nacional del Trabajo (CNT) indulged in open combat, each organisation employing armed assassins or *pistoleros*.[31]

The main reason for the employers' refusal to accede to the demands of labour was the growing threat of economic recession. In Catalonia this was soon to take the form of a banking crisis. November 1920 saw the collapse of the Bank of Tarrasa following its speculation in foreign currencies. A month later the prestigious Bank of Barcelona suspended payments, while in the ensuing panic a number of other less important financial houses also fell.[32] By April 1921 140 cotton mills had closed down in the Principality owing to the loss of export markets, making 20,000 workers idle. A further 120 mills worked at only half capacity, affecting another 50,000 workers. In addition, half the workforce of the Catalan metallurgical sector was laid off.[33] Vizcaya too felt the shock of post-war recession through its greater contact with the international economy. Exports of iron ore, of which the province was by far the leading producer, slumped from 2,104,000 tons in 1920, to 501,000 tons in 1921, although they afterwards recovered to 1,040,000 tons in 1922 and 1,039,000 tons in 1923. Moreover, falling demand for iron ore in the main markets sent prices tumbling. The price of high-grade Bilbao ore in Middlesbrough fell from 47s a ton at the beginning 1921 to 12s 6d a ton in

November 1922. Furthermore the general decline in the iron trade, plus an increase in fuel and port charges, hit Basque shipping. By 1922 over one million tons of Spanish shipping was moored up.[34]

Faced with the double threat of working-class opposition and declining profit margins, Spanish industrialists rapidly abandoned their 'insurrectionary' tactics in order to seek support wherever they could find it. For its allegiance to central government Catalan business was rewarded during the period from November 1920 to April 1922 with the appointment of a new hard-line Civil Governor, Martínez Anido, who endeared himself to the employers' organisations by his mass arrests of syndicalist leaders and his implementation of the infamous *ley de fugas* by which political undesirables were reported 'shot trying to escape'. The disastrous military defeat in Morocco in 1921 presented Cambó with a further opportunity to put his ideas into practice when in August of that year he became Finance Minister in another Maura coalition. In a further eight months in office he succeeded in introducing a new banking law which aided the reconstruction of the Bank of Barcelona and in increasing the level of tariff protection to the highest in Europe, albeit at the cost of breaking off commercial relations with France.[35]

By this time, however, the aspirations of Spanish big business of modernising the economy had succumbed to finding ways of staving off the depression. Moreover, when the Maura government fell in April 1922, the new Prime Minister, Sánchez Guerra, to the annoyance of Catalan business, preached conciliation with the CNT. Syndicalist leaders arrested by Martínez Anido were released from prison and the 'butcher of Barcelona' was dismissed. The CNT even began to gain the upper hand in Barcelona, as evidenced by the success of the general transport strike of May to June 1923. Most unforgivable of all for the protectionist-minded industrialists, Santiago Alba at the Finance Ministry began to undo the work of Cambó by renegotiating commercial treaties. Thus, disenchanted by the politicians, Catalan business began to court the military. When General Miguel Primo de Rivera staged a military *coup* in Barcelona in September 1923 he received the loyal and enthusiastic support of a number of employers' associations, including the Fomento del Trabajo Nacional, as well as that of Bilbao chamber of commerce.[36]

THE DICTATORSHIP, 1923–30

One of the ironies of the Primo de Rivera dictatorship is that although for the greater part of its existence it was sustained by a period of international prosperity, within Spain Primo de Rivera attracted the bitter emnity of some of his most ardent original supporters. Nowhere is this truer than in the case of the Catalan business community.

In return for their support, Catalan industrialists believed that Primo de

Rivera would satisfy them in three main ways: by suppressing labour unrest, increasing even further the level of tariff protection, and respecting their autonomist views. In this final category, however, fellow officers in Madrid, imbued with traditional anti-Catalanist sentiments, forced Primo to go back on his promise.[37] In 1924 the Mancomunitat was abolished by the Dictatorship. Cambó went into exile, from where he bitterly attacked the regime.

Although in its 'honeymoon' period of 1923–26 the Dictatorship attracted much support—including that of the socialist trade union movement, the Unión General de Trabajadores (UGT)—for ridding Spain of the discredited political parties of the Restoration, Primo de Rivera was reluctant to offend the economic interests of the oligarchy. Thus in the urgent matter of agrarian reform, despite plans to resettle 'colonists' in the south, he could not see his way to provoke a head-on collision with the *latifundistas*. The agricultural policies of the dictatorship favoured the inefficient cereal growers of the large estates. Hence the regime attempted the impossible task of implanting its political economy in the countryside without altering in any way the social structure which it had inherited from the past.[38]

To its credit, the Dictatorship made a conscious attempt to intervene in the economy. Among its achievements was a ten-year plan for the construction of a network of roads and railways, as well as a programme of electrification and public works. These ambitious proposals were to be paid for by a series of financial reforms, much of which was the brainchild of Primo's ambitious young Finance Minister, José Calvo Sotelo. Calvo Sotelo provoked the opposition of more orthodox bankers and industrialists by his attempts to introduce a global tax on income. Other instruments of his policy were the use of the extraordinary budget and of State monopolies, the most famous of which was the petrol monopoly, CAMPSA, established in 1927.

In many areas of Spanish industry the Dictatorship presided over an era of spectacular progress. Electricity output increased from 1·62 million kWh in 1926 to 2·43 million kWh in 1929. The production of iron ore more than doubled in the same period from 3·18 million tons to 6·55 million tons. Foreign trade trebled, although imports considerably exceeded exports. However, the showpiece of the regime was its hydraulic policy, which owed much to the influence of Joaquín Costa, the man who, Primo reminded the nation, had called for an iron surgeon to implement his own policies. The Confederation of the Ebro, under the presiding genius of the hydraulic engineer Lorenzo Pardo, created 72,163 hectares of new irrigation, and improved a further 109,136 hectares.[39]

Nevertheless, it cannot be claimed that the economic prosperity of the 1920s was attributable to the Dictatorship. To begin with, Primo de Rivera had the good fortune to seize power at a time when there was an upturn in the international economy. Moreover, in some sectors of industry the policies of the regime proved something of a failure. The refusal to tackle the problem of agrarian reform condemned the manufacturing industry of Catalonia to a traditionally low level of internal consumption soon after it had lost its wartime export markets.

Yet, even though the regime was not responsible for the economic boom of the 1920s, the collapse of prosperity precipitated Primo de Rivera's demise. Devoid of political support, the Dictatorship came to rely on economic growth as a substitute for the free expression of opinion. From 1928 the economic policy of the Dictatorship started to collapse, while in the following year Spain began to be affected by the world depression. A bad harvest in 1928 coincided with a decline in emigrant remittances, a deteriorating trade balance, and a net export of capital. This in turn led to a depreciation on the value of the peseta which Cambó and the financial community blamed on the inflationary monetary policies of the Dictatorship.[40]

Early in 1930 Primo de Rivera resigned for predominantly political reasons. Most significantly he had lost the support of the army. The monarchy essayed a return to political normality, but within little over a year Alfonso XIII went into exile in France, thus clearing the way for the Second Spanish Republic. Before we analyse the Republic's attempts at economic and social reform it may be instructive to trace the rise of organised labour, for whom many of its policies were designed.

NOTES

1   Raymond Carr, *Spain, 1808–1939* (Oxford, 1966), p. 499.
2   Fernanda Romeu Alfara, 'La crisis de 1917 y sus consecuencias económicas y sociales en la región valenciana', *Saitabi*, xiv, 1964 (1966), pp. 118–21.
3   Ramón Tamames, *Estructura económica de España*, 7th edn (Madrid, 1974), i, p. 45.
4   Fidencio Kischner, *La influencia de la guerra en las industrias catalanas* (Barcelona, 1919), pp. 18–19; Instituto de Reformas Sociales, *Información sobre la emigración española a los países de Europa durante la guerra* (Madrid, 1919), p. 73; Francisco Bernis, *Consecuencias económicas de la guerra* (Madrid, 1923), p. 95.
5   J. A. Torrente Fortuño, *Historia de la Bolsa de Bilbao* (Bilbao, 1966), pp. 280 ff.
6   Santiago Roldán, José Luis García Delgado and Juan Muñoz, *La formación de la sociedad capitalista en España, 1914–20*, 2 vols (Madrid, 1973), 1, p. 37; Kischner, *op. cit.*, p. 26; Instituto de Reformas Sociales, *Información sobre emigración*, p. 75; Pedro Gual Villalbí, *Memorias de un industrial de nuestro tiempo* (Barcelona, 1923), pp. 104–15.
7   Kischner, *op. cit.*, p. 25; Francisco Cambó, *L'acció d'estat i l'acció privada en las industrias que tienen sobre-producció* (Tarrasa, 1919), pp. 5–6.
8   Kischner, *loc. cit.*
9   Instituto de Reformas Sociales, *Informes de los inspectores de trabajo sobre la influencia de la guerra europea en las industrias españolas, 1917–18*, 2 vols (Madrid, 1918), 1, p. 153; and *Información sobre emigración*, pp. 76–7.

10   Roldán et al., op. cit., 1, pp. 46–7.

11   Ibid., pp. 49–50.

12   Ibid., pp. 50–1; Instituto Nacional de Estadística, Principales actividades de la vida española en la primera mitad del siglo XX: síntesis estadística (Madrid, 1952), p. 64.

13   Roldán et al., loc. cit., pp. 51–2.

14   Cámara de Comercio, Industria y Navegación de Bilbao, Memoria comercial del año 1918 (Bilbao, 1919), p. xxi; Roldán et al., op. cit., p. 76.

15   Roldán et al., op. cit., pp. 79–83.

16   Gual Villalbí, op. cit., passim.

17   Jesús Pabón, Cambó, 3 vols (Barcelona, 1952–72), 1, pp. 429–32; El Trabajo Nacional, 1 September 1915; cf. Joseph Harrison, 'Big business and the failure of right wing Catalan nationalism, 1901–25', Historical Journal, 19 (1976), 901–18.

18   El Trabajo Nacional, 15 October 1914, 15 November 1914, 1 December 1914, 1 January 1915; Boletín de la Cámara de Comercio de Barcelona, January 1915; Marcelino Graell, Las zonas neutrales: su importancia para Barcelona (Barcelona,

19   El Trabajo Nacional, 17 July 1915, 1 September 1915.   [1914].

20   Cámara Oficial de Comercio y de la Industria de Zaragoza, Las zonas neutrales (Saragossa, 1914); A. Giménez Soler, Las zonas francas (Sargossa, 1915).

21   Pabón, op. cit., 1, p. 431.

22   El pensamiento catalán ante el conflicto europeo (Barcelona, 1915).

23   Comisión Protectora de la Producción Nacional, Crisis de la producción y del trabajo, información en cumplimiento de encargo del gobierno (Madrid, 1921); Cambó, L'acció d'estat, pp. 15–21.

24   Información, 9 September 1915.

25   Ibid., 2 December 1915.

26   Ibid., 24 February 1916, 9 March 1916.

27   Euzkadi 26–29 January 1917; El Liberal (Bilbao), 27 January 1917; see my article 'Big business and the rise of Basque nationalism', European Studies Review, 7 (1977), 371–91.

28   Santiago Alba, Un programa económico y financiero (Madrid, 1916).

29   Francisco Cambó, Vuit mesos al ministeri de Fomento: mi gestió ministerial (Barcelona, 1919), p. xi.

30   El Trabajo Nacional, March 1918.

31   See below, chapter six.

32   Joan Sardá and Lluc Beltrán, Els problems de la banca catalana (Barcelona, 1933), pp. 20–3; Francesc Cabana, La banca a Catalunya: apunts per una historia (Barcelona, 1965), pp. 6–89.

33   Boletín de la Cámara de Comercio y Navegación de Barcelona, April 1921; El Trabajo Nacional, April 1921.

34   Información 29 January 1921, 28 February 1921, 14 January 1922, 15–29 January 1923, 14 January 1924; Economia y Finances, January 1921, February 1921.

35   El Trabajo Nacional, May 1921.

36   J. G. Ceballos Teresi, Economía, finanzas, cambios; la realidad económica y financiera en los treinta años del presente siglo, 7 vols. (Madrid, n.d.), 5, pp. 174–7.

37   Stanley Payne, Politics and the Military in Modern Spain (Stanford, 1967), pp. 194–5.

38   Juan Velarde Fuertes, Política económica de la dictadura, 2nd edn (Madrid, 1973), p. 38.

39   M. Lorenzo Pardo, La conquista del Ebro (Saragossa, 1931).

40   Francisco Cambó, La valoración de la peseta (Barcelona, 1929), p. 83.

CHAPTER 6

The rise of organised labour

SOCIAL CONFLICTS DURING THE ANCIEN RÉGIME

Until recently it was commonly accepted that after the riots of the mid-seventeenth century in Castile and parts of Andalusia an idyllic calm prevailed throughout the realm which was not interrupted until the peasant disturbances and Luddite outbursts of the 1830s. Over the past few years, however, evidence has come to light of two distinct types of social conflict which took place in Spain in the intervening period: food riots, which occurred in both rural and urban areas, and peasant revolts directed against the excesses of the seigneurial regime.

In his study of the Esquilache revolt of 1766, which at one point threatened to topple the government, Pierre Vilar places Spain within the framework of a general European model of popular revolts brought about by economic crises of the *ancien régime*. These crises were mainly agrarian in character, short-lived, and manifested themselves by the scarcity and resulting high price of basic foodstuffs.[1] Other studies by Enric Moreu Rey and Irene Castells offer detailed accounts of the Barcelona bread riots of 1789.[2] On the question of anti-seigneurial disturbances, Manuel Ardit charts the revolt of 1801, which spread from the city of Valencia to the surrounding countryside. Led by the mythical Pep l'Orta (the Valencian equivalent of Captain Swing), forty villages rose against the tyranny of their *seigneur*. Yet this revolt, possibly like many others as yet unchronicled, soon met with disaster when it was put down by royal troops. Seven of the rebels were hanged and another forty either exiled or sentenced to long terms of imprisonment.[3]

How many more such incidents disturbed the peace of the old order we may never know; but it is important not to confuse these revolts with modern revolutionary phenomena. Mostly they were isolated protest movements, limited both socially and geographically. Encounters between groups of workers and their employers were in general restricted to a particular industry or locality and rarely if ever generated any sense of class consciousness. The vast majority of food rioters did not for a single moment reject the existing social order. Moreover no social group offered any alternative political or economic programme to the *ancien régime*. Thus in March 1789, at a time of pre-revolutionary activity in Paris, the bourgeoisie of Barcelona allied themselves with the privileged classes to suppress a rising of the lower orders.[4]

PEASANT DISTURBANCES IN THE NINETEENTH AND EARLY TWENTIETH CENTURIES

The transfer of land from the Church and the nobility to a new class of bourgeois landowners in the middle decades of the nineteenth century brought an overall deterioration in the living standards of the greater part of the rural population. Among the hardest hit were the poorer sections of the community, who were not only deprived of their traditional rights but, following the sale of communal lands, had to pay municipal taxes on basic items. Prior to the liberal reforms a peasant family could to some extent compensate for lack of income from the land by work in domestic industry. The spread of mass production from the factories increasingly closed this option to them.

From the 1830s onwards there was a sharp increase in the incidence of peasant disturbances, especially in the south. A dramatic increase was recorded in the number of instances of banditry in Andalusia, where the rural population came to regard the bandit as a champion of their rights as long as he directed his attentions on the local landlord. It was to re-establish order in the countryside that in 1844 the Moderate government created the detested Civil Guard, which was organised along military lines. In spite of this, peasant disturbances continued to occur in many parts of Spain, such as the risings in Castile and Aragon in 1855 and 1856. However, the first major outbreaks of peasant unrest in the nineteenth century took place in Andalusia, in the provinces of Seville and Granada.

The Seville revolt in July 1857 was the work of an ill equipped mob of scarcely more than a hundred men who marched through the night from the provincial capital to the neighbouring towns of Utrera and El Arahal. Arriving there at dawn, the peasant army stormed the outposts of the Civil Guard and afterwards set fire to the municipal archives where the records of common land sales were kept. The reaction of the authorities was both swift and excessively brutal. Upon learning of the events in Utrera and El Arahal a strong column of infantry was despatched with cavalry support. Together they massacred twenty-five of the rebels and arrested many others. After a hastily arranged trial, a further twenty-five were made to face the firing squad as a warning to the peasantry against future insurrections.[5] Undeterred by the threat of reprisals, four years later in June 1861 a spontaneous army of six thousand peasants—at one moment it was said to have numbered ten thousand—led by the social republican Pérez del Alamo, occupied the town of Loja in Granada where they remained for five days until the appearance of the military caused the rioters to disperse as quickly as they had gathered.[6]

Despite these and subsequent attempts to precipitate a general uprising among the peasantry, the anticipated social revolution aimed at the breaking up of the *latifundios* and the recovery of the common lands never materialised. In the next few years, the merest show of force on the part of the authorities was sufficient to break up the handful of risings which took place.

Rural anarchism
The growth of peasant self-consciousness in southern Spain was the consequence of the spread of anarchist ideas. These were imported into the Peninsula in 1868 by Bakunin's envoy, Guiseppe Fanelli. The initial success of the anarchist movement in winning over followers among the peasantry of western Andalusia has naturally led many to link its emergence in that region with the existence of the *latifundio*. However, the relationship between rural anarchism and large estates is far from straightforward. *Latifundios*, for example, were just as common in the provinces of Ciudad Real, Huelva, Cáceres and Granada, where anarchism was practically unknown, as they were in the leading provincial strongholds of the movement, Córdoba, Seville and Cádiz. In addition, if we consider the seven municipalities in Córdoba most affected by anarchist strikes in 1903 (Bujalance, El Carpio, Espejo, Fernán Nuñez, Montemayor, Castro del Río and Villafranca), in only four of these did large estates cover more than 70 per cent of the total land surface; in Castro del Río—centre of peasant revolts in that province—the proportion was only 30 per cent; in another it was 14 per cent, while in the remaining one there were no *latifundios* at all. In other districts of Córdoba where *latifundios* covered 90 per cent of the land surface, e.g. Hornachuelos, there were no social conflicts at all in 1903.[7] Similar evidence for the province of Seville suggests that there, too, rural anarchism was most common in districts where large estates occupied betweeen 35 and 40 per cent of the land surface. Only in the province of Cádiz was there a strong correlation between the existence of *latifundios* and the presence of agrarian anarchism. Thus in the best known centres of the movement in Cádiz at this time, Jerez, Arcos, Ubrique and Bornos, *latifundios* accounted for 73·6, 56·8, 54·4 and 79·1 per cent respectively of the total land surface.[8]

Although the relationship between the two phenomena, latifundism and rural anarchism, is not altogether clear, it does appear that it was in the latifundist provinces that the social and political conditions necessary for the gradual reform of society were most glaringly lacking, leaving the peasantry no alternative other than to submit or join in the kind of violent protest movement that was capable of obtaining their main objective, the redistribution of property. As Edward Malefakis shows, the very nature of agricultural production in the *latifundio* region prevented the day labourer from earning a comfortable living and thereby becoming a contented member of rural society. In a typical wheat-growing area nearly three-fifths of the yearly demand for labour occurred during the harvest months from June to August, and a further one-fifth during the October ploughing season. Over three-quarters of the annual demand for labour in olive growing took place in the five months from January to May. The position of the hired hand was, if anything, marginally worse in wine-growing areas, where almost two-thirds of the annual labour demand was confined to three-month pruning season from February to April. It was, of course, always possible to spread out the annual demand for labour by selective planting of various crops which required work on them at different times of the year. Yet, in practice, over most of southern Spain climatological factors and the lack of enterprise on the part of the landlords, many of whom were absent from their estates for the most of the year, condemned vast tracts of land to perennial monocultivation.[9]

For the peasantry the main consequences of this irregular seasonal distribution of employment were twofold: long periods of unemployment and scandalously low wages. The southern *bracero* could only expect to obtain work for between 180 and 250 days of the year. In regions of extreme monocultivation, such as the olive-growing region of south-west Jaén, the total number of days in the year when work was on offer might be as little as 130.[10] Because of this combination of restricted demand for labour and abundant supply, agricultural wages in the south were extraordinarily low: on average the annual income of the day labourer was two-thirds, or even less, of the national industrial wage. In order to keep himself and his family alive through the long jobless winter, all able bodied members of the peasant household had to work long hours at harvest time.

The peculiarities of agricultural production in the south, moreover, severely weakened the bargaining power of the rural labour, rendering the strike weapon practically ineffective for most of the year. At harvest time, the only occasion when production could be seriously threatened by the withdrawal of labour, the landowners strengthened their position and at the same time depressed wages by hiring migrant labourers. These were brought in from near-by mountain villages whose own economies depended on earnings from outside, as well as from further afield. Both Galician and Portuguese migrants were particularly vilified by the Andalusian peasant for this reason. Before the present century agricultural strikes were of little significance; in the last quarter of the nineteenth century, for example, there was only one such strike, which took place during the harvest of 1893.

The agricultural labourer was similarly incapable of improving his lot by political means. On paper, the Spain of the Restoration regime was a model of democracy; universal adult male suffrage was granted as early as 1890. In practice, however, the two main parties, the Conservatives and Liberals, alternated in office on the basis of an intricate system of election rigging within the Ministry of the Interior. That this corrupt and dishonest system should persist into the twentieth century owed much to the apathy of the electorate. In the small isolated villages of Andalusia its survival was also greatly aided by the enormous pressure which the local party magnates were able to exert over the largely illiterate masses.[11]

Despite a growing sense of frustration among the Andalusian peasantry, anarchism was slow to emerge as a powerful force. There was an upsurge of interest in the movement after the visit of Fanelli, which brought 28,000 adherents in Andalusia in 1873. Thereafter membership levelled off, while the wholesale repression of anarchism following the Mano Negra conspiracy of 1883, when the government discovered an alleged plot to murder landowners, served to reduce the number of followers even further.[12] Over the next two decades anarchist protests in the countryside were confined to sporadic outbursts of crop burning, cattle maiming and the destruction of vines, mostly in the provinces of Seville and Cádiz. The only major exception to this phase of general inactivity took place in 1892 with an assault on the town of Jerez de la Frontera by a peasant force numbering four thousand.

The re-emergence of rural anarchism in 1903, incorporating the syndicalist tactic of the general strike, brought the first sustained period of labour agitation in the Andalusian countryside. The strike movement spread from the traditional anarchist centres in Seville and Cádiz into the Guadalaquivir valley of Córdoba, where anarchism gained a foothold for the first time. In 1904, amid a new wave of strikes in the south, peasant associations also began to spring up in Old Castile.[13] However, the policy of arrest and deportation of strike leaders, and the use of Civil Guard protection of blackleg labour, together with the long and debilitating famine of 1904–06, helped to break the strike movement and dampen revolutionary fervour for another decade.

The unprecedented wave of rural unrest in southern Spain during the years 1918–20 had its origin in the sharp fall in peasant living standards caused by wartime inflation and the mounting political awareness in the region following the October revolution in Russia; hence the christening of the period as the *trienio bolchevista*. Information available for a particular village in Córdoba showed that between 1913 and 1919 the average daily wage of an agricultural labourer rose from 2·25 pesetas to 3·25 pesetas; yet at the same time his cost of living rose by twice the increase in his wages, from 2·57 to 4·55 pesetas.[14] Growing discontent in the countryside was shown by the growing circulation of anarchist newspapers and was fanned by the propaganda tours of both anarchist and socialist agitators. One of these so-called 'men of ideas', renowned throughout anarchist circles in Córdoba, was moved to change his name from Cordón to Kordhonief because of his passionate belief in bolshevism.[15]

The propaganda campaign bore fruit in the massive expansion of labour organisations in the south. In his celebrated account of peasant agitations in Córdoba during the *triento bolchevista* Juan Díaz del Moral calculated that at least 70,000 organised labourers, in sixty-one out of the seventy-five towns of the province, took part in the disturbances. In some communities the whole population joined the association.[16] Outside Andalusia the Federación Nacional de Agricultores de España (FNAE), which was founded in 1913 with little initial success, at last managed to organise anarcho-syndicalist locals, especially in the regions of Aragon and the Levante. This was the time in Valencia and Saragossa when anarcho-syndicalism spread from an urban to a rural setting.

By comparison with the earlier upsurge of rural anarchism in 1903–04, the level of strike activity during the *trienio* was much greater. As a measure of the intensity and extent of the second wave of strikes, the statistical section of the government-sponsored Institute of Social Reform found it impossible to keep abreast of events. According to its incomplete records, the number of agricultural strikes in Spain rose from forty-six in 1917 to sixty-eight in 1918, subsequently trebling to 188 in 1919 and 194 in 1920. The Institute's figures for Córdoba in the two years 1918–19 showed thirty strikes; yet these findings are at considerable odds with Díaz del Moral, who drew up a list of 184 such occurrences over the same period.[17]

At first these strikes had a remarkable degree of success, which was no doubt due to the decision of the FNAE to group together all workers, including small tenant farmers and shopkeepers, in a loose syndicate. This was in imitation of a similar decision taken by its industrial counterpart, the CNT, at the Congress of Sans in June 1918. Terrified by the demonstration of revolutionary solidarity among the agricultural labour force, the employers soon gave in to the latter's demands. On the whole these were not unreasonable; at Castro del Río, for instance, the *braceros* asked for a minimum wage of 2·50 pesetas a day, still substantially below the average industrial wage. When their demands were accepted by the landowners, they raised their sights to 3·50 pesetas a day, but later reached a compromise of 3 pesetas. Among other claims was the abolition of piecework. This was initially conceded by the employers, although they later went back on their promise.[18]

The attitudes adopted by successive governments of the period to the demands of the southern peasantry were mutually contradictory. The moderate Conservative Ministry of Eduardo Dato was happy to see an improvement in the appallingly low wages received by the *braceros*. In May 1919, however, the ultra-reactionary Juan La Cierva elected to crush the strike movement in the south. A division of troops under the command of a general were despatched to Córdoba, and agricultural unions were banned. Although a reduced number of strikes continued to take place, La Cierva profited from the knowledge that the most effective way to deal with Spanish anarchism was ruthless suppression.

Rural socialism

Compared with rural anarchism, socialism made a much later appearance in the Spanish countryside. Not until the *trienio bolchevista* did the Spanish Socialist party (the PSOE) begin to make serious headway among the peasantry, while it was not until the Second Republic that the movement became of major importance.

There are a number of theories which seek to explain the failure of Spanish socialism at this time to win over the rural population, some of which do not stand the test of even the most cursory analysis. For example, psychological factors such as the nature of the Andalusian character evidently do not provide the answer, as is demonstrated by the great strides made in the south by the PSOE and the socialist trade union, the FNTT, after 1931.[19] Nor, except in the provinces of Seville, Cádiz and parts of Córdoba, can the poor performance of the Socialists be explained by the relative strength of the anarchists, since, as we have seen, they themselves had great difficulty in breaking out of their own restrictive bounds before the *trienio bolchevista*. Elsewhere the existence of a third party with specific ideological commitments may have taken some support from the Socialists and socialist organisations. Throughout Old Castile and northern Spain, the fact that over two-thirds of the peasant population professed strong Catholic convictions may have accounted for the relative social stability of that area. In Old Castile, moreover, the campaign to obtain tariff protection against cheap wheat imports formed the basis of a common plan of action between the small tenant farmers and the landlords, who divided their support among the two main parties of the Restoration regime.[20]

Another widely canvassed explanation of the failure of the Socialists to capture rural support is the supposed indifference of socialism in general to the historical problems of the peasant population, as instanced by Marx's much quoted comment on 'the idiocy of rural life'. Outside Spain, however, there are numerous examples of socialist parties which made not insubstantial inroads in rural areas, for example the Italian Socialist party among the peasants of the Po Basin, the French Socialist party under Jaurès, and the Bavarian wing of the German Social Democratic party. Nevertheless, although there may have been no insurmountable ideological obstacles to the success of rural socialism in Spain, it was undoubtedly the case that the PSOE was slow to court the peasantry.

The PSOE was founded in 1879; yet seven years elapsed before the party could afford to finance a propaganda tour of Andalusia by one of its leaders, Pablo Iglesias. The visit, moreover, brought no positive results, and prompted the party to concentrate its effort on the districts where it already received some popular support, i.e. in the urban industrial areas. It was not until the PSOE congress of 1912 that the need to elaborate a specifically agrarian policy was recognised, and it took a further six years before the party's agrarian programme was approved.

The result of this policy change was quite surprising in terms of the composition and development of the socialist movement. By May 1920 the Socialists had established 359 agricultural locals in Spain, with a total membership of 61,327, while agricultural labourers comprised nearly one-third of the supporters of the socialist trade union movement, the Unión General de Trabajadores. Equally significant in the long run, the new recruits were to keep a greater faith in the socialist movement than the fluctuating membership of the main anarchist organisations. In order to retain the support of the new converts, in the two years before Primo de Rivera banned the political parties, the PSOE played an important role in attempts to bring about agrarian reform, an activity which it was to continue into the Second Republic.

THE EMERGENCE OF THE INDUSTRIAL PROLETARIAT

Although the level of industrial activity in late eighteenth and early nineteenth-century Spain was limited, both geographically and in numerical terms, it was nevertheless responsible for a series of far-reaching social changes. In common with the more advanced industrial nations of north-west Europe, the combination of improved productivity and falling prices brought about a considerable expansion of the cotton industry, and a simultaneous decline of more archaic textiles. This development was commented upon with regret as early as 1785 by the authorities in Catalonia charged with keeping the peace. In a petition of that year which they sent to Charles III, the *Audiencia de Cataluña*, the mouthpiece of the local magistrates, lamented the abandonment of linens and woollens in the Principality and their replacement by calico manufacture. 'The workers,' argued the document, 'find the working of cotton cleaner and more convenient. They even abandon agriculture for it and, since the handling of calicoes requires neither excessive strength nor great intelligence, everyone chooses to live by this occupation, which in a few hours' work brings in an excessive wage.'[21]

In reality, working conditions were rarely as attractive as the magistrates depicted them. The average working day lasted from twelve to fifteeen hours in generally overcrowded, ill lit and badly ventilated premises. The composition of the labour force in the early cotton industry reflected the nature of the production processes. At the beginning of the nineteenth century between 40 and 45 per cent of the 100,000 workers in the industry were males, with a similar percentage of females. The proportion of child labourers fluctuated between 10 and 20 per cent, increasing as the spread of mechanisation in the 1840s simplified methods of production. To the employers this development permitted a reduction in wage costs, since children of six years and above were expected to work shifts of up to fourteen and fifteen hours for very low wages, frequently on monotonous and debilitating tasks.

Outside the factory, the standard of living of the average working-class family was lamentably poor. In the 1850s the typical working-class family spent over half its income on food with bread accounting for half of this, the remainder of the family food budget going on such items as sardines, beans, potatoes and olive oil. According to a contemporary estimate, the average life expectancy of a poor male in the city of Barcelona between 1837 and 1847 was 19·68 years, compared with 33·83 years for a member of the 'wealthy classes'.[22]

The first labour struggles and early organisation

Among the earliest responses of labouring men in Spain to the emergence of industrial society was machine-breaking. In general the instigators of the Spanish variance of Luddism were artisans and domestic workers protesting against the introduction of mechanised processes which deprived them of work. Most of these incidents occurred in the less advanced textile industries, since there was very little domestic work in the cotton industry.

One of the first recorded instances of the destruction of machinery took place at Alcoy in March 1821, when a group of about 1,200 domestic workers in the woollen industry of that town set fire to seventeen spinning machines before they were stopped by the intervention of the authorities. Three years later an angry mob destroyed the machines in the factory of Micaela Lacot in Camprodón which produced flannels and draperies. We know of this even because it gave rise to a royal order of June 1824 which obliged manufacturers to take on extra hands and to instruct unemployed workers in the use of machinery. Similar destructive acts, of which little detail is known, also took place in Sallent and Segovia.[23] However, the most famous episode in the annals of Spanish Luddism occurred during the anti-clerical agitation of August 1835 during the First Carlist War when, after looting and setting fire to a number of convents in Barcelona, the mob destroyed the El Vapor factory of José Bonaplata. The events surrounding this episode are confused, although one account claims that the incendiarists received the active encouragement of rival manufacturers who feared the effects of cut-throat competition from the more up-to-date establishment.[24]

The earliest known attempt at working-class organisation took place in January 1834, when, on behalf of their fellow workers, a group of six young weavers in Barcelona petitioned the Captain General of Catalonia, General Llauder, as to the width of the standard piece of cloth known as the *pieza*. It was the view of the six that, by increasing the width of the *pieza*, the employers in effect were asking the labour force to take a cut in wages.

Moved by the extent of popular revolutionary sentiments during the disturbances of the following year, the municipal authorities, who at first were inclined towards inaction, finally took the men's complaint seriously. Llauder published a decree which stipulated the width of the *pieza* and also set up a factory inspection commission to consider complaints from both sides of the industry as well as to inspect the factories in order to watch over the length of the *piezas*. The commission, which soon went out of existence, was given the power to fine employers who failed to comply with the decree; it could also hand out sentences of eight days' imprisonment to workers who refused to make use of the arbitration procedure.[25]

Encouraged by this limited concession on the part of the Barcelona authorities to the petition of the weavers, the next two decades saw the blossoming of a number of workers' organisations, first of all among textile workers but spreading later to a number of other occupations. The first organisation to receive official recognition was the Asociación Mutua de Tejedores (Weavers' Mutual Association), headed by Juan Munts, which was founded in May 1840. In the second half of that year the Association embarked upon a series of well organised local strikes with the intention of securing pay increases for its members, an action which persuaded the authorities to set up a joint committee of workers and employers. The ineffectiveness of this body led to a new wave of strikes and the use of lock-out tactics by the employers. Before long, the textile workers' association had 7,000 members in Barcelona and another 8,000 in the rest of the province, while a further consequence of this first example of collective action was a drift towards republicanism among the masses.[26]

Rumours that the central government in Madrid was about to negotiate a free trade agreement with Great Britain in 1842, which would almost certainly have entailed a massive increase in textile imports from Lancashire, led to a brief period of co-operation between the weavers and the local authorities. A municipal loan of 140,000 reales was awarded to Asociación Mutua to set up its own factory, the Compañía Fabril de Tejedores. The latter organisation, although not renowned for its enterprise, still managed to outlive the parent body, which was dissolved by the government in 1843. Despite being restricted by the terms of its constitution to the manufacture of workmen's overalls, it nevertheless survived through times of industrial crisis and served a useful function in providing jobs for the unemployed, especially those on strike. Before it finally succumbed to the depression of 1848 the Compañía Fabril de Tejedores offered a livelihood to a considerable number of workers.

The putting down of a working-class revolt in Barcelona in 1843 heralded a decade of autocratic rule by the Moderates. As workers' organisations went underground the mill owners profited from their temporary eclipse to install steam power and labour-saving machinery. However, with the triumph of the 1854 revolution, in which the industrial proletariat of Barcelona played a major part, trade unionism began to re-emerge from its clandestine phase.

In the midst of the revolutionary events a new federation of all textile workers was founded, known as the Unión de Clases. At the end of 1854 this federation approached the Barcelona employers and demanded the scrapping of individual contracts and their replacement by collective agreements. During the following year working-class agitation was stepped up and a wider federation, the Junta Central de Directores de la Clase Obrera, of which the cotton industry formed a central core of support, soon claimed a membership of 80,000 in Catalonia. Labour militancy reached a fever pitch when the leader of the textile workers, José Barceló, was arrested on trumped-up charges of robbery and murder and subsequently garrotted. A general strike was declared which soon spread throughout the province of Barcelona, where 40,000 workers laid down their tools. As a reprisal for Barceló's death, a number of employers met with the same end. In an attempt to calm the situation the Progressive government of Espartero despatched a delegation to Barcelona which was successful in persuading the workers to call a halt to the strike by promises that the government would take notice of their petitions and mediate between labour and capital. In October 1856 the Progressives went so far as to present to the Cortes a modest Bill of social legislation. The Bill, however, in no way satisfied the workers, who insisted, among other things, on the basic right of association. At the end of the year a petition signed by 33,000 workers, two-thirds of them from Catalonia, was sent to the government, urging it to keep its promises. In despair a number of mills were attacked, leaving a trail of damage and resulting in numerous arrests. Throughout 1856 the Barcelona workers maintained the offensive and intervened actively in a fresh series of revolts after the Moderates returned to power in July. Large number of workers began to swell the ranks of the Federal Republican party, attracted by its demands for universal suffrage, while another indicator of the heightening sense of proletarian consciousness was the circulation of a considerable number of socialist newspapers and pamphlets brought across the frontier from France.[27]

In an attempt to dampen revolutionary sentiments the Narváez government again suppressed working-class associations in Catalonia in April 1857. Yet strikes continued to take place in support of workers' demands, and by 1860 the societies began to function in a state of effective legality, a factor which provoked a new decree of 1861 banning them once again. Despite this new measure working-class organisations, although officially prohibited, continued to act more or less openly, tolerated by the authorities, until they were granted legal status by the revolution of 1868.

The First International and the split in the labour movement
At the same time that the tireless efforts of the associationists were

rewarded by the granting of the basic freedoms of speech, the press and association, the September revolution also generated and encouraged new currents of thought aimed not so much at the achievement of gradual reforms as the total destruction of the capitalist system. The struggle between Marx and Bakunin for control of the First International led to the simultaneous introduction into Spain of two rival doctrines of social revolution, Marxism and anarchism. After learning of the events of 1868 Marx had high hopes of achieving the revolution south of the Pyrenees, but before long was forced to admit that 'the working classes of Spain now have very little to be congratulated on'.[28] In contrast, Bakunin's envoy in Spain, Fanelli, was successful in founding sections of the Alliance for Social Democracy in Madrid and Barcelona, where he deposited the programme and statutes of the organisation. Upon their return from the Basle conference of the International in December 1869 the two main leaders of the Barcelona anarchists, Rafael Farga Pellicer and Gaspar Sentiñón, began an all-out campaign to win over the Catalan proletariat to Bakunin's ideas. At the first congress of the Spanish region of the International, held in Barcelona in June 1870, the delegates showed themselves opposed to political activity and all forms of government, whether monarchical or republican. In addition, the congress also adopted the structure of local and regional association organised on an industrial basis, thus blending together the theories of Bakunin and the Catalan experience of association.[29]

Despite the activities of the First International, prior to the first world war Catalan anarchism was never a mass movement. Outlawed by the government in January 1874, the movement spent the next seven years underground. The first resolute effort to set up a mass organisation took place in 1881, when, in an attempt to stave off the movement's collapse, the moderates threw out the revolutionaries and embarked upon a policy of trade union activity within a legal framework. The moderates founded the Federación de Trabajadores de la Región Española (FTRE), which within a year of its foundation had 58,000 members. However, the success of the new trade union federation was only fleeting, while large sections of the Catalan proletariat remained outside its influence. Within the textile industry, for example, the strongest trade union, the Tres Clases de Vapor, was led by reformist socialists. The differences between these two organisations, moreover, were accentuated by the campaign of the Catalan mill owners for tariff protection, aimed at offsetting the crisis experienced by the cotton industry during the late 1880s. On this occasion the Tres Clases de Vapor seconded the efforts of the employers in order to safeguard jobs. At the end of the decade the FTRE was dissolved. The extremists withdrew from the unions and undertook a campaign of terror which was to result in their systematic repression by the authorities. By the mid-1890s what remained of the organisation was destroyed and large numbers of anarchists were forced into exile, where many of them remained for the rest of their lives.[30]

During the first decade of the twenieth century a sizable proportion of the Barcelona workers came to support the faction of the Republican party led by Alejandro Lerroux. Lerroux has been depicted as the puppet of Restoration politicians, paid to discredit the Catalan nationalists of the Lliga Regionalista; indeed, there is evidence that he took bribes from Liberal leaders. Nevertheless recent research by Joaquín Romero Maura shows that Lerroux's Republicans were a genuine working-class party offering a political solution to the problems of the proletariat.[31] The anarchists, faced with the mounting success of this new phenomenon at the ballot box, returned to terrorism in the false belief that only by a more extremist alternative could they hope to win over the support of the workers. Their insurrectionary tactics were again proved to be mistaken when in July 1909 the Maura government took only a week to put down a working-class revolt in protest against the conscription of Catalan troops to fight in the war in Morocco. The disastrous effects of the so-called Tragic Week led to the founding of the anarcho-syndicalist Confederación Nacional del Trabajo in 1910 in a further attempt to defend the interest of the proletariat through trade union activity.

In common with the CNT, the socialist trade union organisation, the Unión General de Trabajadores, was also founded in Barcelona. The year of the UGT's foundation was 1888, when the Restoration regime again legalised trade unions. In the early years of the organisation the Catalan section of the UGT comprised its principal grouping, providing one-fifth of the national membership in 1893. Subsequently, partly owing to the greater organising skills of Lerroux and later to the formation of the CNT, Catalan socialism dwindled almost to insignificance. In 1910, for example, when the UGT had 40,000 members throughout Spain, only 635 of these were in Barcelona.[32]

It is interesting to note that outside Catalonia the rise of organised labour was a much later development. This is particularly true in the regions where socialism came to predominate, Madrid, Vizcaya and Asturias. The working class of Vizcaya showed few signs of activity in the spheres of either politics or trade unionism before 1890, while Asturias remained without workers' organisations until the beginning of the present century. Detailed figures for 1907 show that 17,000 of the 30,000 members of the UGT came from Madrid, which contained various groups of organised workers in the craft trades, from printers and bank clerks to stonemasons.

Despite the large concentration of mines and steelworks in Vizcaya and Asturias, both regions experienced a remarkably low level of working-class organisation prior to the first world war. The first socialist associations in Asturias were established not by the miners but by the metal-workers and dockers in the port of Gijón. Moreover, commenting upon the profound changes brought about by the war, a local trade union leader stated in the socialist newspaper *El Socialista* in 1916 that in the previous twenty-five years the metalworkers of Vizcaya 'demanded nothing from the employers'.[33] Indeed, so weak was the tradition of association in these two regions that much of the initial impulse and organisation of the unions came from the local leaders of the PSOE. In Vizcaya before 1910 the Socialists retained the support of the workers by a policy of militant action which was to lead to five general strikes in the mines in a period of twenty years. That all but one of these strikes resulted in victory for the workers owed much to the willingness of successive governments to intervene on the men's behalf. In contrast, disputes in Asturias over the same period rarely displayed signs of violence, the strike weapon being used only as a last resort.

Throughout the first quarter-century of the organisation the leadership of the UGT pursued a policy of cautious pragmatism which brought a steady if unspectacular increase in membership from 15,000 in 1900 to 77,749 in 1911, thereafter doubling to 147,729 in 1913. The reformist tendency of its leaders led to UGT to collaborate with a small group of Restoration politicians, prominent among whom were the Liberal leader, José Canalejas, and the future Conservative premier, Eduardo Dato, who took a keen interest in the formulation and enacting of social legislation. After 1904 two prominent *ugetistas*, José Mora and Francisco Largo Caballero, represented the working class on the newly formed Institute of Social Reform, which was responsible for drafting a series of Bills aimed at improving the lot of Spanish labour. Among its earliest proposals to reach the statute book were the law on arbitration and conciliation of 1908, the strikes law of 1910 and the law on the number of hours worked in the mines of 1910. In the midst of the serious labour upheavals of 1919 the Institute was responsible for drafting the Act for an eight-hour working day—the major historical demand of Spanish labour. However, before the outbreak of the European war the UGT was greatly disappointed by the ineffectiveness of the Institute, which, five years after its foundation, had only eight inspectors to enforce the new laws and a total annual budget of only 325,000 pesetas.[34] In the same year (1909) UGT collaborationism was severely shaken by the repressive attitude of the Maura government to the events in Barcelona, above all the execution in September 1909 of the anarchist leader and educator Francisco Ferrer. Díaz del Moral, for example, comments that the bloody aftermath of the Tragic Week led to a marked change in outlook within the organisation, which 'descended from its ivory tower, full of passion and vigour'.[35]

Revolution and reform, 1909–31
In the wake of the Tragic Week a number of important developments took place in the history of the labour movement. With the avowed aim of

toppling the hated Maura government in the coming elections, in 1909 the PSOE entered into a series of alliances with republican groupings, a consequence of which was the election of the first Socialist deputy, the party's leader, Pablo Iglesias. With this initial whiff of success the prestige of the PSOE rose considerably. For the first time in its history its ranks were swelled by intellectual recruits, among them Luis Araquistáin, Julián Besteiro, Oscar Pérez Solis and Manuel Nuñez de Arenas.

The miners' strike in Vizcaya in the summer of 1910 showed that the newly elected Liberal government of Canalejas was willing to intervene on the side of the workers. As a result the number of strikes in Spain rose from 147 in 1909 to 256 in 1910, and 311 in 1911. In September 1911 a general strike was declared in Bilbao which received the reluctant support of the leadership of the PSOE. As the strike movement spread, the newly formed CNT, not wishing to be outflanked by the usually stolid Socialists, added its support, a decision which in the short run was to do great harm to the infant organisation. The response of Canalejas to the general strike was to declare a state of martial law throughout Spain and to close down the local and regional centres of the CNT. A month later a Barcelona judge banned the CNT altogether, sending it underground for the next three years. These decisions were to trigger off a state of civil strife during which Canalejas was assassinated by an anarchist gunman in November 1912. For its part, the UGT was forgiven its supposed indiscretions and allowed to function as before.[36]

On the eve of the first world war one factor in particular accounted for the relative weakness of organised labour both politically and economically: this was that the great majority of Spanish workers belonged to neither socialist nor anarchist trade unions. Compared with a total active population of 1·1 million industrial workers and 1·7 million agricultural labourers, the UGT had 127,804 members in 1914, a substantial decline from the previous year, while the outlawed CNT had a mere 15,000 adherents. The PSOE, moreover, with the solitary figure of Pablo Iglesias in the Cortes, seemed the permanent victim of the failure of the parliamentary process to improve the lot of the working class. A dramatic change in this situation, however, was brought about by the mounting wartime inflation, which seriously hit working-class living standards. Starting in 1915, a new wave of strikes erupted throughout Spain, while in the following year strike activity not only increased but also betrayed signs of more effective organisation.

In May 1916 the Asturian delegates to the UGT congress in Madrid called for a national general strike in alliance with the CNT, aimed at forcing the Romanones government to take action against inflation and rising unemployment. Faced with a further drop in membership to 110,000 in 1916, Julián Besteiro accepted the Asturian proposal on behalf of the leadership. The response of the CNT was mixed. Although moderates like Salvador Seguí and Angel Pestaña expressed interest in an alliance with the UGT, more specifically anarchist circles within the organisation ruled out the question of a merger. Despite these difficulties, in July 1916 the UGT and the CNT formally signed the Pact of Saragossa, by which they agreed to work together to put pressure on the government to tackle the problem of the rising cost of living, arguing in favour of a general strike as the most effective means of bringing this about.[37]

The resulting national general strike on 18 December 1916, the first of its kind in the history of the Spanish labour movement, was by any standards a tremendous success. The number of men who struck work exceeded the combined membership of the UGT and the CNT. The Spanish capital was brought to a standstill; even the middle classes took part, closing down shops and cafés.[38] In the long run, however, despite sending a delegation led by Besteiro to the Ministry of the Interior, the one-day stoppage had little effect; inflation and unemployment continued unabated. Nevertheless the closing of the Cortes by Romanones in February 1917 was the signal for a further meeting between the UGT and the CNT in the following month, after which they issued a joint manifesto threatening an indefinite general strike unless remedial action was quickly taken.

The general strike was finally called in August 1917, for political rather than economic reasons. Led by the Socialists, the Spanish workers resolved to help the middle classes, represented in the Assembly movement, carry out the bourgeois revolution which they themselves lacked the strength to undertake. In its manifesto, drawn up by Besteiro on 12 August, the strike committe demanded only moderate concessions: the establishment of a republic, the creation of a provisional government, and honest elections. Nowhere was there any mention of more extreme measures such as social revolution. The strike's chances of success, however, were seriously undermined when, on the day after its declaration, the signatories of the manifesto, Largo Caballero, Besteiro, Anguiano and Saborit, were arrested in their secret headquarters in Madrid. Even so, despite the defection of Cambó's Lliga Regionalista and the less than enthusiastic support of the republicans, the strike soon spread to large areas of Spain. There were violent demonstrations in Madrid, Barcelona and Vizcaya. Yet owing to the lack of leadership the strike was broken by the end of August; only the Asturian miners and the railwaymen resisted for any greater length of time. Another factor which undoubtedly proved decisive was the passivity of the agricultural labourers of the south, who refused to co-operate on the grounds that the strike was political.[39]

On 4 October a military tribunal handed down sentences of life imprisonment to the strike committee, who were sent to Cartagena prison. There they remained until the general election of February 1918, when all four were elected to the Cortes, Largo Caballero with the aid of anarchist votes in Barcelona. As to the anarcho-syndicalists of the CNT, they could hardly have been more disillusioned by the events of 1917. Having abandoned anarchist doctrines and temporarily accepted the leadership of the Social- ists in order to bring about the transitional stage to a bourgeois democracy, they found themselves left high and dry. In future they would reinforce their apoliticism and restructure their organisation. Thus it was that at the Congress of Sans in June 1918 the Confederación Regional del Trabajo, the Catalan branch of the CNT, agreed to do away with craft organisation and adopt compulsory industrial unionism in the shape of the sindicato único. This decision was the culmination of a process of centralisation and unification begun in 1915, when the CNT was once again permitted to function normally by the government.

The next few years saw a phenomenal expansion in CNT membership. In 1918 the local federation of Barcelona boasted 54,572 affiliated members, a figure which quadrupled by the autumn of 1919 to reach 205,642. By the end of 1919 the total membership of the CNT throughout Spain was 714,028. Even regions previously considered Socialist preserves such as Vizcaya and Asturias were now penetrated by the CNT. The UGT, which suffered a considerable setback following its routing in the general strike of 1917, was totally eclipsed by the rival organisation, and by 1920 had only 211,342 adherents, less than one-third of total CNT membership. Meanwhile the centres of labour agitation in Spain passed from Vizcaya to Barcelona.[40]

The prelude to the new era of industrial turmoil was an attempt in January 1919 by the management of the Anglo-Canadian hydro-electric enterprise La Canadiense of Barcelona to reduce the wages of clerical staff. The CNT, spoiling for a confrontation with the employers in order to show off its new-found strength and organisation, declared a strike which before long became general throughout Catalonia and other parts of Spain. The effects of the strike were almost immediately visible to the authorities as Barcelona was plunged into darkness at night-time and public transport throughout the province was brought to a standstill. Within three weeks the strikers claimed victory as individual employers began to concede the men's demands. Finally, on 3 April 1919, the Romanones government decreed an eight-hour day to come into effect from 1 October.

However, the harshness of the Catalan employers' counter-offensive, together with the repressive policies of the State after the departure of the conciliatory Romanones government, had the effect of widening an already existing rift within the CNT between anarchists and syndicalists. Before long, moderate syndicalist leaders like Pestaña and Seguí lost control of the movement under the pressure of events to younger and more violent elements. The ensuing civil war in Barcelona from 1919 to 1923 between anarchist gunmen and the hired assassins of the sindicatos libres, paid by the employers, marked the end of the CNT as a mass movement of organised labour. Seguí himself was the victim of one such assassination attempt, and his death meant the removal of a substantial obstacle to the adoption of overtly insurrectionary tactics by the CNT.

When Primo de Rivera seized power in September 1923 with the backing of the employers, it came as no surprise that the CNT was again outlawed. A more surprising development within the Spanish labour movement at this juncture was the willingness of the rival UGT to co-operate with the dictatorship in order to safeguard its own interests. The PSOE having survived the crisis of 1920–21, when only a small fraction of its membership split off to found the Spanish Communist party, the Socialist trade union wing decided that, instead of overthrowing what the far left saw as a proto-fascist regime, they should seek to benefit from a monopoly of worker representation. By a number of criteria their decision was vindicated by future developments. Between 1923 and 1927 UGT membership actually rose from 210,617 to 223,349. Socialist centres (Casas del Pueblo) were established in a number of new localities. Meanwhile Francisco Largo Caballero, after twenty years' apprenticeship as a delegate to Institute of Social Reform, became a Counsellor of State, in which capacity he was able to exert considerable influence on labour matters. These included a system of equal representation committees known as comités paritarios which, although hardly established before Primo was overthrown, formed the basis for the mixed juries or jurados mixtos of the Second Republic.[41] Hence it came about the when Alfonso XIII fled the country in April 1931 the Socialists had consolidated their political and trade union organisations to the point where they were able to play an active role in any attempt to build a new, democratic Spain. The CNT, in marked contrast, was now, in the main, violently hostile to any form of government, whether it was a military dictatorship or a liberal democracy.

NOTES

1   Pierre Vilar, 'El motín de Esquilache y las crisis del Antiguo Régimen', Revista de Occidente, 107 (1972), 199–249.

2   Enric Moreu Rey, Revolució a Barcelona el 1789 (Barcelona, 1967); Irene Castells, 'El rebomboris del pa de 1789 a Barcelona', Recerques, 1 (1970), 51–81.

3   Manuel Ardit Lucas, 'Los alborotos de 1801 en el reino de Valencia', Hispania, 29 (1969), 526–42.

4   Josep Fontana, 'Nacimiento del proletariado industrial y primeras etapas del movimiento obrero', in Cambio económico y actitudes políticas en la España del siglo, XIX, pp. 57–95.

5   Constancio Bernaldo de Quirós, El espartaquismo agrario andaluz, new edn (Madrid, 1974), pp. 40–3.

6   Rafael Pérez del Alamo, Apuntes sobre dos revoluciones andaluzas, new edn (Madrid, 1971), pp. 69–77.

7   Juan Díaz del Moral, Historia de las agitaciones campesinas andaluzas—Córdoba (Antecedentes par una reforma agraria), new edn (Madrid, 1973), p. 221;

Pascual Carrión, *Los latifundios en España: su importancia, origen consecuencias y solución* (Madrid, 1932), pp. 199–214; Juan Pablo Fusi, El movimiento obrero en España, 1876–1914', *Revista de Occidente*, 131 (1974), 208.
  8 Fusi, *El movimiento obrero*, loc. cit.
  9 Malefakis, op. cit., pp. 98–9.
 10 *Ibid.*, pp. 100–1; Carrión, op. cit., pp. 363–7.
 11 Joaquín Romero Maura, 'El caciquismo: tentativa de conceptualización', *Revista de Occidente*, 127 (1973), 15–44.
 12 Clara Lida, 'Agrarian anarchism in Andalusia: documents on the Mano Negra', *International Review of Social History*, XIV (1969), 315–52.
 13 Instituto de Reformas Sociales, *Memoria acerca de la información agraria en ambas Castillas* (Madrid, 1904).
 14 Instituto de Reformas Sociales, *Información sobre el problema agrario en la provincia de Córdoba* (Madrid, 1919), pp. 166–7.
 15 Díaz del Moral, op. cit., p. 271.
 16 *Ibid.*, pp. 281 and 491–4.
 17 Instituto de Reformas Sociales, *Estadística de las huelgas, memorias de 1917–20*, 4 vols (Madrid, 1918–21); Díaz del Moral, op. cit., pp. 314–29.
 18 Vizconde de Eza, *El problema agrario andaluz* (Madrid, 1919).
 19 See below, chapter seven.
 20 Fusi, *El movimiento obrero*, p. 211.
 21 Torrella, *El moderno resurgir textil de Barcelona*, pp. 220–5.
 22 Ildefonso Cerdá, 'Monografía estadística de la clase obrera de Barcelona de 1856', in *Teoría general de la urbanización*, 2 vols (Madrid, 1867), II, p. 304.
 23 Emili Giralt, Josep Termes and Alberto Balcells, *Bibliografia dels moviments socials a Catalunya, País Valenciá i les iles* (Barcelona, 1972), p. 11; Biblioteca de Catalunya, *Folletos Bonsoms*, No. 10, 188.
 24 Archive des Affaires Etrangères, Paris, *Correspondances politiques des consuls, Espagne*, vol. 9, 339.
 25 M. Raventós, *Els moviments socials a Barcelona durant el segle XIX* (Barcelona, 1925), pp. 25–7; Vicens Vives, *Cataluna en el siglo XIX*, p. 218.
 26 Izard, op. cit., p. 95.
 27 Casimiro Martí, 'Las sociedades obreras en Barcelona y la política en junio de 1856', in *Homenaje a Jaime Vicens Vives*, 2 vols (Barcelona, 1967), II, pp. 373–81; Josep Termes, *Anarquismo y sindicalismo en España: la Primera Internacional (1864–81)* (Barcelona, 1972), pp. 20–2.
 28 Casimiro Martí, *Orígenes del anarquismo en Barcelona* (Barcelona, 1959), pp. 77–8.
 29 Anselmo Lorenzo, *El proletariado militante*, 2 vols (Toulouse, 1949), I, pp. 85–120.
 30 Joaquín Romero Maura, 'Anarchism: the Spanish case', in David Apter and James Joll (eds), *Anarchism Today* (London, 1971), pp. 60–82.
 31 Joaquín Romero Maura, *La Rosa de Fuego: republicanos y anarquistas: la política de los obreros barceloneses entre el desastre colonial y la semana trágica, 1899–1909* (Barcelona, 1975) pp. 270 ff.
 32 Fusi, *El movimiento obrero en España*, pp. 217–18.
 33 *El Socialista*, 26 June 1916, cited in Fusi, *El movimiento obrero en España*, p. 221.
 34 Angel Marvaud, *La question sociale en Espagne*, p. 289. See my article 'The beginnings of social legislation in Spain, 1900–19', *Iberian Studies*, 3 (1974).
 35 Díaz del Moral, op. cit., p. 163.

36   M. Buenacasa, *El movimiento obrero español, 1886–1926* (Paris, 1966), pp. 52–3.
37   Gerald Meaker, *The Revolutionary Left in Spain, 1914–23* (Stanford, 1974), p. 41.
38   Francisco Largo Caballero, *Mis recuerdos: cartas a un amigo* (Mexico, 1954), p. 52.
39   Díaz del Moral, *op. cit.*, pp. 266–7.
40   Balcells, *El sindicalismo–Barcelona* (Barcelona, 1965), pp. 15 and 52; Buenacasa, *op. cit.*, pp. 81–2.
41   Joaquín Maurín, *Los hombres de la dictadura*, pp. 197–9.

CHAPTER 7

The Second Republic and the international depression, 1931–39

The Second Spanish Republic was proclaimed on 14 April 1931. During the first two years of its troubled existence, commonly referred to as the *bienio reformador*, or reformist biennium, a left-of-centre coalition comprising the Socialist party and diverse Republican groups sought to enact a series of moderate reforms reflecting the common ground which supposedly existed between the reformist wing of the working class and more progressive elements within the bourgeoisie. The Church and the military were singled out for attack as traditional institutions with excessive power and influence over the State. In an attempt to reduce the overcentralisation of the Restoration as well as to buy off the separatists in Catalonia an autonomy statute was granted to that region in October 1932. Yet the most significant initiative of the *bienio reformador* was the long-awaited assault on the iniquitous distribution of land and the problem of rural unemployment, particularly in the south.[1]

Although the regionalist policies of the Republican–Socialist alliance cemented lasting popular support for the new regime in Catalonia, in most other respects these minimalist reforms failed to achieve their desired objectives. The anti-Catholic legislation of the period, which allowed for divorce, civil marriage and secularised burial, and aimed to curb the influence of the teaching orders, had the counter-productive effect of serving as a focal point for Conservative opposition to the infant Republic.[2] At the same time the intended beneficiaries of the legislation, the great mass of the rural population, were soon to become bitterly disappointed by the slowness and utter ineffectiveness of the Republic's attempt at agrarian reform. From the very outset of the Republic the anarcho-syndicalists, admittedly stronger in the industrial towns than the countryside, rejected the policy of bourgeois reformism advocated by their Socialist rivals. Indeed, by the spring of 1933 the Socialists too, who were beginning to replace the CNT as the leading expression of peasant grievances, began to get disenchanted by the failure of their armchair intellectual partners.[3]

The breakdown of the working relationship between the Socialists and Republicans permitted a shift to the right in the general election of

November 1933. Thereafter Spain was governed by a centrist coalition based on the Radical party, the least reform-minded of the parties represented in the governments of the *bienio reformador*. The attitude of the Socialists to the new regime was conditioned by the increasing dependence of the Radicals on the Catholic CEDA (Spanish Confederation of Autonomous Right-wing Groups), with its corporatist ideology, provocative language and the strong admiration of its leadership and rank and file for both Mussolini and the Austrian chancellor Dollfuss. Dollfuss, as the PSOE were only too aware, was responsible in the spring of 1934 for the destruction of their Austrian counterparts. The entry of three CEDA Ministers into Radical Lerroux government in October 1934 was the signal for the declaration of a revolutionary general strike by the socialist trade union movement, the UGT. Spain's October revolution, however, was easily defeated by the authorities, with the single exception of Asturias, where African troops had to be brought in to put down the northern miners. Repression afterwards was harsh: some 30,000–40,000 political prisoners were taken, including many of the leading personalities of the *bienio reformador*. Others were forced to flee the country. Catalonia too was punished for having declared itself a separate republic by the indefinite suspension of its autonomy statute.[4]

The two years of Conservative rule were dubbed by the left the *bienio negro*, or black biennium. Prior to October 1934 the liberal reforms of the previous years were slowed down and in some cases suspended. After the crushing defeat of the left, Spain entered a period of reaction; many of the reforms of 1931–33 were reversed as the extreme right clamoured for the overthrow of parliamentary democracy. Yet the final attempt by the right to gain power by legal means in the elections of February 1936 saw them narrowly defeated by a Popular Front coalition committed to restoring the programme of the reformist biennum. There were, however, important differences between the Popular Front administration and that of 1931–33. Most significantly the PSOE, although prepared to back the new government with its votes, refused to compromise its socialist ideals by accepting ministerial responsibility a second time. The peasantry were no longer content to wait for land to be handed down to them and began to think and act in terms of the seizure of estates. During the spring and early summer of 1936 a sharp polarisation of Spanish politics took place as the ranks of the PSOE and the CEDA were depleted by desertions to the Communists on the left and the Falange on the extreme right. In an attempt, as they claimed, to restore law and order to an anarchic situation the military embarked on what was to become a brutal and destructive civil war during which foreign intervention made Spain the battleground of Europe.

SPAIN AND THE WORLD ECONOMIC CRISIS

Spain's seemingly insurmountable problems of the 1930s cannot be seen in isolation. The politicians of the Second Republic aimed to carry out their legislative programme at the time of the most profound eonomic crisis that the capitalist system has ever experienced. Thus it is reasonable to ask to what extent the events of the 1930s in Spain were the product of external conjunctural factors and how far they were due to the Republic's endeavour to replace a repressive and anachronistic social structure by one which attempted to serve Spaniards as a whole.

The relationship between the Spanish crisis and the world economic recession received detailed attention from a number of authorities. Commenting in 1934, the Bank of Spain was not alone in suggesting that Spain had fared less badly than elsewhere. 'It does not require a great analytical effort,' the bank argued, 'to be convinced that if in some sectors the Spanish economic crisis is intimately connected with the world crisis (foreign trade, shipping, steel, iron, etc), in general, however, substantially national trends and characteristics have predominated. The Spanish depression had been, in general, notably less profound than the world depression, paralleling the latter neither in its beginnings nor its final stages, nor in its most lasting and typical fluctuations. The complete and closed nature of our economy, our limited industrialisation [and] our totally rudimentary system with its small-scale financing and businesses has brought about our relative isolation from the capitalist world and contributed to make the crisis more superficial.'[5]

The level of unemployment, a strong indicator of social discontent, was much lower in Spain than in the more advanced economies which had greater links with the international capitalist system. The number of jobless in the United Kingdom rose to 23 per cent of the working population in August 1932. This coincided with the bottom of the depression in Germany, when 45 per cent of trade union members were without work and a further 23 per cent on short time. Across the Atlantic the number of unemployed in the United States reached a peak at about 25 per cent in 1933. In Spain, meanwhile, where the out-of-work population rose steadily from 1930 to the end of 1933, unemployment still accounted for only 12·8 per cent of the insured population at the latter date. Elsewhere, though, recovery measures began to reduce the number of unemployed, while the situation in Spain stabilised in 1934 and 1935; in 1936 political unrest was an important factor in a further sharp rise in unemployment. Catalonia, however, which had little contact with world markets, never experienced an unemployment rate over 6·5 per cent, a level which was reached only in the spring of 1936.

The overall figure for Spain, moreover, obscured important regional and sectoral variations. The deep concern shown by early Republican governments for Andalusia reflected the disproportionate level of unemployment among the southern peasantry. Rural unemployment in the south was a perennial problem: in the autumn of 1930 it assumed serious proportions following an exceptional drought and the failure of the olive crop in parts of the region. A government report of 1931 put the number of out-of-work agricultural labourers throughout the region of Andalusia at 100,000, or 12 per cent of the total. The agrarian reformer Pascual Carrión claimed that in certain months of 1930 and 1931 as many as 200,000 were unemployed in lower Andalusia alone.[6] For Spain as a whole agricultural unemployment continued to occupy a disproportionately high level throughout the Second Republic. In June 1932, a time of bumper harvests, 258,570 out of the 446,263 jobless were classified as agricultural workers. From them on to the outbreak of civil war agriculture continued to provide between three-fifths and two-thirds of the registered unemployed.[7]

Table 31   The level of unemployment in Spain, 1932–36

	Fully unemployed	Short time	Total
January 1932	–	–	389,000
June 1932	–	–	446,263
December 1933	351,804	267,143	618,947
December 1934	406,743	261,155	677,898
December 1935	416,198	257,963	674,161
June 1936	–	–	801,322

Source.   Alberto Balcells, Crisis económica y agitación social en Cataluña (1930–36), (Barcelona, 1971), p. 53.

As the Bank of Spain conceded, the recession in world trade hit Spanish exporters severely. Between 1930 and 1935, while other nations drew up bilateral trading arrangements which excluded Spain, the level of the country's foreign trade fell by nearly three-quarters. Sales of individual items slumped disastrously. Table wines, which earned 291 million pesetas in 1928, brought in only 13 million in 1935. Exports of oranges fell in value from 257 million pesetas to 103 million over the same period; almonds from 70 to 34 millions; rice from 39 to 4 million; and olive oil from 36 to 7 million. This sharp decline brought hardship to the producers of the Levante, Andalusia, Catalonia and La Rioja. Galicia bore the brunt of the fall in the value of exports of fish preserves from 64 million pesetas to 19 million. The Basque region was among those areas hit by the decline in exports of iron-ore from 91 to 33 million pesetas between 1928 and 1935.[8]

Demographic developments
The nature and intensity of the economic crisis in Spain were significantly affected by demographic factors. In particular the problems of the coun-

Table 32   Foreign trade of Spain, 1928–35 (million pesetas)

Year	Imports	Exports	Total
1928	3,005·0	2,183·5	5,188·8
1929	2,737·0	2,112·9	4,849·9
1930	2,447·5	2,456·8	4,904·3
1931	1.175·9	990·3	2,166·2
1932	957·7	742·3	1,718·0
1933	836·6	673·0	1,509·6
1934	855·0	612·5	1,467·5
1935	876·1	588·2	1,464·3

Source. Jordi Nadal, Jaime Vicens Vives and Casimiro Martí, 'Les mouvements ouvriers en Espagne en temps de dépression économique (1929–39), in *Mouvements ouvriers et dépression économique de 1929 à 1939* (Assen, 1966), p. 106.

tryside were exacerbated by the decline of employment prospects in the industrial towns and the closed-door policy of the Latin American nations, previously the main recipients of surplus agricultural labour from the Peninsula.

According to the population census of 31 December 1930, Spain, on the eve of the Second Republic, had a population of 23,563,867 inhabitants, a net increase of almost 10 per cent over the 1920s. In the intervening years the drift away from the countryside to the towns continued unchecked. The proportion of the active labour force employed in agriculture fell by over one-fifth from 57·30 per cent to 45·51 per cent.

The final years of the Dictatorship witnessed a sharp acceleration in the process of urbanisation. From 710,000 inhabitants in 1921 Barcelona expanded to 1,005,000 in 1931, overtaking Madrid, which also grew in the same period from 751,000 to 952,000. Altogether the seven largest cities in Spain—Barcelona, Madrid, Valencia, Seville, Málaga, Saragossa and Bilbao—increased their population by 23 per cent at this time, from 2,320,000 to 3,026,000. The expansion of the leading provincial capitals coincided with a slowing down in emigration. Between 1921 and 1925 outward

Table 33   Occupation of the active labour force according to census data, 1910–40 (%)

Year	Agriculture	Industry	Services
1910	66·00	15·82	18·18
1920	57·30	21·90	20·31
1930	45·51	25·51	27·98
1940	50·52	22·52	27·35

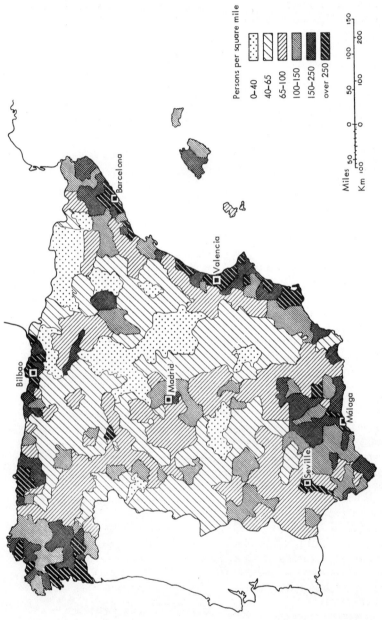

Map 4 The density of population, according to the 1930 census. (From Admiralty Naval Intelligence Division, Geographical Handbook series, *Spain and Portugal*,

Persons per square mile

0–40
40–65
65–100
100–150
150–250
over 250

Miles
Km

Barcelona

Valencia

Bilbao

Madrid

Seville

Málaga

passages of Spanish migrants, mainly to Latin America, exceeded return passages by an annual average of 25,730 persons, falling to an average of 6,232 a year between 1926 and 1930.[9]

Beginning in 1931, however, these demographic trends were slowed down or reversed. The most dramatic turn-about affected overseas migration. The Latin American Republics, themselves subject to the world economic recession, imposed restrictions on further immigration and banned the remittance of savings. Spaniards therefore returned home in large numbers, the net balance of immigration into Spain in the four years from 1931 to 1934 being 106,243.

Although not reversed, the movement of population away from the countryside to the towns experienced a pronounced deceleration. In the five years before the military rising (1931–36) Barcelona grew at only one-quarter of its rate of growth of the previous quinquennium and Madrid grew at half its previous rate.

The net effect of these two developments was an expansion in the relative size of the agricultural population, which increased by more than a tenth between 1930 and 1940. A substantial proportion of those repatriated chose to resettle in their place of origin, while large numbers of workers dismissed from the mines and factories returned to the land. Thus regions least equipped to deal with the social problems of unemployment, such as Galicia and the Levante, were transformed overnight from net exporters of population to net recipients.[10]

In addition, the situation in those families where the breadwinner found himself out of a job was often far graver in Spain than elsewhere owing to the rudimentary state of social security south of the Pyrenees. Following the disastrous financial experiments of the Dictatorship, Republican Finance Ministers were obsessed with financial orthodoxy. Both the Socialist Indalecio Prieto and his Catalan Republican successor Jaime Carner had as their prime objective the stabilisation of the peseta in order that they might restore Spain's international credit. This was achieved by the middle of 1932. The deficits of the Carner budgets of 1932 and 1933 were substantially smaller than those of the Dictatorship.

The sole national agency set up initially to combat unemployment was the Caja Nacional del Seguro contra Paro Forzoso, established in 1931. By 1933 the sum allotted to it was no more than one million pesetas annually, less than 0·5 per cent of the national budget. All it was able to do was offer financial support to those workers' associations which offered unemployment insurance. In 1935 a new institution known as the Junta Nacional contra el Paro was set up to co-ordinate public works projects, yet in the following year it received only 2 per cent of budgetary expenditure when unemployment was at its height.

In spite of the serious problems created by the coming of the world economic crisis at the time of the establishment of the Republic it is generally agreed that neither the left-inspired Asturian revolt of 1934 nor the military uprising of 1936 can be explained primarily in these terms. Their origins were to be found in the Spanish past.[11]

THE AGRARIAN PROBLEM

The agrarian problem, the most explosive issue of the early years of the Republic, was a consequence of the scandalous neglect of the countryside by successive Restoration governments. Prior to the fall of the monarchy the only major piece of State intervention on the land in the twentieth century was the Besada law of 1907, which set up a junta for the Colonisation and Repopulation of the Interior aimed at resettling the countless thousands of half-starved peasants. In practive this well intentioned measure of Catholic paternalism proved to be little more than a dead letter. Between 1908 and 1926 no more than 1,679 peasant families were settled on a total of 11,243 hectares of land.[12]

The earliest initiative for reforms on the land during the Second Republic came from the Socialists, the one party in the governing coalition with a clearly defined agrarian programme. In April 1930 the socialist UGT established a land workers' federation, the Federación Nacional de Trabajadores de la Tierra (FNTT). The provisional government which ruled Spain from April to July 1931 while a constitution was being drafted included as Labour Minister the veteran trade union leader Francisco Largo Caballero. Accused by his political opponents of abusing his ministerial office to consolidate the position of the FNTT, Largo Caballero nevertheless played a vital part in enacting a series of measures aimed at tackling some of the most pressing problems of the countryside.

Faced with the immediate problem of rural unemployment and social upheaval as well as the need to ensure the year's harvest, the provisional government resorted to the device of rule by decree. Two of the six decrees that were issued dealt primarily with tenant farmers, while the remaining four concerned landless labourers.

In the first of these measures the provisional government forbade the expulsion of small tenant farmers save in the cases of failure to cultivate or non-payment of rent. The aim of this decree was to prevent the widespread cancellation of leases by landlords who feared that the new legislation would hit leased property.

The second series of measures concerning tenant farmers gave priority to legally constituted workers' associations in the sub-leasing of land on large properties. Although this legislation drew accusations of favouritism on the Socialists, it had long been advocated by Catholic reformers.[13]

The remainder of Largo Caballero's measures sought to ameliorate the condition of the *bracero*. A decree of 1 July 1931 established parity between rural and industrial workers by providing for an eight-hour day in agriculture. In practice this was equivalent to a wage increase, since landlords would be obliged to pay overtime during the harvest. Another decree, scorned in anarchist circles, since it appeared to continue the agrarian policy of the Dictatorship, allowed for the creation of arbitration boards or 'mixed juries' whose main purpose was to carry out collective bargaining and act as an inspectorate with regard to labour legislation. Inevitably during the *bienio reformador* the Socialists came to play a leading part on these boards, where they exerted considerable influence because of their ability to levy fines on erring landlords. During the *bienio negro* roles were reversed as the landlords came to dominate the mixed juries.

Yet the most contentious pieces of legislation enacted by the provisional government were the law of municipal boundaries (*términos municipales*) of 28 April and the compulsory cultivation decree (*laboreo forzoso*) of 7 May. The former drew up boundaries around each of the 9,000 municipalities of Spain from within which landlords were required to recruit their hired labour. Not until local labour had been fully taken up could farmers look outside the municipality. The decree aimed to reduce rural unemployment in the south, where it was greatest, but at the expense of migrant labour from Galicia and Portugal. It also had the unforeseen consequence of denying work to many thousands of equally deserving peasants from mountain villages outside the boundaries of the municipalities who depended for their livelihood on selling their labour on the plains at harvest time. The decree created numerous other difficulties, including declining productivity, since local labourers soon discovered that they could maximise their incomes by deliberately going-slow, and the entry of less skilled labour from the towns, attracted by the greater guarantee of jobs in their native municipalities. An admission of the initial failure of this legislation was the later decision to amend it, particularly to take into account migrant labour from the surrounding villages.

The *laboreo forzoso* decree was possibly the most controversial of all the decrees of the provisional government. The aim of the legislators was to prevent hostile landlords from declaring an economic strike against the new regime by abandoning cultivation. It was decreed that if landowners refused to cultivate according to what was termed the normal 'uses and customs' of the region their lands would be confiscated and handed over to workers' associations. Inevitably Largo Caballero's opponents accused him of playing politics. Yet the decree was careful to stipulate that it was to be administered not by any Socialist-dominated mixed jury but by a group of technicians appointed on a provincial basis. Moreover the legislation was envisaged purely as a preventive measure and not as a *passe-partout* to the wholesale seizure of land. In economic rather than social terms, however, the measure was certainly mistaken. At a time of decreasing world prices for cereals the Republic would have been better advised to have encouraged pastoral farming along the lines advocated earlier by the agrarian reformer Antonio Flores de Lemus.[14]

Despite the bureaucratic nature of many of these decrees, above all the law of municipal boundaries, this series of measures represented a clear statement on the part of the Republic that the State intended to safeguard the interests of the peasantry, hitherto unprotected. In no way did they constitute a long-term solution to the problem of rural unemployment, which with regard to export crops was worsened by the deteriorating international situation.

Towards an agrarian reform act
It was to tackle the problem of endemic rural unemployment and to draft future legislation that in May 1931 the provisional government set up a technical commission under the chairmanship of the lawyer Felipe Sánchez Román. The commission presented its report on 20 July 1931, six days after the opening of the Constituent Cortes.

The argument of the report was unnervingly simple. Agrarian reform should be restricted to the *latifundio* zones, whose problems, including seasonal unemployment, were gravest. To avoid the expense of indemnifying landlords, with all its contingent delays, land should not be expropriated but occupied temporarily. No differentiation should be made as to the type of land thus affected; all persons owning 300 hectares of cereal land within Spain or holding property which yielded over 10,000 pesetas would have any surplus forcibly seized. So as not to provoke a conflict between collectivists and individualists, the commission recommended that the land be handed over to 'peasant communities' whose members would be allowed to vote on the issue of land distribution. The aim of the commission was to resettle between 60,000 and 75,000 peasant families annually, thereby completing the reform within twelve to fifteen years. The cost of this process, mostly grants for livestock and equipment along with credit to settlers, was estimated at betweeen 200 to 250 million pesetas a year, or 7 per cent of the annual budget.

Sánchez Román advised that the recommendations of his commission be put into effect immediately by decree, since he feared that a prolonged Cortes debate might weaken the proposals and subject them to unnecessary delay. Yet within a week the proposals of the technicians were rejected out of hand by nearly all sections of political opinion. The hostility of the landowners was only to be expected. Mendizábal, the spokesman of the landlords of Cuenca, accused Sánchez Román of proposing a Russian reform without making the revolution.[15] Martínez Velasco of the Agrarian party also referred to the measure as bolshevik. Nevertheless, what really sank the report was the criticism it aroused from within the governing coalition. Both conservative Republicans and Radicals con-

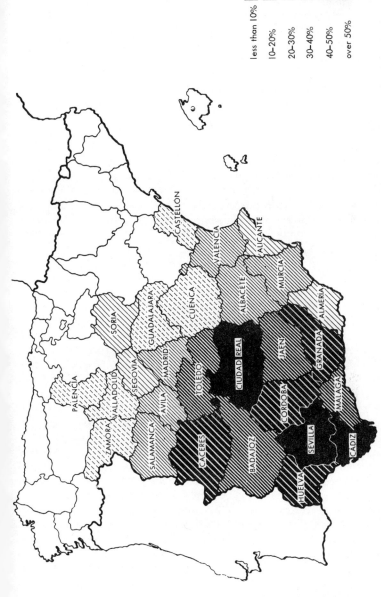

Map 5 Percentage of land holdings over 250 hectares, by province, according to the Catastral survey of 1932. The unshaded provinces were not surveyed. (After International Bank for Reconstruction and Development, *The Economic Development of Spain* (Baltimore, 1963), facing p. 259.)

less than 10%

10–20%

20–30%

30–40%

40–50%

over 50%

sidered the proposals too advanced, while in the opinion of the Socialists they did not go far enough. The worry of the PSOE was that the 'temporary' nature of the projected reform might mean that a future government less committed to agrarian change would undo the legislation and throw the peasantry off the land. It would appear that by underestimating their own ability to influence future events the Socialists missed a golden opportunity. Only briefly in the autumn of 1932 was the initiative for reform, for which they had fought so hard, regained.

In the seven months, from August 1931 to March 1932, which followed the abandonment of the technical commission's recommendations the Constituent Cortes debated seven Bills and counter-projects. It was a further five months before the Domingo Bill, named after its sponsor, the Agriculture Minister, Marcelino Domingo, became law. The new Bill, moreover, was far less ambitious than the scheme of the technical commission. Although the commission's recommendation of temporary occupation was dropped in favour of confiscation, the only properties to be touched were so-called 'illigitimate' properties which had been auctioned off in the nineteenth century. Compensation was proposed for both noble and non-noble property, mostly in the form of semi-negotiable bonds, while, in order to reduce the level of financial support needed from the State, the target of resettling 60,000 to 75,000 peasants a year was scrapped. Another divergence from the proposals of Sánchez Román's commission was that legislation by decree was rejected in favour of open debate on the floor of the democratically elected Constituent Cortes.

Adherence to the democratic process meant that the progress of Domingo's Bill was painfully slow. By the beginning of August 1932 the obstructionary tactics of the Agrarians, together with a large measure of indifference from the Radicals and bourgeois Republicans, saw to it that only four of the Bill's twenty-four articles had been approved. However, an abortive military coup on 10 August led by General Sanjurjo allowed Prime Minister Azaña to regain the initiative. With the right in disarray following the rapid collapse of the revolt, the left temporarily closed ranks to force through the remaining clauses of the Bill in under a month.

The failed Sanjurjo revolt provided the reformers with a ready-made scapegoat in the shape of the nobility. Attributing responsibility for the revolt to the Sevillian aristocracy, an assertion not entirely borne out by the evidence, Azaña argued that the simplest way to destroy the enemies of the Republic was to rid them of their landed base. Later discussion substantially modified earlier proposals, so that in the end the wrath of the Republicans was directed not at the nobility in its entirety but at its upper échelon, the grandees. Even so, this group was allowed to hold on to its woodlands and pastures as well as between 300 and 600 hectares of cereal lands.[16]

Passing the Domingo Bill into law was one matter; its application was another. The Agrarian Reform Law of 9 September 1932 provided for the creation of an Institute of Agrarian Reform charged with enforcing legislation. The lack of power of the Director General of the Institute, along with its enormous bureaucratic council, contributed to the frittering away of the great impetus for reform that had been gained by Azaña in the wake of the collapse of the Sanjurjo revolt. This loosely constituted body proved hesitant and confused, while Domingo, who was later to combine the roles of Agricultural Minister and Director General, was little short of incompetent.[17] By the end of 1933 no more than 4,399 peasants had been resettled on 24,203 hectares of land, while a further 20,133 hectares were confiscated from the alleged supporters of Sanjurjo.[18]

The inability of the politicians to get to grips with the problem of long-term unemployment in the countryside and carry out their proposed reforms was reflected in the high degree of social unrest which dogged the Republic throughout its existence. In the *latifundio* zone, especially the provinces of Cádiz, Córdoba, and Seville, where the tradition of revolt was most developed, the peasantry immediately put pressure on the new regime to implement its agrarian reform proposals.

The entry of the PSOE into the government, the occupation of the Labour Ministry by Largo Caballero and the early Socialist domination of the mixed juries greatly strengthened the FNTT, providing it with a formidable recruiting base. It has been estimated that within three years of its foundation the FNTT increased its membership to 451,000 establishing over three thousand local branches. Moreover, not only did the socialist land workers' federation extend its influence in existing rural strongholds of the movement such as Extremadura, but it also began to compete for recruits in regions traditionally dominated by the CNT, in particular the Levante and Seville.

Table 34   Expansion of FNTT membership, 1930–33

	Local unions	Membership
April 1930	157	27,340
June 1930	275	36,639
April 1932	2,233	308,579
June 1932	2,541	392,953
June 1933 (estimated)	3,319	451,337

Source. J. and G. P. Moch, *L'Espagne républicaine* (Paris, 1933), p. 228.

Estimates vary as to the strength of the CNT, although a recent study accepts the figure of about 800,000 members in 1934.[19] Despite the inroads made elsewhere by the Socialists the CNT continued to dominate the valley of the lower Guadalquivir and parts of the Levante, while in the north anarcho-syndicalist influence spread from the city of Saragossa to the surrounding countryside of Aragon and La Rioja.

Pursuing the revolutionary path which it had followed since 1919, the CNT soon announced its hostility to the bourgeois Republic. At an extra-ordinary congress held in Barcelona in June 1931 the organisation declared upon war against the State, which it considered, like the Restor-ation monarchy, an enemy of the working class. As an expression of its revolutionary purity moderates like Pestaña and Peiró, who advised cau-tion and called for better preparation before issuing a call to arms, were later expelled.[20]

Purged of its moderates, the CNT launched three separate putsches during the first two and a half years of the Republic: the first, in January 1932, centred on the upper Llobregat valley in Catalonia; the second, in January 1933, spread from Barcelona to other large cities; and a third, which began in Aragon in December 1933, had a somewhat wider impact. All three ill fated revolts were essentially urban phenomena; in relatively few cases did they spread to the countryside. The most publicised excep-tion was the notorious Casas Viejas affair, which took place on 11 January 1933 when news of the uprising in Catalonia sparked off a spontaneous rebellion in a tiny hamlet of that name in the province of Cádiz which was put down with great brutality by a local unit of Assault Guards, allegedly with the collusion of Azaña.[21] The only CNT revolt to receive significant support from the peasantry was the Aragon uprising of December 1933, but even on this occasion the response was limited to La Rioja and parts of the Aragonese countryside.

The lack of success of rural anarcho-syndicalism at this time can be ascribed to a number of factors. Ever since the post-first world war labour agitation Andalusia had been overshadowed as a centre of the libertarian movement by Catalonia and later by Saragossa. The new leaders of the CNT–FAI, such as Durruti, García Oliver and the Ascaso brothers, were schooled in the industrial towns of the north. Inevitably these men devoted less attention to agrarian problems. More significant was the decision of the Republic, taken somewhat reluctantly although later accepted as a necessary evil, to crush any manifestation of peasant rebel-lion on the part of the CNT. Even after fears of open insurrection in Andalusia had subsided in the first year of the new regime, extra con-tingents of Civil and Assault Guards (who were created in 1931 speci-fically to deal with anarcho-syndicalism) were maintained in the region in order to suppress strikes and the burning of crops, farms and machines. In the long run the overtly repressive attitude of the Azaña government towards a section of the underprivileged, most glaring at Casas Viejas, did much to alienate liberal as well as Socialist opinion and contributed to an erosion of its support.[22]

In contrast to the CNT, which saw the Republic's Agrarian Reform Law as nothing but a hoax, the Socialist FNTT acted with remarkable restraint during the first two years of the Republic. By the spring of 1933, however, many FNTT supporters had themselves become highly critical of the tactic of class collaboration. The rapid expansion of the agrarian wing of the UGT brought an increased militancy to the usually staid Socialists. Therefore, well before the arrival of the Lerroux government in September, a large section of the Socialists was talking in semi-revolutionary terms.[23]

Reaction and revolution on the land, 1934–36

The events of the *bienio negro* confirmed the maximalist wing of the Socialists in their belief that agrarian reform could not be legislated from above. Not only were the new laws enforced with less enthusiasm but Lerroux further enraged the Socialists by altering the appointees on mixed juries and sabotaging the law of municipal boundaries. To oppose what they saw as a concerted attack on the rural community the FNTT took the lead in declaring harvest strikes in June 1934 and banned the use of harvest machinery. This wave of strikes spread to 1,563 municipalities where the peasants passively laid down their tools without resort to any revolutionary activity whatsoever. Lerroux's Interior Minister, Salazar Alonso, nevertheless ruthlessly put down the strikes declaring the harvest to be 'sacred'. Arrests and imprisonments weakened the FNTT leadership and seriously undermined the morale of the peasantry, rendering it ineffective during the urban-led October revolution, which was directed against the entry of the CEDA into the government.

With the Spanish working class in disarray after the collapse of the October revolution, the new Agriculture Minister, Jiménez Fernández, one of the three CEDA representatives in Lerroux's government, attempted to introduce an element of social catholicism into agrarian reform. The intended beneficiaries of two major proposals by Jiménez Fernández were not in this case the landless labourers but small tenant farmers, the supposed bulwark against anarchism and communism. A decree of 2 January 1935 proposed the creation of small homesteads to be settled on a temporary basis, with preference being given to tenants and sharecroppers who could furnish their own tools. A target of 10,000 settlers a year was established. In addition the White Bolshevik, as he was dubbed by the extreme right, drew up a Bill to oblige owners to extend those leases of the *yunteros*[24] of Extremadura which were about to lapse. On this occasion it would appear that Jiménez Fernández was not acting entirely out of altruism but also in response to the demands of the FNTT, which still had considerable strength in that region.[25] Lack of government backing, however, forced a courageous man out of office in March 1935 and ushered in a period of bleak reaction in the countryside. Agrarian reform was virtually killed off, the Institute of Agrarian Reform starved of funds and the *yunteros* evicted, while wages plummeted.[26]

The hostility of the maximalist wing of the Socialists and of the land workers' federation to the 'sham' of agrarian reform continued even after the electoral defeat of the right and the arrival in office of the Popular Front government in February 1936. With a weak left Republican government powerless to stop them, the FNTT encouraged the peasantry to take the law into their own hands by entering landed estates and seizing property. The first land seizures occurred in the tiny village of Cenicientos in the province of Madrid on 3 March and soon extended to the provinces of Toledo, Salamanca and Murcia. The Agriculture Minister, Ruiz Funes, fearing a series of farm invasions, above all by the well organised *yunteros* of Extremadura, sought to negotiate, promising on 12 March that 40,000 *yunteros* could be settled within a week. The *yunteros* meanwhile decided to act for themselves, and on 25 March the Badajoz federation of the FNTT supervised the occupation by 60,000 peasants of 3,000 farms, an act which was later legalised by Ruiz Funes.

From May to July 1936 the peace of the Republic was further shattered by a wave of harvest strikes aimed at forcing up wages from the low level of the previous year. A feature of these strikes was the high degree of co-ordination betweeen the three main left-wing groups, the Socialists, the anarchists and the expanding Communists. To appease the strikers, who on occasions numbered 100,000, new mixed juries were appointed which straightway doubled the 1935 wage. The government also satisfied long-standing peasant demands by instituting a *turno rigoroso* whereby land-owners were forced to hire workers from local labour exchanges in the order in which they had been registered, thereby avoiding victimization.

This desperate attempt by the Popular Front government to still peasant grievances enabled it to claim that it had gained control of the situation. The end of the ploughing season brought a sharp reduction in the number of occupations, while the government appeared to have taken charge of land distribution.[27] Such a hypothesis, however, cannot be tested, since on

Table 35 Land settlements under the Popular Front, 1936

	Peasants settled	Area occupied (hectares)
March	72,428	249,616
April	21,789	150,490
May	5,940	41,921
June	3,855	55,282
July	6,909	74,746
Total	110,921	572,055

Source. *Boletín del Instituto de Reforma Agraria*, 4 (March–July 1936), cited in Edward Malefakis, *Agrarian Reform and Peasant Revolution in Spain* (New Haven, 1970), p. 377.

18 July 1936 the military revolted, and in so doing provoked a further wave of revolutionary activity in one part of Spain while permitting further counter-revolutionary activity in another.

Preoccupation with the *latifundio* zone tended to eclipse the various problems that beset the agricultural population elsewhere in the Peninsula. The troublesome leases (*foros*) of Galicia were scarcely touched. In Catalonia the left-controlled regional government passed a law in 1934 known as the *ley de cultivos* which allowed tenant farmers (*rabassaires*) to acquire the land which they had cultivated for fifteen years or more. Yet the *rabassaires*, plagued by falling wine prices on world markets during the 1920s and '30s, saw the law rejected by the Madrid government following opposition from the landlords.[28] Small growers in Valencia meanwhile received no aid whatsoever to compensate for their decreased earnings from exports.

DECLINING INDUSTRIAL PRODUCTION

There can be little doubt that the great burden of Spain's economic depression was borne by the agricultural community. Out of the 618,947 unemployed in December 1933, 414,640 were classified as agricultural workers; a year later agriculture provided 404,000 out of the 667,698 jobless. Only in the construction industry, where there were 76,000 unemployed in December 1933 and 93,000 in December 1934, did Spain experience similar levels of urban unemployment. The numbers of jobless in the metallurgical and textile industries in December 1934 were 30,000 and 9,000 respectively.[29]

Significantly all three industries experienced a reversal in their fortunes. From the end of 1929 in the case of construction, and the fourth quarter of 1930 with respect to metallurgy, the scrapping of public works projects inaugurated by the Dictatorship sent these prosperous sectors into recession. The iron and steel industry received a further setback when the Republic decided to switch from railway construction to road building. In contrast, the stagnating textile industry of Catalonia, which relied on domestic consumer demand rather than orders from the State, at last experienced a brief phase of prosperity due to an increase in spending power.

Industrial production continued to rise until 1931; thereafter production *per capita* fell by approximately one-sixth until the depression bottomed out in 1933. By 1935, the last full year for which statistical data are available, the index of production had almost regained the 1931 level.

The region whose industry was most seriously affected by the inter-war crisis was the Basque country, with its strong dependence on metallurgy. Sheltered behind high tariff walls since 1906, production of iron and steel increased steadily over the next two decades, with record figures of

Table 36   Index of industrial production per capita, 1929–35 (1913 = 100)

1929	130·4
1930	132·1
1931	133·7
1932	121·2
1933	111·2
1934	122·1
1935	129·1

Source. Nadal, Vicens Vives and Martí, art. cit., p. 111.

771,900 tons of cast iron and 1,021,600 tons of crude steel produced in 1929—levels which were not surpassed for a quarter of a century. Six years later, in 1935, output of iron had been more than halved to 344,200 tons, with steel production also substantially cut back to 637,200 tons. Six thousand men were thrown out of work in the iron ore mines and steelworks of Vizcaya by May 1932, while a total of 26,572 workers in the province were either unemployed or on short time in December 1933. The profits of the steel companies fell sharply after 1930; those of Altos Hornos de Vizcaya tumbled from 11·2 million pesetas in 1930, to 4·5 million in 1931, 5 million in 1932, 6·2 million in 1933 and 4·1 million in 1934.[30]

Catalonia, during the early 1930s at least, presents us with the country's clearest example of a slump-proof region. Catalan industrialists went so far as to argue that Spain was experiencing no economic crisis at all, simply a political crisis.[31] Indeed, the good fortunes of the textile industry went a long way to soften the blow of hard times in other industries such as construction. Ever since the loss of Cuba, Catalan textiles had become overwhemingly dependent for their sales on the Spanish market, the tendency towards autarky being reinforced by the tariffs of 1906 and 1921. In the 1930s the Principality produced 63 per cent of all woollen goods and 90 per cent of all cottons manufactured in Spain.[32]

When looms and spindles lay idle throughout the world four factors favoured the development of textiles in Catalonia; the low price of raw cotton, the maintenance of a high level of industrial production until 1932, the increase in agricultural wages and the bumper wheat crop of 1932.[33] Together these factors accounted for the relative stability of the industry until 1933. Prices held firm until that year, the general price index dropping less than one point between 1929 and 1932, from 100 to 99·2, before falling to 90·5 in 1933. Textile production began to fall significantly only in the second half of 1932, the index bottoming out at 81·3 in September 1933 (September 1929=100). What these indicators show is the early buoyancy of consumer spending power in the Peninsula despite the fall in agricultural exports and the contraction of iron and steel production. Yet from the middle of 1933 the textile industry failed to compensate in the home market for the continued fall in agricultural exports. Despite the record harvest of 1934 landlords took advantage of the *bienio negro* to introduce wage cuts, thereby reducing consumer spending power.

The contraction of production resulted in a sharp increase in unemployment in the textile industry. In the five months from July to December 1933 the number of unemployed textile workers in the province of Barcelona jumped from 5,667 to 9,793. Machines fell idle; the number of inactive spindles in the whole of Catalonia rose from 5·7 per cent in 1933 to 17·04 per cent in 1934, while the number of looms standing idle increased from 18 per cent in 1933 to 28·57 per cent in 1934 and 36·23 per cent in 1935.[34]

Industrial labour and the economic crisis

The period from 1929 to 1933 witnessed an enormous increase in labour militancy in Spain. In 1929 only ninety-six strikes were recorded, as against 1,127 in 1933. Over the same period the number who struck work increased from 55,576 to 843,303 and the number of days lost from 313,965 to 14,440,629. The proportion of successful strikes more than doubled, from 18 per cent in 1929 to 40 per cent in 1933. After 1933 the strike movement lost momentum until by 1935 it was practically insignificant, the number of workers on strike falling from 843,303 in 1933 to 32,500 in 1935.

Table 37   Strikes in the period 1929–35

	No. of strikes	Days lost ('000)	Workers on strike ('000)
1929	96	313·1	55·6
1930	402	3,745·4	247·2
1931	734	3,843·3	236·2
1932	681	3,589·3	269·1
1933	1,127	14,440·6	843·3
1934	594	11,115·3	741·8
1935	–	–	32·8

Source. *Anuario Estadístico de 1933: Pequeño Anuario Estadístico de 1936;* cited in Nadal, Vicens Vives and Martí, *art. cit.,* p. 119.

From the above data alone it would be easy to reach the conclusion that the high degree of labour militancy in 1933 was a reflection of the depth of the economic crisis, since in that year industrial production in Spain was at its lowest. Other evidence suggests that fluctuations in strike activity during the Second Republic owed much more to the revolutionary orientation of the working class and the ability or otherwise of the employers to resist its demands.

The tailing off in the number of strikes after 1933 coincided not so much with an economic recovery, which was certainly not reflected in the unemployment figures, as with the victory of the Right in the November elections. The defeat of the left encouraged the hitherto demoralised employers to launch a counter-offensive in 1934, when the proportion of successes gained by the strikers fell from 40 per cent (the 1933 figure) to 22 per cent of all conflicts. Moreover there can be little doubt that the diminutive number of workers on strike in 1935 was due to the string of repressive measures which followed the humiliation of the working class in the October revolution of 1934. Workers' organisations were rendered ineffective as their leaders languished in prison or in exile, and many union branches were shut down by the authorities.

The lack of any direct correlation between industrial production and strike activity is illustrated by the mixed fortunes of the textile and metallurgical industries. In the textile industry production of fibre doubled between 1932 and 1933 from 524 to 1,059 tons. Yet, instead of reflecting the general economic progress of the industry, the number of days lost in strikes increased elevenfold, from 217,000 to 2,399,000. Over the same period production of iron and steel increased slightly between 1932 and 1933, while the number of days lost in strikes fell significantly.[35]

Table 38   Industrial production and days lost in strikes in the textile and metallurgical industries, 1930–33

	Textile Industry		Metallurgy	
	Production (tons)	Days lost ('000)	Production ('000 tons)	Days lost ('000)
1930	1,014	260·0	1,577·8	286·3
1931	1,479	197·5	1,224·6	1,056·1
1932	524	216·8	832·8	701·1
1933	1,059	2,399·0	858·8	159·1

Source. Nadal, Vicens Vives and Martí, *art. cit.,* p. 121.

THE SPANISH CIVIL WAR, 1936–39

The failure of the military rebels to achieve an immediate victory in July 1936 left Spain divided geographically into two armed camps; the legal 'Republican' zone and the insurgent or so-called 'Nationalist' zone. In a matter of days the nation found itself split into two autonomous economic regions each with its distinct socio-political system.

At the beginning of August 1936 the Republican government in Madrid controlled all the major industrial regions: Catalonia, the Basque region and Asturias. In addition the Republican zone also contained the agricultural regions of New Castile and the Levante as well as eastern Andalusia, Aragon and part of Extremadura. Demographically the Republic had slightly over half the country's population at the outbreak of the civil war—12,712,181, as compared with 12,280,000 in the Nationalist zone. Moreover, within its bounds were the major urban conglomerations of Madrid, Barcelona, Valencia and Bilbao. Thus the Republic had a near-monopoly of light and heavy industry, yet to feed its large city population it had to count on farmlands which specialised in the production of horticultural products, olives and citrus fruits.

The economic problems of the Nationalist zone were quite distinct. There was an abundance of food production in the area under the control of Burgos. Nationalist Spain produced two-thirds of the nation's wheat, over half its potatoes and vegetables and nine-tenths of its sugar. In livestock farming, too, the rebel zone had the edge over the Republic. To combat deficiencies in industrial production the Burgos government launched a major assault on the north in August 1936 aimed at acquiring the much-needed mineral resources of Vizcaya. Victory in the north in October 1937 was a turning point in the Nationalist war effort, since it brought with it 36 per cent of total national production, including 60 per cent of Spain's coal production and 40 per cent of steel.[36]

With their greater population and industrial wealth the provinces that remained loyal to the Republic were better placed to contribute to the financing of what turned out to be a costly war. In 1935 those same provinces had contributed 70 per cent to the national Exchequer (esti-mated at 5,000 million pesetas), while the provinces which supported the Nationalists contributed only 30 per cent. If we accept the findings of the Commissariat of the Plan of 1963 that the total cost of military operations on both sides, calculated at 1935 prices, was 30,000 million pesetas, we arrive at the conclusion that the cost of fighting the three-year war was approximately six times the annual budget of 1935, which included expenditure on items besides defence. Other means of raising revenue had to be found.

In a partial attempt to remedy the situation the Republican zone resorted to the orthodox procedure of increasing public debt by the issue of bonds. The failure of the July 1938 issue, however, showed that after two years of war lack of public confidence in the legal government rendered this method of war finance unproductive. Fortunately for the Madrid gov-ernment, it was able to make use of the metallic reserves of the Bank of Spain, which were valued at 4,675 million pesetas ($575 million) in 1935. By a decree of 13 September 1936 the reserves of the bank, 510 tons of gold in 7,800 boxes, were shipped to Moscow for safe keeping. Thereafter purchases of armaments and war *matériel* from the Soviet Union were offset against this figure until eventually, according to one disputed source, Spain's credit was used up.[37]

The most important internal monetary device employed by Burgos was the creation of a new central Bank of Spain, which advanced over 9,000 million pesetas to the Nationalists. Yet the decisive factor with regard to the supply of arms and munitions to the rebel camp was the accumulation of debt to its Italian and German supporters. It has been variously estimated that the Italians, who received little in return, gave $263 million in aid to Franco, while Nazi Germany, which showed a strong interest in Spanish mineral resources to satisfy the requirements of Goering's second Four Year Plan, provided the Nationalists with arms worth $215 million.[38]

On the domestic front, despite its industrial and revenue-raising inferiority, the regime of General Franco was able to count on a far greater degree of political cohesion than the Republic. The outbreak of the civil war brought about a remarkable transformation in the Republican camp. The Madrid government lost much of its control in the early months to local groups of the PSOE, the CNT–FAI and the Communists. In Catalonia and the Levante in particular there was an intense campaign for the collectivisation of private enterprises, each under the control of workers' committees. Plans for workers' collectives, however, were often confused and contradictory, reflecting as they did the differing ideologies of the political groups. Despite the Republic's industrial superiority there was little or no co-ordination between the two main industrial regions of Catalonia and the Basque country, both of which were now governed by their own autonomy statutes. By early 1937 a state of chaos reigned in Spanish industry over which the anarchist Industry Minister Juan Peiró had no control.[39]

In the field of agriculture, Republican governments during the civil war aimed to accelerate agrarian reform. By a decree of 10 August 1936 the Giral government confiscated land from all those who abandoned exploitation, while in two further decrees of 10 August 1936 and 7 October 1937 the Communist Agriculture Minister, Vicente Uribe, ordered the expropriation without indemnity of the lands of all those who supported the military insurrection. Between October 1936 and the spring of 1938 46,896 estates were expropriated and a total of 4,086,386 hectares handed over to the peasantry, equivalent to half the land sown in the Republican zone as it was at the beginning of 1937. Faced, however, with providing for such a large urban population with inferior food resources, the Republic was undoubtedly handicapped by the collectivist experimentations of the anarchists, whose lack of organisation proved disastrous, particularly in Aragon.

With the formation of the Negrín government in May 1937 the Republic placed the emphasis on the creation of a centralised State whose aim was to win the war rather than to bring about a social revolution. After two further years of civil strife the Republic was to defeated by the even greater determination of the Nationalists.

Nationalist Spain was a totalitarian semi-fascist State which adapted many of its laws from Mussolini's Italy. Its Bill of Rights was the so-called *Fuero del Trabajo* of 1938, based on the Italian *Carta del Lavoro*. Counting on the support of the landlords, big business and the banks, the new State revoked much of the legislation of the Republic. In April 1937 it set up an institute known as the Servicio Nacional de Reforma Económica y Social de la Tierra which reversed most of the legislation of the Institute of Agrarian Reform. Yet ideology was not allowed to dominate, and dissident Falangists were imprisoned. The Republic had to be overthrown at all costs.

NOTES

1 *Cf.* Gabriel Jackson, 'The Azaña regime in perspective, 1931–3', *American Historical Review*, LXIV (1959).
2 Richard Robinson, *The Origins of Franco's Spain: the Right, the Republic and Revolution, 1931–36* (Newton Abbot, 1970), pp. 59–60.
3 Malefakis, *Agrarian Reform and Peasant Revolution in Spain*, pp. 391–3.
4 Paul Preston, 'The "moderate" right and the undermining of the Second Republic in Spain, 1931–33', *European Studies Review*, 3 (1973), 369–94; and, by the same author, 'Spain's October revolution and the rightist grasp for power', *Journal of Contemporary History*, 10 (1975), 555–78.
5 Servicio de Estudios del Banco de España, *Ritmo de la crisis económica española en relación con la mundial* (Madrid, 1934), p. 354.
6 Ministerio de Trabajo, *La crisis agraria andaluza de 1930–31* (Madrid, 1931), pp. 9–35; Pascual Carrión, *Los latifundios en España*, p. 366.
7 Jules Moch and G. P. Moch, *L'Espagne républicaine* (Paris, 1933), p. 269; Malefakis, *op. cit.*, p. 286.
8 Jordi Nadal, Jaime Vicens Vives, and Casimiro Martí, 'Les mouvements ouvriers en temps de dépression économique (1929–39): leurs consequences d'ordre politique et social', in *Mouvements ouvriers et dépression économique de 1929 à 1939* (Assen, 1966), pp. 106–7.
9 Ramón Tamames, *La República: la era de Franco* (Madrid, 1973), pp. 56–61.
10 *Boletín del Instituto de Reforma Agraria*, 1 (April 1933), 425–31.
11 Nadal, Vicens Vives and Martí, *art. cit.*, pp. 103–23.
12 Cristóbal de Castro, *Al servicio de los campesinos* (Madrid, 1931), p. 193.
13 Malefakis, *op. cit.*, p. 167.
14 *Ibid.*, p. 169; Antonio Flores de Lemus, 'Sobre una dirección fundamental de la producción rural española', *Hacienda Pública Española*, 42–3 (1976), 471–85.
15 Arturo Mori, *Crónica de las Cortes Constituyentes de la Segunda República española*, vol. 7 (Madrid, 1932–33), 415–21.
16 Malefakis, *op. cit.*, pp. 193–4 and 204.
17 *Ibid.*, pp. 243–50.
18 *Boletín del Instituto de Reforma Agraria*, 1 (December 1933), 20 and 202–3.
19 Malefakis, *op. cit.*, p. 293.
20 José Peirats, *La CNT en la revolución española*, 1 (Paris, 1971), 51–73; Antonio Elorza, *La utopía anarquista bajo la Segunda República española* (Madrid, 1973), pp. 351–468.
21 Peirats, *op. cit.*, 1, pp. 68–71.

22   Gabriel Jackson, The Second Republic and the Civil War in Spain, 1931–39 (Princeton, 1965), pp. 101–2.
23   Malafakis, op. cit., pp. 326–7.
24   See above, chapter one.
25   Jacques Maurice,'Problemas de la reforma agraria en la Segunda República (1931–36), II', M. Tuñón de Lara and J-F. Botrel (eds), Movimiento obrero, política y literatura en la España contemporánea (Madrid, 1974), p. 91.
26   Malefakis, op. cit., pp. 355–63.
27   Ibid., p. 379.
28   Joaquín Maurín, 'El problema agrario a Cataluña', Leviatán, 4 (August 1934), 42–50; Balcells, El problema agrarí a Cataluñya, pp. 135–70.
29   Alberto Balcells, Crisis económica y agitación social en Cataluña (1930–36) (Barcelona, 1971), pp. 59–60.
30   Manuel Tuñón de Lara, La España del Siglo XX (Paris, 1966), p. 316.
31   See especially Juan Ventosa y Calvell, La situación política y los problemas económicos de España (Barcelona, 1932), pp. 19–20.
32   Balcells, Crisis económica y agitación social en Cataluña, p. 101.
33   Ibid., p. 109.
34   POUM, Ponències: resolucións de la conferència de la indústria textil del POUM (Barcelona, 1937), p. 61, cited in Balcells, Crisis económica y agitación social en Cataluña, p. 123.
35   Nadal, Vicens Vives and Martí, art. cit., pp. 120–1.
36   Hugh Thomas, The Spanish Civil War (Harmondsworth, 1965), p. 611.
37   Joan Sardá 'El Banco de España (1931–62)', in El Banco de España: una historia económica (Madrid, 1970), pp. 401–79; Angel Viñas, El oro español en la guerra civil (Madrid, 1976).
38   J. R. Hubbard, 'How Franco financed his war', Journal of Modern History, xxiv (1953), 390–406; Glenn T. Harper, German Economic Policy in Spain during the Spanish Civil War, 1936–39 (The Hague and Paris, 1967); Robert Whealey, 'How Franco financed his war—reconsidered', Journal of Contemporary History, 12 (1977), 133–52.
39   Juan Peiró, Mi gestió en el Ministerio de Indústria (1937), p. 276, cited in Leandro Benavides, Política económica en la II República española (Madrid, 1972), p. 181.

CHAPTER 8

From autarky to economic liberalism, 1939–75

DEMOGRAPHIC DEVELOPMENTS

A recent estimate puts the number of deaths due to the civil war at 675,000. In addition, during the first two months of 1939, as the Nationalist forces converged on Catalonia, around 400,000 Republican sympathisers crossed over the French border into exile. By the end of the second world war approximately 100,000 of these refugees had been repatriated, some forcibly by the German army of occupation but most of them voluntarily, a net loss to Spain of some 300,000 individuals. Adding the two totals together, we arrive at the conclusion that as a direct consequence of the civil war the Spanish nation was deprived of almost one million inhabitants.[1] Eighty per cent of all losses came from the Republican side, and included a significantly high proportion of skilled workers, scientists and technicians, who emigrated in large numbers. Most were young men with a long working life ahead of them; the new regime could ill afford to do without their services.

At first these population losses were replaced only slowly. The early 1940s, however, brought something of a matrimonial boom, following wartime postponments, the full fruits of which were felt a generation later in the 1960s. Between 1960 and 1975 the population expanded at an unprecedented rate, from 30·4 millions to 35·0 million inhabitants.

Table 39   Evolution of births, deaths and marriages, 1930–75 (per thousand inhabitants)

Year	Population (millions)	Births	Deaths	Marriages
1930	23·7	28·5	17·8	7·6
1940	25·9	24·3	16·5	8·4
1950	28·1	20·0	10·8	7·5
1960	30·4	21·6	8·6	7·2
1965	31·8	21·1	8·5	7·2
1970	34·0	19·5	8·3	7·4
1975	35·0	18·9	8·4	7·7

Source. Instituto Nacional de Estadística. 1975 figures are provisional.

The most significant feature of the active population during the Franco period was the sharp drop in the relative size of the agricultural sector. Between 1940 and 1975 it fell from 50·52 to 22·91 per cent of the total active labour force. The steepest decline in the agricultural population came after 1960; between that date and 1975. Five million Spaniards quit the land for the industrial towns and the tourist regions, while in 1965 the factory finally overtook the farm as the leading employer of labour.

Table 40   Occupation of the active labour force in Spain according to census data, 1930–75 (%)

Year	Agriculture	Industry	Services
1930	45·51	26·51	27·98
1940	50·52	22·13	27·35
1950	47·57	26·55	25·88
1960	39·70	32·98	27·32
1965	34·30	35·20	31·20
1970	29·11	37·28	33·61
1972	27·06	37·75	35·19
1973	25·15	36·09	38·76
1975	22·91	36·77	40·32

Source. Instituto Nacional de Estadística; Banco de Bilbao, Renta nacional de España y su distribución provincial, 1975 (Bilbao, 1977), pp. 148–50.

After the civil war the highest natural rate of population increase (excluding migration) occurred in the agricultural areas of Galicia, the two Castiles, Andalusia and Extremadura. From these regions there was a constant stream of migrant labour to provinces with higher per capita incomes. Especially since the spread of industrialisation in the 1950s, Barcelona and Madrid received massive numbers of workers from the rest of Spain. Between 1951 and 1970 the net balances of migration to the provinces of Barcelona and Madrid were 946,800 and 1,030,000 persons respectively.

Table 41   Immigration to Barcelona and Madrid, 1951–70 (annual averages)

	1951–60	1961–65	1966–70
Barcelona	47,961	62,751	30,691
Madrid	41,170	70,921	52,728

Source. Ramón Trias Fargas, Introducció a la economia de Catalunya (Barcelona, 1972), p. 77.

Following the disruptions caused by the second world war, the late 1940s brought an increase in the rate of emigration, mostly in the direction of Latin America. Initially, shortages of employment and entry restrictions meant that a substantial proportion of those emigrating were dependants of male workers already living abroad. The Spanish regions participating most strongly in this current were Galicia and the Canary Islands.

From 1959, however, Latin America was suddenly and dramatically eclipsed as the most popular destination for Spanish emigrants by Western Europe. In 1961 France alone overtook the whole of Latin America in terms of the number of emigrants received, while significant numbers also went to West Germany, Switzerland and the Netherlands. The main areas of origin of this new wave of migrants were Galicia and Andalusia, which at last began to export its surplus labour.[2]

The decision by mounting numbers of Spaniards to try their luck north of the Pyrenees was in response to both pull and push factors. For their part the Western European countries, their own populations depleted by the second world war, required large numbers of migrant workers to maintain their high levels of economic growth. While West Germany looked to the east as a source of cheap labour before the construction of the Berlin Wall, France began to recruit in Italy, North Africa and the Iberian Peninsula. Yet much of the responsibility for Spain's first wave of emigration to Europe lay with the Franco regime's earliest attempt at economic planning—the Stabilisation Plan of 1959, which made it considerably easier for Spaniards to emigrate.[3] The planners reasoned that the export of surplus

Table 42   Total Spanish emigration, 1959–76

Year	Departures	Returns	Balance
1959	55,130	41,309	13,821
1960	73,431	35,308	38,123
1961	115,372	7,815	107,557
1962	142,505	45,844	96,661
1963	134,541	52,230	82,311
1964	192,999	112,871	80,128
1965	181,278	120,678	60,600
1966	141,997	143,082	−1,085
1967	60,000	85,000	−25,000
1968	85,662	67,622	18,000
1969	112,205	43,336	68,869
1970	105,538	40,000	65,674
1971	120,984	60,000	70,348
1972	110,369	70,000	40,369
1973	100,992	110,000	−9,073
1974	55,347	140,000	−84,473
1975	24,477	70,000	−45,485
1976	15,642	70,000	−54,358

Source. Instituto Español del Emigración.

labour would not only reduce the level of unemployment within Spain but, with the help of emigrant remittances, would also contribute to a reduction of the nation's balance-of-payments deficit. According to official estimates, Spanish migrant workers sent home over $700 million in 1975.

The economic recessions of the late 1960s and middle '70s brought a sharp reduction in the number of emigrants. In 1966 and 1967 there was a net balance of immigration, while in the last two years of Franco's rule nearly 130,000 more Spaniards returned home than emigrated. In addition, after 1969 France received large contingents of Portuguese labourers, and Switzerland became the first choice for Spanish migrants.[4]

Table 43   Emigration from Spain, by country of destination, 1970–76

	1970	1971	1972	1973	1974	1975	1976
Germany	40,685	30,317	23,271	27,919	245	95	30
France	22,727	24,266	21,795	11,631	5,601	1,151	477
Switzerland	26,777	51,751	55,746	53,284	42,029	17,992	11,244
Others	7,495	7,368	3,044	3,254	2,820	780	373
Europe	97,657	113,702	103,856	96,088	50,695	20,618	12,124
Overseas	7,881	7,282	6,513	4,904	4,652	3,859	3,518
Total	105,538	120,984	110,369	100,992	55,347	24,477	15,642

Source. Instituto Español del Emigración.

PHASES OF ECONOMIC POLICY DURING THE FRANCO REGIME

In the course of the Franco era (1939–75) Spain underwent at least four distinct phases of economic policy making which reflected the change from the proposed autarky of the 1940s to a growing degree of eonomic liberalism and the adoption of the planning mechanism in the 1950s and 1960s. In political terms, the successive phases were in step with the slow downfall of the quasi-fascist and xenophobic Falange and the emergence of a new breed of technocratic decision-makers attached to the Catholic lay group Opus Dei.

The first stage of economic policy making, the striving for self-sufficiency, persisted throughout the 1940s. In an attempt to explain away the ubiquitous stagnation and poverty of this decade, government sources stressed the 'terrible destruction and widespread loss' produced by the civil war. According to the preamble to the First Development Plan, published in 1964, as well as the many public buildings that were destroyed during the conflict a quarter of a million dwellings were ruined and a similar number rendered uninhabitable. Destruction, argued the plan, was especially marked in 192 towns and cities where three-fifths of all buildings were wrecked. Moreover, in the domain of transport, two-fifths of all locomotives and freight wagons and nearly three-quarters of all railway carriages were said to have been destroyed and 225,000 tons of merchant shipping sunk.[5] Such evidence, nevertheless, tends to be misleading, especially since the main centres of population, including Madrid, Barcelona, Seville and Valencia, suffered relatively minor damage, apart from the effects of air raids and hand-to-hand fighting in such areas as the University in Madrid. An earlier official publication compared the destruction of dwellings during the civil war with similar losses in Europe produced by the second world war. Losses in Spain were calculated at no more than 0·5 per cent of the total number of dwellings, compared with 2 per cent in Great Britain and Belgium, 3 per cent in France, 4 per cent in Italy and 24 per cent in Germany during the major conflict.[6]

Another reason generally adduced for Spain's disastrous economic performance during the 1940s was her exclusion from the world trading community. Apart from wartime contacts with the Axis, and post-war relations with Perón's Argentina and Salazar's Portugal, Spain was virtually isolated. After the war she was excluded from membership of the United Nations and of other international organisations, nor did the country receive Marshall Aid.

Autarky, although forced upon Spain, was also a matter of choice, embarked upon enthusiastically by the regime's political and economic advisers. As early as June 1940 the New State was offered a substantial loan of $100 million by the United States in order that she might purchase essential raw materials. This generous offer was, however, rejected out of hand, since acceptance would have run counter to the politically motivated aim of the regime of developing import substitutes.[7] By the end of the decade the deficiencies of this mistaken policy were all too apparent: Spain suffered constantly from a scarcity of raw materials, resulting in persistent crises of production. At the same time real incomes failed to rise above pre-civil war levels, while the rate of private capital accumulation was disappointingly low. The subordination of economics to political ambitions had manifestly failed. Fortunately, it was at this time that the United States came to the rescue with the offer of economic aid which would allow Spain to abandon the false goal of self-sufficiency for a more open economy.

The outbreak of the Korean war in 1951, together with the evolution of the Cold War, forced the United States to search out allies with proven anti-communist credentials. To the Eisenhower administration Franco's Spain, which in 1941 had sent its Blue Division to fight with the Axis on the Russian front while formally remaining non-belligerent, easily filled the bill. In September 1953 the two nations signed a mutual defence treaty. During the next eight years (1953–61) Spain received $618·2 million in grants and $404 million in loans in the economic sphere alone, as well as $436·8 million of military aid. From 1962 to 1968 the level of US aid fell considerably, while the loan element was seven times the total of gifts. Nevertheless in this period Spain, with $420·4 million in loans and $59·8 million in grants, ranked second only to Japan in terms of US credits received.

Unlike the earlier Marshall Aid, American support for the Franco regime came with strings attached. The greater part of US grants in the 1950s was in the form of raw materials which were surplus to domestic requirements, in particular raw cotton and soya bean oil. Furthermore, over a third of all loans ($154·3 million out of $404 million) were made as a contribution to the US security system. During the period 1962–68 all United States aid to Spain was linked to purchases from the major partner. Part of the loans was to buy expensive military equipment, including aeroplanes and control systems, at the expense of Spain's indigenous defence industries. Nevertheless this gesture of reconciliation made possible a substantial increase in imports of such items as petroleum, chemical products, machinery and iron and steel goods, which finally enabled Spain to overcome the many bottlenecks in production resulting from the pursuit of autarky.[8]

The second phase of Spanish economic policy-making was not without its problems. The paths followed were ambiguous and never fully pursued. From as early as 1953 signs of disequilibrium began to appear in the home market, bringing the threat of over-production in certain consumer industries, above all in the textile sector. The response of the government was to issue two decrees in 1954 and 1956 which raised wages in the public sector in an attempt to stimulate domestic consumption. The inevitable result of the two decrees was inflationary pressure leading to a balance of payments crisis and a flight of capital from Spain. By the winter of 1958 the country was on the verge of bankruptcy, with only $10 million in reserves and a net deficit of $60 million, counting current obligations. Government Ministers also feared a recurrence of the wave of strikes which had broken out in Asturias, the Basque region and Catalonia earlier in that year.[9]

To tackle the mounting social and economic problems of the day Franco ordered a clean sweep of the economic Ministries, introducing his new team of Opus Dei technocrats. Under their leadership Spain was to embark upon a third phase of economic policy-making, that of neo-liberalism. The first appointments in 1957 were followed in 1958 by a series of initiatives which eventually bore fruit in the Stabilisation Plan of 1959. In 1958 Spain joined a number of international organisations; the Organisation for European Economic Co-operation (OEEC), later to become the Organisation for Economic Co-operation and Development (OECD), the International Monetary Fund (IMF) and the International Bank for Reconstruction and

Development (World Bank). At home great interest was shown in the French Stabilisation Programme of 1958 with which Spain's neighbour attempted to combat her own severe financial and economic problems. In that year the architect of the French plan, Jacques Rueff, was invited to visit Spain, as also were delegations from the OEEC and the IMF. The result of their deliberations was a series of decrees issued in July and August 1959 which formed the basis of the Spanish Stabilisation Plan.

The main features of the Stabilisation Plan of 1959 were cuts in public expenditure, increases in taxation and a wage freeze, all of which were directed against inflation, while to tackle the problems of the balance-of-payments deficit and the flight of capital there was an effective devaluation of the peseta, which was fixed at sixty to the dollar. In recognition of the recent Italian experience that it was easier to conquer inflation by a combination of domestic savings and outside capital, the regime promulgated the first of a series of laws directed towards the encouragement of foreign investment.[10] The plan's success was guaranteed by foreign support, which totalled $420 million, including $100 million in credits from the OEEC, $75 million in IMF drawing rights, $70 million in commercial credits from the Chase Manhattan and First National City banks, and $30 million in loans to foreign companies from the US Import–Export Bank.[11]

Although the immediate after-effects of the introduction of the Stabilisation Plan were renewed stagnation rather than the sought-after economic growth, the regime kept faith with its new policy approach. In 1961 a commission of experts from the World Bank visited Spain and in their report urged upon the country the need to aim for a high rate of growth based on transfers of labour and capital from areas of low productivity to areas of high productivity.[12] The First Development Plan of 1964, however, owed less to the World Bank than to the French system of 'indicative planning'.

The French planning system was copied by the Spaniards, lock, stock and barrel, even down to the designation of the smallest bureau. A variety of factors contributed to this desire to imitate, including the favourable reception of the Spanish Stabilisation Plan of 1959, the high esteem in which French institutions were held in Britain and the United States, and the rapid rate of economic growth which France was then experiencing. It was also hoped that the adoption of the policies followed by a Common Market country would make Spain more readily acceptable as a future partner in the European Economic Community.[13] The Common Market had been formed by the signing of the Treaty of Rome in 1957, and Spain had applied for membership in 1962. Even so, her first application was shelved in 1964 largely owing to disquiet within the 'Six' at the absence of basic political and intellectual freedoms under the Franco regime.

For the 1960s as a whole Spain could boast the most rapidly expanding economy in Western Europe. The rate of growth in real gross national

product averaged 7·4 per cent for the decade, varying in individual years
from 4·5 per cent to 11·4 per cent. Yet it is a matter of opinion whether the
so-called 'Spanish miracle' can be attributed to indicative planning. There
can be little doubt that the acceptance of economic planning was pre-
ferable to autarky or the pursuit of arbitrary and often conflicting policies.
However, the very existence of the 'plan' served as an excuse for the refusal
on the part of the regime to undertake even the most elementary structrual
reform which might have upset vested interests. It has been argued that the
much vaunted economic growth of the 1960s occurred in spite of the
efforts of the planners and that the motivating force of the Spanish
economy was not the plan but tourism, which earned the necessary foreign
currency to pay for essential imports of foodstuffs and capital goods.[14]
From a total of 4,194,000 tourists visiting Spain in 1959, numbers rose to
34,559,000 in 1973, an eightfold increase; while receipts from holiday-
makers rose more than twentyfold from $128·6 million in 1959 to a record
$3404·3 million in 1975. By the early 1970s receipts from foreign tourism
more or less wiped out an otherwise huge balance-of-trade deficit, a factor
which was dramatically reversed after 1973.

Table 44   The contribution of tourism to Spain's balance of payments, 1959–76

Year	Tourists ('000)	Receipts of foreign currency from tourism ($ millions)	Balance of trade deficits ($ millions)
1959	4,194	128·6	253
1960	6,113	297·0	57
1961	7,445	384·6	279
1962	8,668	512·6	634
1963	10,931	679·3	1,004
1964	14,102	918·6	1,056
1965	14,250	1,156·9	1,737
1966	17,251	1,292·5	1,964
1967	17,858	1,209·8	1,745
1968	19,183	1,212·7	1,548
1969	21,682	1,310·7	2,333
1970	24,105	1,680·8	2,360
1971	26,758	2,054·4	2,025
1972	32,506	2,486·3	2,911
1973	34,559	3,091·2	4,405
1974	30,343	3,187·9	8,340
1975	30,122	3,404·3	8,516
1976	30,014	3,083·3	8,723

Sources. Ministerio de Información y Turismo; Ministerio de Comercio, Balanza
de pagos de España, 1972; trade figures from 1969 onwards from Banco de Bilbao,
Informe económico, 1976 (Bilbao, 1977), p. 177.

Although the First Development Plan (1964–67) was entitled the 'Plan for Economic and Social Development', the 'social' element was added only as an afterthought when earlier drafts were in circulation. This inclusion was manifestly for political reasons.[15] The Second and Third Plans (1967–71 and 1972–75) did indeed lay greater stress on such items as housing and the unequal distribution of wealth by provinces; yet efficiency rather than equity remained the dominant goal of both national and regional policy.[16] Public sector investment aimed at tackling these problems failed to meet its target in any of the stipulated years. Furthermore the two later plans were driven irreversibly off course by unforeseen external factors, not least of which were the devaluation of sterling in 1967, which in turn brought down the peseta, and the massive increases in the price of oil after 1973.[17] Finally, with the assassination of Admiral Carrero Blanco in December 1974 the Opus Dei technocrats, previously encouraged by the former Premier, were dismissed from the Cabinet and the Third Plan was abandoned.

THE DECLINE OF THE AGRICULTURAL SECTOR

Throughout the first decade of the Franco era agriculture continued to play a dominant role in the Spanish economy, a fact that was underlined by the persistent failure of the nation's farmers to grow enough foodstuffs to meet the requirements of the population. As late as 1948 the Bank of Bilbao, which had always maintained the strongest links with Spanish industry, was to exclaim that 'a year of good harvests is a year of prosperity'.[18] Yet not until the bumper crop of 1951 did agricultural yields exceed pre-civil war levels.

The aim of the government's agrarian policy during the 1940s was to intervene in the economy through rationing and price control to try to ensure the production and equable distribution of certain staple items, most specifically wheat and olive oil. As a corollary of this policy, little official support was given to export crops, for example oranges, nor to livestock farming.

In the case of wheat, however, government interference brought disastrous consequences. Yields fell from an average of 128 for the period 1931–35 to 72·2 in the quinquennium 1941–45 (base year 1910=100). Throughout the latter period the nation's needs could only be met by massive imports, which accounted for 15·6 per cent of total consumption, while in 1947–48 Spain was only saved from widespread famine by imports from Argentina totalling 10–13 per cent of domestic consumption. Despite the foreign purchases, the great majority of the population went hungry during the 1940s.[19]

Its plan for autarky in ruins, the regime tried to apportion the blame on a number of external factors, above all the weather and difficulties in obtain-

Table 45   Index of agricultural production, 1940–51 (1953–54 = 100)

1940	77·85	1946	95·70
1941	86·83	1947	89·10
1942	91·72	1948	82·36
1943	86·91	1949	80·98
1944	91·90	1950	81·60
1945	65·06	1951	108·00

Source. Consejo de Economía Nacional.

ing imported agricultural machinery and fertilisers.[20] Yet these excuses were clearly at odds with the evidence, as a minority of economists and policy-makers readily stressed. Only in 1945 and 1949 (and later in 1953) were weather conditions abnormally detrimental to Spanish farmers. Moreover the scarcity of tractors and phosphates, although contributing to some drop in productivity, could not have accounted for such a drastic slump in output. Responsibility for the subsistence crisis of the 1940s lay with the mistaken policies of the government with regard to wheat. By its intervention to fix the purchasing price for the crop at a level unremunerative to the farmer, the State merely succeeded in bringing about the abandonment of cereal cultivation in favour of alternative crops, or persuaded the farmer to hoard part of his crop for later sale on the black market.[21]

The agrarian ideology of the Franco regime
During the formative years of the Franco regime certain of its ideologically committed supporters argued vociferously in favour of agriculture as the firmest base upon which to construct the New State.[22] The regime, too, while pursuing its own distinctive industrial policy, showed a preference for rural as against urban values. In practical terms this was understandable, since during the civil war the industrial proletariat of the towns remained overwhelmingly loyal to the Republic, displaying thereafter little enthusiasm for the victors.

The agrarian policy of the Franco regime took on an entirely different character to that of the defeated Republic. Immediately following the cease-fire the new government set about dismantling the highly contentious Institute of Agrarian Reform in the newly conquered territories, just as it had done in the Nationalist zone after the outbreak of civil war. In October 1939 the buildings and part of the staff of the Institute were incorporated into the newly constituted National Institute of Colonisation (INC). Concern for the problems of the landless labourer of the *latifundio* belt was relegated to a secondary position. The INC was to be preoccupied with the new agrarian priority of the regime, interior colonisation coupled with irrigation.

Although the origins of the new approach to agriculture were to be found in the little-observed Besada Law of Interior Colonisation of 1907, current interest stemmed from the theory developed in fascist Italy in the 1930s that intensive irrigated cultivation was the best way of absorbing surplus rural labour. The desired objective was the creation of passive communities of self-sufficient peasant farmers, living in harmony with the New State.

In reality the regime's ideology proved superior to its achievements During the first twenty years of its existence no more than 49,645 persons were resettled by the INC, of whom only 22,403 were offered irrigated land, while the remaining 27,062 peasants were settled on dry land.[23]

Prior to the early 1950s the State scarcely possessed an irrigation policy. The first major schemes which it promoted were the Badajoz plan of April 1952 and the Jaén plan of April 1953, which were incorporated into Spain's earliest attempt at regional planning. The construction of monumental dams was aimed not only at bringing water to the fields but also electricity and industry to designated areas. Although considerable propaganda value was derived from these and subsequent projects, they were to prove expensive when measured by results. In the late '60s and early '70s about one-fifth of total agricultural investment was directed towards irrigation; yet in 1971 irrigated land covered only 2·4 million hectares, or no more than 12 per cent of the cultivated land surface. Moreover, in the majority of irrigation schemes undertaken the anticipated 'industry' element failed to materialise.[24]

Minifundios, latifundios and the flight from the land
From the early 1950s the aspect of the Franco regime's agricultural policy to receive widest acclaim was the attempt to redistribute the fragmented plots of land which characterised the landscape of northern Spain. Laws of 1952, 1955 and 1962 (*leyes de concentración parcelaria*) aimed to reduce the number of farming units and provide reconstituted plots, each with access to means of communication. The law applied to any municipality where its enforcement was solicited by three-fifths of all proprietors who between them owned a similar proportion of the land. In each area affected by the law the authoritites established a 'minimum unit of cultivation' below which size no new plot of land could be created. Proprietors with less than this amount of land were offered the necessary credit to acquire additional land up to that level. The resulting plot was then considered indivisible.

There can be little doubt that *concentración parcelaria* allowed for considerable economies of scale, particularly in terms of a more rational use of fertilisers and agricultural machinery and a reduction in the time spent working on the land. The measure, however, was applied with some timidity, since each proprietor was reallocated exactly the amount of land

that was taken away from him, whereas for its most effective functioning
the scheme required a certain amount of redistribution of property. Rely-
ing on the support of powerful landed interests, the regime refused to
antagonise them. Even so, between 1953 and 1972 3,601,400 hectares of
land were reconsituted, slightly over half the amount that was
petitioned.[25]

One area where the Franco regime manifestly failed to fulfil its professed
objectives was on the question of the *latifundios* of the south. Large estates
which comprise one per cent of all holdings still occupy 49 per cent of the
cultivated land surface in Spain. With the exception of Portugal on the eve
of the 1974 revolution, Spain possessed the most unequal distribution of
land in Europe after World War II.[26] An act of December 1953 'concerning
land capable of improvement' provided for the expropriation of all
under-utilised land; however, a joint report of the FAO and the World
Bank suggested that as late as 1966 it had hardly, if indeed at all, been
applied.[27] In 1971 this law was superseded by a further piece of legislation
with a similar title: ample proof of the inadequacy of the 1953 Act. Two
years later, in January 1973, the cornerstone of agricultural policy, the
National Institute of Colonisation, was itself absorbed into a new organisation, the National Institute of Agrarian Reform and Development
(IRYDA). Critics noted with irony the half-hearted manner in which the
destructors of the Republic avoided re-creating the old Institute of
Agrarian Reform (IRA).[28] Nevertheless these two developments demonstrated the willingness of some elements within the dying Franco regime
to pursue a cautious, conservative agrarian policy. What was missing was
an overall plan for the agricultural sector as a whole.

The inadequacies of Spanish agricultural policy in the 1960s were
highlighted by the massive exodus from the land. By this time, however,
the policy of interior colonisation in order to soak up excess rural man-
power had been discarded in favour of the planners' vision of transferring
labour to areas of higher productivity. Beginning with the Stabilisation
Plan of 1959 the agricutural sector was deliberately run down and surplus
labour given greater facilities to emigrate.

In the late '50s and early '60s the great majority of those leaving the land
were wage-earners. Their departure provoked a spectacular increase in
agricultural wages, which rose by 269 per cent between 1957 and 1969.
Wherever possible, landlords attempted to offset increased labour costs by
employing more capital. In cereal growing it was a simple matter to
replace the hired hand by agricultural machinery. On dry land of average
quality a combine harvester could reduce the total number of hours spent
gathering in the crop from between 100 and 130 hours per hectare to no
more than three or four hours. Similarly, sowing time could be cut down
from eighteen hours per hectare using an ox-drawn plough to little more
than one hour with the aid of a tractor. With other crops, such as the olive

and the vine, mechanisation proved a more difficult task, a factor which resulted in a sharp increase in prices. In the case of the olive, where there are a number of substitutes for olive oil, marginal lands disappeared from production altogether.[29]

The spread of mechanisation was possibly the outstanding development in the agricultural sector during the 1960s; the number of tractors quadrupled from 53,000 in 1960 to 229,000 in 1969, rising to 337,000 in 1975. Economies of scale resulting from mechanisation were more easily obtained on large estates; yet if small farmers were to survive they too were compelled to purchase expensive machinery. To pay for their acquisitions, many small farmers had to look for additional work, either as a wage labourer on a neighbouring estate or in one of the newly emerging agroindustries. By the end of the 1960s this group also began to leave the countryside, thereby compounding the crisis of traditional agricultural society which the Franco regime had originally aimed to preserve but eventually ignored.[30]

THE INDUSTRIAL SECTOR

The period immediately after the civil war was characterised by a strong element of government interference in Spanish industry. Foremost among the industrial priorities of the New State was the creation of a number of import substitutes. In common with national agriculture at this time, the model for industrial policy was to be found in the fascist experience in Italy.[31] The main instruments of this policy were the industry of 1939 and the Instituto Nacional de Industria (INI) founded in 1941 and copied from the Italian Istituto per la Riconstruzione Industriale (IRI).

The aim of the industry laws of 1939 was to provide a framework for the development of private capitalism. To strengthen existing enterprises and encourage the establishment of new firms, Spanish industrialists were promised a variety of incentives ranging from tax reductions to guaranteed returns on investment. Without doubt, this legislation stimulated the development of infant industries, such as the manufacture of nitrogenous fertilisers.[32]

The Instituto Nacional de Industria was set up as a State holding company with the purpose of creating new industries, especially where such industries would strengthen national defence and facilitate self-sufficiency. As a concession to anti-capitalist sentiments within the Falange it was also proposed that INI would set about breaking up private monopolies, although in practice this policy was never implemented. Its allotted role within national industry was to venture into areas that were unattractive to private capitalism owing to low profit margins or the scarcity of funds for investment. Between 1942 and 1945 INI participated in twenty different companies, of which five could be classified as military or strategic in origin and seven as aimed at autarky. Despite its clearly defined objectives, INI's policies have often seemed to reflect little more than the private whims of its directors. Consequently it proved impossible to use the organisation as a basis for economic planning. Over the years INI was permitted to cast its nets over a wide range of industries, acquiring many often competing interests which it did little to restructure, becoming in the process an inefficient bureaucratic monster. A number of its undertakings were wound up.

At the end of 1975 INI had a direct participation in fifty-nine companies, of which sixteen were wholly owned, and a stake in two hundred others. The Institute had a dominant weight in a number of sectors; for example, it controlled 90 per cent of all shipbuilding, 45 per cent of steel production, 60 per cent of laminates and 57 per cent of aluminium. INI also had important holdings in oil refinery, car manufacture, air transport, aircraft manufacture, chemicals and tourism, while it provided 10 per cent of Spain's gross industrial product and employed 4 per cent of the total work force.

During the economic crisis of the mid-1970s successive governments attempted to use INI as a stabilising factor to help check cyclical movements. In particular, when private industry refused to invest, INI kept up its own progress in the hope of maintaining general economic activity. However, the Institute attracted much hostility from managers in the private sector because of the favourable terms on which it obtained credit and the preference which it received from the State. There now exists a strong body of opinion in favour of splitting up INI into a number of individual companies.

The level of industrial production

On numerous occasions during the 1940s Spanish entrepreneurs were exhorted to produce more to ensure that the nation's industrial needs were met without resort to imports. Yet, despite the incentives offered, industrial growth remained at a low level throughout the decade. The main reason for poor industrial performance was the lack of energy sources and basic raw materials, particularly cement, steel and non-ferrous metals. The result was disastrous bottlenecks in production.

After 1950 the leading indicators show a marked upturn in industrial activity, with a doubling of production during the succeeding decade. The change in fortunes can be ascribed to a number of factors. The improved harvests of the early 1950s stimulated consumer spending among the rural population, while the flow of labour from the countryside to the industrial towns meant that wages rose less rapidly than in the agricultural sector, thus permitting industrial growth without a commensurate increase in labour costs. The State too assigned a high priority to industrial development.[33] The decision to accept foreign aid from the United States in return for military bases allowed Spain to abandon the none too successful policy of import substitution and purchase much-needed raw materials.[34] Thus between 1950 and 1954 the proportion of capital goods within the range of imports rose from 13·51 per cent to 27·07 per cent. At the same time, attention was paid to the development of new energy sources.

Table 46   Indices of industrial production, 1940–59

	INE (1929 = 100)	CEN (1953–54=100)	INE (1942 base)	CEN
1940	–	60	–	97
1941	–	59	–	96
1942	112	62	100	100
1943	120	54	107	88
1944	122	62	108	101
1945	114	59	102	97
1946	134	69	120	112
1947	137	69	122	111
1948	140	70	125	112
1949	133	76	119	113
1950	152	76	136	123
1951	172	79	153	128
1952	196	91	175	147
1953	206	94	184	153
1954	214	105	191	169
1955	240	115	214	186
1956	265	123	236	198
1957	279	134	249	216
1958	305	150	272	254
1959	319	185	282	298

Source. Instituto Nacional de Estadística and Consejo de Economía Nacional.

Between 1942 and 1959 industrial production rose by 6·3 per cent per annum, while from 1959 to 1972 it increased at an annual rate of 7·9 per cent. During the latter period Spain became the fifth industrial power in Europe, with a rate of industrial growth surpassed only by Japan among member States of the OECD. The 1960s brought an elevenfold increase in car production; shipbuilding increased by 4·5 times, petroleum refinery by 4·5, steel production by 3·8 and cement by 3·2. The contribution of industry to gross domestic product rose during the decade from 28·9 per cent to 35·6 per cent. This expansion was reflected in Spain's trade statistics; no longer did exports of foodstuffs and raw materials loom largest. In 1975 industrial exports (including raw materials) accounted for 78 per cent of the total.[35]

The high level of industrial development, particularly since 1960, can be largely attributed to two factors: the availability of cheap credit and the active encouragement of foreign investment in Spain. Between them the nation's bankers and foreign investors determined the shape of contemporary capitalism in Spain.

Banking and industrial concentration
As part of their endeavours to control wartime finances, the Nationalists imposed a ban on the establishment of any further banking institutions in August 1936. This policy, known as the 'status quo', was continued after the ending of hostilities and later ratified in 1946. As a result, existing large-scale financial institutions were able substantially to consolidate their power and influence.

Between 1940 and 1950 the five largest banks (Bilbao, Vizcaya, Hispano Americano, Español de Crédito and Central) expanded at an unprecedented rate, while their profits increased sevenfold. This momentum was maintained during the '50s, when the profits of the 'big five' rose from 439·5 million pesetas to 1,890·9 million. From 1940 to 1960 the combined reserves of these banks grew from an insignificant sum to 7,471·6 million pesetas.[36] In their concern at the monopolistic position acquired by the 'big five', the Opus Dei Ministers abolished the 'status quo' in April 1962, thus preparing the way for the setting up of new banks, a policy which had some limited success.

Geographically, the main feature of Spanish banking since the civil war was its growing centralisation, more than half a century after similar developments took place in the major European economies. By 1967 52 per cent of all finance capital was controlled from Madrid, while Bilbao came to play only a secondary role, with 14·5 per cent of finance capital. Madrid-based banks controlled 67 per cent of bank branches in Spain and 61·9 per cent of deposits. Meanwhile Catalan banks, in a decline since the collapse of the Bank of Barcelona in 1920, became almost insignificant nationally. Even within the Principality the great majority of firms are today financed by banks domiciled outside the region. In 1976 the leading Catalan bank occupied only thirteenth place in the Spanish banking league.[37]

The existence of credit restrictions during the 1950s allowed the banks to gain almost absolute control over industrial finance; companies independent of banks practically ceased to exist. In their search for funds, industrial companies found it increasingly expedient to shift their headquarters to within close proximity of the banks. This factor contributed to the spread of industrialisation in and around the Spanish capital, a development not entirely unwelcome to the regime, since it eroded the economic power bases of Catalan and Basque nationalism. By the mid-'60s 55 per cent of Spain's largest companies were based in Madrid.

From the early 1960s Spanish economists voiced their concern as the emergence of a new financial oligarchy, centred on Madrid, which controlled huge sectors of national industry. In 1965, for example, the 300 leading Spanish financiers controlled 98 per cent of steel production, petroleum refinery and electricity generation.[38]

Although anti-monopoly legislation was on the statute books in the 1940s and 1950s, the regime made little attempt to encourage competition. Indeed, the quest for autarky sought to remove foreign competition, while the industry laws of 1939 established a series of privileges for those industries declared to be of national interest. Hence for the next twenty years a considerable degree of concentration was permitted to develop among Spain's leading industries, to a large extent determined by the banking groups which controlled them. A clear illustration of this phenomenon is provided by the electricity supply industry. In 1962 eight enterprises, all linked to the major banks, possessed 51 per cent of productive capacity, generating 53 per cent of electricity; the remaining capacity and production were shared by 230 firms. Similar developments took place in sugar refinery, where five major companies controlled 71·65 per cent of production, and also in the fields of fertilisers, cement and metallurgy.[39]

A new law of 1963 attempted to prohibit restrictive practices, proposing a series of fines in order to curb them. However, in order to encourage competition, Spain needed much more than preventive legislation. Although theoretically an advance, the law proved ineffective in practice, since the necessary anti-monopolistic institutions took a long time to establish.[40]

Foreign investment

The Stabilisation Plan of 1959 has been described as an SOS, for foreign capital. There is an agreement that without the presence of direct and indirect foreign investment Spain would not have experienced her so-called 'economic miracle of the 1960s'. Spanish savings alone, argued the Governor of the Bank of Santander in 1967, were insufficient to meet the needs of the economy: it was therefore necessary to find new sources of finance.[41]

Official statistics cover only those companies in which foreign capital accounts for more than one-half of the total. From these data, however, it can be clearly seen that between 1960 and 1974 four countries accounted for three-quarters of all foreign investment: the United States, with 34·78 per cent; Switzerland, with 18·64 per cent; West Germany, with 11·80 per cent, and Great Britain, with 11·28 per cent. The Swiss figure is probably misleading, as it may include both funds from the United States and those kept by Spaniards in Swiss bank accounts. With regard to the United States, a Common Market business report of 1969 showed that of the world's 400 largest companies 200 were North American, and that, of these, ninety-two had 101 affiliates in Spain of which sixty-one were majority holdings. Out of the remaining 200 non-American firms only fifty had Spanish affiliates, numbering sixty-three, of which forty-two had major holdings.[42]

The industrial sectors with the largest foreign participation at the end of the Franco era were chemicals, food processing, iron and steel and non-ferrous metals. With its low level of scientific and technical expertise, the chemical industry was particularly keen to receive foreign support; in 1967 it was calculated that chemicals accounted for 26·72 per cent of all foreign investment.[43] Among the main reasons given by United States companies for their growing involvement in Spain after 1960 were a rapidly expanding market, an atmosphere favourable to investment, relatively cheap labour, low levels of taxation, and the political, economic and financial stability of the country.[44]

Following the publication in France of Jean-Jacques Servan Schreiber's work on United States capitalism abroad, *Le Défi Américain*, a strong critical current emerged south of the Pyrenees against the so-called American challenge in Spain, and once again Spanish writers began to refer to their country as a colonial economy controlled by American-based multinational companies.[45]

REGIONAL IMBALANCE WITHIN THE SPANISH ECONOMY

One of the most serious results of the nature of Spanish economic development all through the modern period is the enormous discrepancies in wealth which still exist between the various regions that make up the country. In 1973 the highest levels of income *per capita* were found to be in the three Basque provinces of Vizcaya, Alava and Guipúzcoa, together with Madrid and Barcelona. These five provinces, which contained 28·7 per cent of the population, produced 40·0 per cent of the nation's wealth. At the bottom end of the scale, the five lowest-ranking provinces—in order of ascendance, Lugo, Cáceres, Badajoz, Granada and Orense—had *per capita* incomes of well under a half that of Vizcaya. With 8·0 per cent of the total number of inhabitants, these backward provinces produced a mere 4·7 per cent of net national income. Since regional income data were first collected in 1956 there appears to have been only a slight narrowing of the gap between rich and poor areas; even this took place largely as a result of internal migration.[46]

Apart from the Badajoz and Jaén plans of the 1950s, regional planning in Spain dates only from the First Development Plan of 1963. Yet, from the very beginning, the emphasis in regional planning was always on the achievement of a high rate of growth rather than on equity factors. Where backward regions were selected for development the criterion was always that of future growth potential. Moreover, Spanish regional policy always reflected the strong preoccupation of the State with national policy goals.[47]

It was this centralist preoccupation of the Franco regime that led to the incorporation into the First Development Plan of the strategy of growth poles, first developed in the mid-'50s by the French economist François Perroux. Growth pole theory emphasised the multiplier effect of leading industries. These were to be set up in areas with a high growth potential, usually in regional capitals with a population of between 150,000 and 200,000 inhabitants, since such sites were already provided with a basic infrastructure of roads, housing and educational establishments, including higher education, which was considered necessary for future diversified growth.

The First Development Plan created two types of growth pole, so-called industrial development poles which numbered five in the cities of Corunna, Seville, Valladolid, Saragossa and Vigo, and two industrial promotion poles, Burgos and Huelva. In addition, comprehensive plans were also produced for the Canary Islands, aimed at expanding its tourist and fishing industries, and for the Campo de Gibraltar—the area immediately behind the Rock—largely for political reasons. Five new poles were designated in the Second Development Plan, Granada, Córdoba, Oviedo, Logrōno and Villagarcía de Aroso.

By the end of 1972, 381 new firms had been established in the designated growth poles, providing an additional 54,000 jobs. In general, however, for every two jobs that were lost in these areas only one was created in their place. The new firms that were attracted to Seville only partly filled the gap caused by the failure of existing establishments. Despite massive government support, the Campo de Gibraltar scheme did not provide enough jobs for the thousands thrown out of work when Spain closed the border with the British colony in 1969.

The success story of the growth pole strategy was the southern city of Huelva, with its huge chemical complex. By 1972 Huelva had received 43 per cent of all government subsidies, while the chemical industry as a whole received about three-quarters of the total investment in growth poles. Yet the case of Huelva typifies the limitations of restricting developments to specific poles, since the city developed few links with the rest of the province and remains an enclave of industrial development located in a backward agrarian region.[48]

THE SPANISH ECONOMY AFTER THE FRANCO ERA

The final year of the Franco regime coincided with the lowest increases in GNP in Spain since the days of autarky. The 1975 rate of increase of 0·5 per cent, moreover, was only raised to 1·8 per cent in the following year. As the final eclipse of the Opus Dei Ministers bore witness, the so-called Spanish economic miracle was gone for ever.

A whole series of indicators illustrate the depths of the economic crisis into which Spain was flung. The nation was particularly hard hit by the increase in the world's oil prices; in 1976 her energy deficit was $4,500 million (9 per cent more than in 1975). As a symptom of the European depression, receipts from tourism fell by 12 per cent in 1976, and emigrant remittances slumped as a further 54,000 migrant workers made the home-ward trek across the Pyrenees. These unfortunates joined the growing numbers of unemployed, which at the end of 1976 reached nearly one million, or 7·5 per cent of the active labour force. Exacerbated by the oil price rise, Spain's balance of payments deficit worsened from $3,500 million in 1975 to $4,300 million in 1976; in the latter year exports covered only 46 per cent of the cost of imports, as against 52 per cent in 1975.

To worsen the problems of the Arias Navarro and Suárez governments which held power after the dictator's death in November 1975, inflation rose to 20 per cent in the following year and stood at 27 per cent for the twelve months prior to the free elections which Prime Minister Suárez called for 15 June 1977. The Madrid stock exchange registered its disquiet with a fall in share prices of 28 per cent in 1976 and a continued decline into the first half of 1977.

It was obvious to all after the death of Franco that tough measures were required to tackle a deteriorating situation. The economist José Ramon Lasuén spoke for many when he argued despairingly that 'Spain has the least possibility of growth and the greatest likelihood of inflation in the OECD'.[49] Yet for political reasons neither of the first two administrations of the new monarchy felt capable of coming to grips with the immediate problems, let alone tackling the profound structural problems that need to be solved in order to bring about lasting recovery.[50] A much heralded pay policy and price freeze proved a dismal failure, while in the year before the election the government preferred to let the money supply rise by 22 per cent rather than incur the wrath of the newly emergent labour movement.

On 12 July 1977, less than a month after Prime Minister Suárez had won a renewed mandate, his Economics Minister and Deputy Prime Minister, Enrique Fuentes Quintana, introduced his first economic package, announcing plans for sweeping fiscal reforms and at the same time bring-ing about a devaluation of the peseta roughly of the order of 20 per cent. Despite a new political agreement signed in October 1977 (the *Pacto de Moncloa*) between all the major parties, including the Communists, aimed at overcoming economic and social difficulties, early results have been disappointing. Following grumbles on the right, Fuentes Quintana and his whole economic team resigned on 22 February 1978. After so much neglect by the heirs of fascism the government's task is a daunting one which may stretch the newly established Spanish democracy to the full.

NOTES

1 Tamames, *La República, la era de Franco*, pp. 350–3.
2 Jesús García Fernández, *La emigración exterior de España* (Barcelona, 1965), p. 19; Javier Rubio, *La emigración española a Francia* (Barcelona, 1974), p. 37.
3 See below, pp. 154–5 and 160.
4 Rubio, *op. cit.*, p. 296.
5 *Economic and Social Development Program for Spain, 1964–67* (Baltimore, 1965), p. 9.
6 *Semanas Sociales de España* (Burgos, 1945), p. 212, cited in J. Clavera, J. M. Esteban, M. Antònia Monés, A. Montserrat and J. Ros Hombravella, *Capitalismo español: de la autarquía a la establización*, 2 vols, 1939–59 (Madrid, 1973), 1, p. 168.
7 Clavera *et al.*, *op. cit.*, 1, 102.
8 Manuel Vázquez Montalbán, *La pentración americana en España* (Madrid, 1974), pp. 140–4.
9 Charles W. Anderson, *The Political Economy of Modern Spain: Policy Making in an Authoritarian System* (Wisconsin, 1970), p. 118; Max Gallo, *Historia de la España franquista* (Paris, 1971), pp. 257–99.
10 Ramón Tamames, *Estructura ecónomica de España*, 3 vols, 7th edn (Madrid, 1974), 3, p. 256.
11 Anderson, *op. cit.*, pp. 130–1.
12 International Bank for Reconstruction and Development, *The Economic Development of Spain* (Baltimore, 1963); cf. Enrique Fuentes Quintana, *El desarrollo económica de España: juicio crítico del Informe del Banco Mundial* (Madrid, 1963).
13 Anderson, *op. cit.*, pp. 164–7.
14 See esp. José Luis Sampedro, 'Le plan de développement espagnol dans son cadre social', in L'Espagne à l'heure du développement, *Revue Tiers Monde* (Paris, 1967), pp. 1033–41.
15 *Ibid.*, p. 1034.
16 Harry W. Richardson, *Regional Development Policy and Planning in Spain* (Farnborough, 1975), pp. 35–6.
17 R. Tomàs *et al.*, *La crisis económica y sus repercusiones en España* (Barcelona, 1975), pp. 167–98.
18 Cited in José Luis Leal *et al.*, *La agricultura en el desarrollo capitalista español, 1940–70* (Madrid, 1975), p. 17.
19 Clavera *et al.*, *op. cit.*, 1, pp. 48 and 260.
20 Cf. Higenio París Eguilaz, *Diez años de política económica* (Madrid, 1949), p. 49.
21 Manuel de Torres, *El problema triguero y otras cuestiones fundamentales de la agricultura española* (Madrid, 1944); A. García González, *El trigo: su economía y legislación actual* (Madrid, 1946).
22 For an early expression of these views see Editora Nacional, DEPYP, *La nueva España agraria* (Bilbao, 1937).
23 Tamames, *Estructura económica de España*, 1, 80.
24 Anderson, *op. cit.*, pp. 44–6; John Naylon, *Andalusia, Problem Regions of Europe* (London, 1975), pp. 24–9; Organisation de Cooperation et de Développement Economiques, *La politique agricole en Espagne* (Paris, 1974), p. 23.
25 Tamames, *Estructura económica de España*, 1, pp. 82–4.
26 Leal *et al.*, *op. cit.*, p. 37.

27   Banco Internacional de Reconstrucción y Fomento—FAO, El desarrollo de la agricultura en España (Madrid, 1966), pp. 92–6.
28   See, for example, Tamames, Estructura económica de España, 1, pp. 121–4.
29   José Manuel Naredo, La evolución de la agricultura en España: desarrollo capitalista y crisis de las formas de producción tradicionales (Barcelona, 1971), pp. 32–40.
30   Ibid., p. 101; E. Barón, El final del campesinado (Madrid, 1971); Javier Gorosquieta, El campo español en crisis (Bilbao, 1973).
31   See Antonio Robert, Un problema nacional: la industrialización necesaria (Madrid, 1943), p. 126.
32   Demetrio Carceller Segura, La situación económica de España (Madrid, 1943), p. 46–7.
33   José María de Areilza, Presente y futuro de la economía industrial española (Bilbao, 1954), p. 10.
34   Manuel de Arburúa, Cinco años al frente del Ministerio de Comercio (Madrid, 1956), p. 199.
35   José María Ordeix Gesti, España hacia una economía industrial (Barcelona, 1972), pp. 16–17; Banco de Bilbao, Informe económico, 1976 (Bilbao, 1977), p. 187.
36   Juan Muñoz, El poder de la banca en España (Madrid, 1969), pp. 60–5.
37   Ibid., pp. 111–22; Servicio de Estudios del Banco de Bilbao, Situación, 5 (May 1977), 22.
38   Ibid., pp. 307–10; Ramón Tamames, La lucha contra los monopolios en España (Madrid, 1970), pp. 323–52.
39   Tamames, La lucha contra los monopolios en España, pp. 356–416.
40   Ibid., pp. 429–30.
41   Emilio Botín, ABC, 28 December 1967, cited in Eliseo Bayo, El 'desafío' en España (Madrid, 1970), p. 313.
42   Ibid., pp. 67–8.
43   Ibid., p. 85.
44   Stanford Research Institute, Las inversiones norteamericanas en España (Barcelona, 1972), pp. 16–21.
45   See Bayo, op. cit., p. 46.
46   Banco de Bilbao, Renta nacional de España y su distribución provincial, 1973 (Bilbao, 1975), pp. 38, 48 and 59.
47   Richardson, op. cit., p. 21.
48   Naylon, op. cit., pp. 31–5.
49   The Economist, Survey 3, 'The new Spain', 2 April 1977.
50   Financial Times, 13 July 1977.

ORGANISATIONS AND POLITICAL TERMS

Bieno negro Period of right-wing rule from November 1933 to the end of 1935, dubbed by the left the 'Black Biennium'.

Bienio reformador First two years of the Second Republic (April 1931–November 1933), when a series of leftist governments attempted to carry out basic reforms.

Casa del pueblo Workers' club and educational centre, the most important of which were run by the Socialist party.

CEDA Confederación Española de Derechas Autónomas; federation of right-wing groups formed during the Second Republic, led by Gil Robles.

Constituent Cortes Parliament elected in June 1931 which drew up the constitution of the Second Republic.

CNT Confederación Nacional del Trabajo; anarcho-syndicalist trade union federation founded in Barcelona in 1910.

CRT Confederación Regional del Trabajo; Catalan branch of the CNT.

FAI Federación Anarquista Ibérica; organisation of intellectuals and activists set up by anarchist militants in 1927 to prevent the CNT from concentrating on trade union activities.

Falange Española Fascistic party founded by José Antonio Primo de Rivera in 1933; merged with Carlists in April 1937 to become the single authorised political party of Franco's Spain.

FNAE Federación Nacional de Agricultores de España; founded in 1913 as the agricultural counterpart of the CNT.

FNTT Federación Nacional de Trabajadores de la Tierra; agrarian wing of the UGT, founded in April 1930.

Fomento del Trabajo Nacional Catalan employers' group founded in 1889 to secure tariff protection.

FTRE Federación de Trabajadores de la Región Española; first attempt by the anarchists to set up a mass trade union organisation; founded in 1881.

INC Instituto Nacional de Colonización; institute set up by Franco in October 1939 to carry out the regime's agricultural policy.

INI Instituto Nacional de Industria; main instrument of the Franco regime's industrial policy in the early years, founded in 1941; permitted to become a slumbering giant.

Liga Nacional de Productores; pressure group set up by Spanish chambers of agriculture to attack the economic policies of the Restoration after the loss of Cuba.

Lliga Regionalista Political party founded by Catalan big business in 1901.

Mancomunitat Catalan regional government established in 1914.

Mesta Guild of sheep farmers of medieval origin which in return for payments to the State was granted the privilege of pasturing its flocks wherever it wished during the annual migrations, to the detriment of Spanish agriculture. Abolished in 1836.

MZA Compañía de Ferrocarriles de Madrid a Zaragoza y Alicante; railway company founded in Spain by Rothschild's in 1856.

Opus Dei Catholic lay group which occupied important economic Ministries in Franco's Spain during the late 1950s.

PSOE Partido Socialista Obrero Español; Spanish Socialist party, founded in 1879.

Sindicatos libres Scab unions founded by the Catalan employers in 1919 to oppose the CNT.

Trienio bolchevista Bolshevik triennium of 1917–19; period of profound social unrest in Spain.

UGT Unión General de Trabajadores; socialist trade union movement founded in 1888.

GLOSSARY OF SPANISH WORDS

behetría Form of government in medieval Castile, distinguished from feudalism in that the local inhabitants elected their *seigneur*.

bracero Landless field worker most common on the large estates of the south. Literally, an 'arm'.

cacique Used in a derogatory sense to denote a local political boss, especially during the Restoration. Derived from the American Indian word for 'chief'.

censo Either a census or an empyteutic lease, i.e. a long-term lease usually inherited.

concentración parcelaria Policy of the Franco regime to unify small scattered plots of land into a single farm.

concierto económico Local agreement by which the State permitted a region to raise its own taxes and allocate expenditure as it saw fit, apart from such national items as defence and foreign policy. Such an agreement was granted to the Basque provinces in 1876 after the abolition of their *fueros*. An important demand of the Catalan business community after 1900.

cortijo Term used, especially in the south, for a farm.

diezmo Source of rural income for the Church during the *ancien régime*. Literally one-tenth of the annual yield.

febre d'or The golden age of Catalan agriculture during the 1880s following the outbreak of phylloxera in France and the commercial treaty of 1882 which opened the French market to the region's wine growers.

foro A permanent and unalterable empyteutic lease common in Galicia. The subject of litigation during the late eighteenth century, when rising grain prices led to sub-leasing.

fueros Used here to denote the old laws of the Basque provinces taken away from them in 1876 as a reprisal for Basque support for the Carlists in the Third Carlist War.

fuerzas vivas The active elements in a community, often used with reference to industrial entrepreneurs.

huerta A plot of irrigated land usually yielding more than one crop a year. A feature of the Levante.

latifundio A large landed estate, most common in the south.

ley de laboreo forzoso Decree of the provisional government of the Second Republic which forced landlords to cultivate their estates according to the 'normal uses', thereby aiming to avert an economic strike against the infant Republic.

ley de términos municipales Decree of the provisional government of the Second Republic which aimed to curb the flow of migrant labour into rural villages in order to strengthen the local unions and raise wages.

minifundio Fragmented small property common in Galicia. The opposite of a *latifundio*.

política hidráulica Phrase coined by the agrarian reformer Joaquín Costa in the late nineteenth century for a policy of State encouragement for irrigation in order to regenerate Spanish agriculture.

pósitos Local granaries created during the Middle Ages which also served as credit institutions. By the nineteenth century they were generally thought to be riddled with corruption.

rabassaire Catalan peasant farmer who sharecropped land, often for the purpose of vine cultivation. During the Second Republic the rabassaires came into conflict with the central government when they sought full ownership of their lands.

sindicato único Anarcho-syndicalist union which grouped together all workers in a particular establishment into one organisation so as to heighten revolutionary fervour.

turno riguroso Socialist demand that landlords be obliged to hire labourers in the order in which they signed on at the local employment office so as to prevent discrimination against militants.

ugetista Member of the UGT.

yuntero Tenant farmer common in Extremadura, so called because he owned a team of oxen, or 'yunta', which he hired out.

BIBLIOGRAPHY

Sources. Collections of data from before the present century must be treated with extreme caution. After 1786 the Secretaría de la balanza de comercio began to collect statistics on the agricultural and industrial wealth of Spain. Their first census was published in 1787, but a second and much more complete census for the year 1799 was published in 1803 under the title Censo de frutos y manufacturas de España e islas adyacentes. The many weaknesses of this document are explained by Josep Fontana in 'El "Censo de frutos y manufacturas" de 1799: un análisis crítico', Moneda y Crédito, 101, 1967, 54–68. Despite much contemporary criticism, the mistakes of the Censo were faithfully reproduced in the two best-known statistical surveys of the nineteenth century, Moreau de Jonnès, Statistique de l'Espagne, Paris, 1834, and Pascual Madoz, Diccionario estadístico-histórico de España y sus posesiones de Ultramar, Madrid, 1845–50, 16 vols. Official statistics on Spanish foreign trade were collected after 1849, see Cuadro (later Estadística) General del Comercio Exterior de España, published by the Dirección General de Aduanas. For statistics on Spanish mining see the Estadísticas mineras, published after 1861. An invaluable guide on how to use these and other mining data is Jordi Nadal, El fracaso de la Revolución industrial en España, 1814–1913, Barcelona, 1975. On general price movements see E. J. Hamilton, War and Prices in Spain, 1651–1800, Cambridge, Mass., 1934, based on the account books of convents and hospitals; G. Anes, Las crisis agrarias en la España moderna, Madrid, 1970, who used local market prices (mercuriales), for the eighteenth century; and for the second half of the nineteenth century N. Sánchez Albornoz, Materiales para la historia económica de España. Los precios agrícolas en la segunda mitad del siglo XIX, vol. 1, Trigo y cebada. Recopilación, análisis y estudio preliminar, Madrid, 1975. Older collections of historical statistics include La riqueza y el progreso de España, published by the Banco Urquijo in 1920 and 1924, and Principales actividades de la vida española en la primera mitad del siglo XX, published by the Instituto Nacional de Estadística, Madrid, 1952. Also published by the same institute is Publicaciones estadísticas de España, Publicaciones del primer centenario de la estadística española, Madrid, 1956. Invaluable sources on contemporary Spain are published by the Banco de Bilbao. See the Informe(s) Económico(s), published for separate years, and the Renta Nacional de España y su distribución provincial, which has come out at regular intervals since 1956, giving a province-by-province breakdown of national income.

General works. The best general economic history of Spain available in English is J. Vicens Vives, An Economic History of Spain, Princeton, 1969. For the eighteenth century a clear account of economic and social developments is found in G. Anes, El Antiguo régimen. Los Borbones, Madrid, 1975. See also the same author's brilliant monograph on the agrarian crises of the eighteenth century, Las crisis agrarias en la España moderna, Madrid, 1970, and A. Domínguez Ortiz, La sociedad española en el siglo XVIII, Madrid. 1955. The breakdown of the old order is well set out in J. Fontana, La quiebra de la monarquía absoluta (1814–20), Barcelona, 1971. There is an excellent survey of Spanish economic history in the nineteenth century, J. Nadal, El fracaso de la Revolución industrial en España, 1814–1913, Madrid, 1975 (for an abridged translation see 'The failure of the industrial revolution in Spain, 1830–1914', in C. M. Cipolla, ed., *The Fontana Economic History of Europe*, vol. 4 (2), London, 1973, pp. 532–626). The nineteenth century is also amply covered in a number of recent works including: N. Sánchez Albornoz, *España hace un siglo: una economía dual*, Barcelona, 1968; G. Tortella, *Los orígenes del capitalismo en España*, Madrid, 1973; Servicio de Estudios del Banco de España, *Ensayos sobre la economía española a mediados del siglo XIX*, Madrid, 1970; and *El Banco de España: una historia económica*, Madrid, 1970. A fine range of articles on agriculture, colonial trade and economic growth is published in the proceedings of the first colloquium of Spanish economic historians held in 1972: see J. Nadal and G. Tortella, eds, *Agricultura, comercio colonial y crecimiento económico en la España contemporánea*, Barcelona, 1974. A wide selection of readings is available in R. Aracil and M. García Bonafé, eds, *Lecturas de historia económica de España*, Barcelona, 1976, 2 vols. The best accounts of twentieth-century Spanish economic and social history are to be found in S. Roldán, J. L. Delgado and J. Muñoz, *La formación de la sociedad capitalista en España, 1914–20*, Madrid, 1973, 2 vols; J. Velarde Fuertes, *Política económica de la dictadura*, new edn, Madrid, 1973; J. Clavera et al., *Capitalismo español: de la autarquía a la establización (1939–59)*, Madrid, 1973, 2 vols; R. Tamames, *La República. La era de Franco*, Madrid, 1973; and R. Tamames, *Estructura económica de España*, new edn, Madrid, 1974, 3 vols. There is a brief and succinct account in English in J. Fontana and J. Nadal, 'Spain, 1914–70', in C. M. Cipolla, ed., *The Fontana Economic History of Europe*, vol. 6 (2), London, 1976, pp. 460–529.

Regional studies. There are a number of excellent studies on the economic and social history of Catalonia, for example: P. Vilar, *La Catalogne dans l'Espagne moderne: recherches sur les fondements économiques des structures nationales*, Paris, 1962, 3 vols; P. Vilar, 'La Catalogne industrielle: réflexions sur un démarrage et sur un destin', in P. Léon et al., eds, *L'Industrialisation en Europe au XIXᵉ siècle*, Paris, 1972; J. Vicens Vives, *Cataluña en el siglo XIX*, Barcelona, 1961; E. Escarra, *Le Développement industriel de la Catalogne*, Paris, 1908; J. Solé Tura, *Catalanismo y revolución burguesa*, Madrid, 1970; A. Balcells, *Crisis económica y agitación social en Cataluña (1930–36)*, Barcelona, 1971; and J. M. Bricall, *Política econòmica de la Generalitat (1936–39)*, vol. 1, *Evolució i formes de la producció industrial*, Barcelona, 1970. See also J. Carrera Pujal, *La economía de Cataluña en el siglo XIX*, Barcelona, 1961, 4 vols, and G. Graell, *Historia del Fomento del Trabajo Nacional*, Barcelona, 1911. On the Basque region the standard of scholarship is not as high, but see J. F. de Lequerica, *La actividad económica de Vizcaya en la vida nacional*, Madrid, 1956; A. de Churruca, *Minería, industria y comercio del País Vasco*, San Sebastian, 1951; *Un siglo en la vida del Banco de Bilbao: primer centenario (1857–1957)*, Bilbao, 1957; J. M. Pérez Agote, 'Orígines del capitalismo en Vizcaya', *Boletín de Estudios Económicos*, 13, 1953, 26–65; and P. de Alzola, *Progreso industrial de Vizcaya*, Bilbao, 19Cᵬ. Outstanding among recent works is J. P. Fusi, *Política obrera en el País Vasco (1880–1923)*, Madrid, 1975. Other regional studies of merit include E. Giralt, 'Problemas históricos de la industrialización valenciana', *Estudios Geográficos*, 29, 1968, 369–95; R. Aracil and M. García Bonafé, *Procés industrial d'Alcoi*, Valencia, 1974; J. Nadal, 'Industrialización y desindustrialización del sureste español, 1817–1913', *Moneda y Crédito*, 120, 1972, 3–80; L. G. San Miguel, *De la sociedad aristocrática a la sociedad industrial en la España del siglo XIX*, Madrid, 1973, a study of society in Asturias in the nineteenth century; R. Fuertes Arias, *Asturias industrial: estudio del estado actual del industrialismo* asturiano, Gijón, 1902; D. Ruiz, El movimiento obrero en Asturias: de la industrialización a la Segunda República, Oviedo, 1968; J. Díaz del Moral, Historia de las agitaciones campesinas andaluzas—Córdoba (Antecedentes para una reforma agraria), new edn, Madrid, 1973; and A. M. Bernal, La propiedad de la tierra y las luchas agrarias andaluzas, Barcelona, 1974.

Demography. The outstanding work on Spanish population history is J. Nadal, La población española: siglos XVI a XX, Barcelona, 1971. See also M. Fuentes Martiáñez, Despoblación y repoblación de España, 1482–1920, Madrid, 1929; J. Nadal and E. Giralt, La Population catalane de 1553 a 1717: l'immigration française et les autres facteurs de son développement, Paris, 1960; F. Bustelo García del Real, 'Algunas reflexiones sobre la población española de principios del siglo XVIII', Anales de Economía, 15, 1972, 89–106; F. Bustelo García del Real, 'La población española en la segunda mitad del siglo XVIII', Moneda y Crédito, 123, 1972, 54–104; M. Livi Bachi, 'Fertility and nuptiality changes in Spain from the late eighteenth to the early twentieth century', Population Studies, 22, 1968; J. A. Lacomba, 'Notas sobre la demografía española durante el primer tercio del siglo XX', in Ensayos sobre el siglo XX español, Madrid, 1972; Instituto de Reformas Sociales, Información sobre emigración española a los paises de Europa durante la guerra, Madrid, 1919; A. Arbelo, La mortalidad de la infancia en España, 1901–50, Madrid, 1962; W. J. Leasure, 'Factors involved in the decline of fertility in Spain, 1900–1950'; Population Studies, 16, 1963, 271–85; A. García Barbancho, Las migraciones interiores españoles 1900–60, Madrid, 1967; J. García Fernández, La emigración exterior de España, Barcelona, 1965; and J. Rubio, La emigración española a Francia, Barcelona, 1974.

Agriculture. In recent years a number of first-rate studies have appeared on Spanish agriculture. For the eighteenth century there is nothing to rival G. Anes, Las crisis agrarias en la España moderna, Madrid, 1970. The same author has also published a collection of essays, Economía e ilustración en la España del siglo XVIII, Barcelona, 1969. See also A. García Sanz, 'Agronomía y experiencias agroeconómicas durante la segunda mitad del siglo XVIII', Moneda y Crédito, 131, 1974, 29–54, and R. Herr, 'Hacia el derrumbe del Antiguo régimen: crisis fiscal y desamortización bajo Carlos IV', Moneda y Crédito, 118, 1971, 37–100. For the nineteenth century there is a first-rate synthesis of general developments in Spanish agriculture in G. Anes, 'La agricultura española desde comienzos del siglo XIX hasta 1868: algunos problemas', in Servicio de Estudios del Banco de España, Ensayos sobre la economía española a mediados del siglo XIX, Madrid, 1970. Recent research on the disentailing legislation of the mid-nineteenth century is well reviewed in F. Tomás y Valiente, 'Recientes investigaciones sobre la desamortización, intento de síntesis', Moneda y Crédito, 131, 1974, 95–160. The same author has also written a concise work on the topic, El marco político de la desamortización en España, Barcelona, 1971. See also S. de Moxó, La disolución del régimen señorial en España, Madrid, 1965; A. Lazo, Les desamortización de las tierras de la Iglesia en la provincia de Sevilla, 1835–45, Seville, 1970; and F. Simón Segura, Contribución al estudio de la desamortización de España: la desamortización de Mendizábal en la provincia de Madrid, Madrid, 1969. (A similar study on the province of Gerona was published in the same year by this author.) Of the studies of the late nineteenth-century crisis of Spanish agriculture see especially R. Garrabou. 'La crisi agrària espanyola de finals del segle XIX', Recerques, 5, Barcelona, 1975, and J. Fontana, 'La gran crisi bladera del segle XIX', Serra d'Or, second series, 11, November 1960, 21–2. The best

contemporary accounts are *La crisis agaria y pecuaria, 1887–89*, Madrid, 7 vols, and
J. Sánchez de Toca, *La crisis agraria y sus remedios en España*, Madrid 1887. On the
early twentieth century see S. C. Méndez Bortolomé, *Consideraciones sobre los
factores del problema agrario de España*, Santiago, 1910. There is a good account of
agricultural policy since 1920: see J. López de Sebastián, *Política agraria en España,
1920–70*, Madrid, 1970. For the Second Republic the most invaluable work is E.
Malefakis, *Agrarian Reform and Peasant Revolution in Spain: Origins of the Civil
War*, New Haven, 1970. Two classic contemporary sources on the agrarian crisis of
the 1930s are P. Carrión, *La reforma agraria: problemas fundamentales*, Madrid,
1931, and, by the same author, *Los latifundios en España: su importancia, origen,
consecuencias y solución*, Madrid, 1932. The Franco period is amply covered in J.
M. Naredo, *La evolución de la agricultura en España*, Barcelona, 1971, and J. L. Leal
et al., *La agricultura en el desarrollo capitalista español, 1940–70*, Madrid, 1975.

Mining. For coal see L. de Adaro, *Los carbones nacionales y la marina de guerra*,
Madrid, 1911, and I. Herrero Garralda, *La política del carbón en España*, Madrid,
1944. There are two classic late-nineteenth-century works on iron-ore mining in
Vizcaya, M. de Basterra, *Vizcaya minera: su historia, legislación foral y derecho
vigente*, Bilbao, 1894, and Círculo Minero de Bilbao, *Las minas de hierro en la
provincia de Vizcaya: progresos realizados en esta región desde 1870 a 1899*,
Bilbao, 1900. See also J. Alcalá Zamora y Quiepo de Llano, 'Producción de hierro y
altos hornos en la España anterior a 1850', *Moneda y Crédito*, 128, 1974, and M. W.
Flinn, 'British steel and Spanish ore, 1871–1914', *Economic History Review*, second
series, 8, 84–90. Among the works on lead are E. González Llana, *El plomo en
España*, Madrid, 1949, and F. Quirós Linares, *La minería en la Sierra Morena de
Cuidad Real*, Oviedo, 1970. Copper is dealt with in I. Pinedo Vara, *Piratas de
Huelva, su historia, minería y aprovechamiento*, Madrid, 1963; S. G. Checkland,
The Mines of Tharsis: Roman, French, and British Enterprise in Spain, London,
1967; and D. Avery, *Not on Queen Victoria's Birthday: the Story of the Rio Tinto
Mines*, London, 1974. For zinc see *La Compagnie Royale Asturienne des Mines
1853–1953*, Paris, 1954, while for mercury there is an excellent monograph, J.
Zurraluqui Martínez, *Los almadenes de azogue (minas de cinabrio): La historia
frente a la tradición*, Madrid, 1934.

The iron and steel industry. For the early period see the monograph of J. Alcalá
Zamora y Quiepo de Llano, *Historia de una empresa siderúrgica española: los altos
hornos de Liérganes y la Cavada, 1622–1834*, Santander, 1974. The reader should
beware of the numerous mistakes and pitfalls in the often cited F. Sánchez Ramos,
*La economía siderúrgica española: vol. 1, Estudio crítico de la historia industrial de
España hasta 1900*, Madrid, 1945. The mid-nineteenth century is brilliantly
covered in J. Nadal, 'Los comienzos de la industrialización española (1832–68): la
industria siderúrgica', in *Ensayos sobre la economía española a mediados del siglo
XIX*, Madrid, 1970. On the accumulation of capital in Vizcaya and the origins of the
industry see M. González Portilla, 'El desarrollo industrial de Vizcaya y la acumula-
ción de capital en el último tercio del siglo XIX', *Anales de Economía*, 24, 1974,
43–83. Contemporary accounts of the early years of the Vizcayan industry are to be
found in B. de Alzola, *Estudio relativo a los recursos de que la industria nacional
dispone para la construcción y armamentos navales*, Madrid, 1886, and P. de
Alzola, *Memoria relativa al estado de la industria siderúrgica en España*, Bilbao,
1896. For Asturias see the excellent L. de Adaro, *Criaderos de Asturias*, vol. 2 of
Criaderos de hierro de España, Madrid, 1916, and L. Adaro Ruiz Falcó, *175 años de*

la sidero metalurgía asturiana, Gijon, 1968. Other works include Altos Hornos de Vizcaya, Bilbao, 1952, and R. N Chilcote, Spain's Iron and Steel Industry, Austin, Texas, 1968.

Textiles. For the eighteenth century see J. C. La Force, The Development of the Spanish Textile Industry, 1750–1850, Berkeley and Los Angeles, 1965; M. Garzón Pareja, La industria sedera en España: el arte de la seda en Granada, Granada, 1962; C. Bueno Aguado, Del obrador a la fábrica: vicisitudes de los centros textiles no catalanes, Bejar, 1973; and E. Herrera Oria, La real fábrica de tejidos de algodón de Avila y la reorganización de esta industria en el siglo XVIII, Valladolid, 1922. On the origins of the Catalan textile industry the following should be consulted: J. Vila Valentí, 'El origen de la industria catalana moderna', Estudios Geográficos, 78, 1960, 5–40; R. Alier, 'La fàbrica d'indianes de la família Canals' Recerques, 4, Barcelona, 1974; R. Grau and M. López, 'Empresari i capitalista a la manufactura catalana del segle XVIII: introducció a l'estudi de les fàbriques d'indianes', Recerques, 4, Barcelona, 1974; and F. Torrela, El moderno resurgir textil de Barcelona, Barcelona, 1961. The fortunes of the industry in the nineteenth century are covered in J. Fontana, Aribau i la indústria cotonera a Catalunya, Barcelona, 1963: J. Nadal and E. Ribas, 'Una empresa algodonera catalana: la fábrica "De la Rambla" de Vilanova, 1841–61', Annales Cisalpines d'Histoire Sociale, 1, 1970, 71–104; and M. Izard, Revolució industrial i obrerisme: Les Tres Classes de Vapor a Catalunya, 1869–1913, Barcelona, 1970. For later developments see also L. Beltrán Flores, La industria algodonera española, Barcelona, 1943, and E. Bertrand y Serra, 'Un estudio sobre la industria textil algodonera, Boletín de la del Comité Regulador de la Industria Algodonera, 1931. The Valencian silk industry is dealt with in V. M. Santos Isern, 'Sederia i industrializió: el cas de Valencia, 1750–1870', Recerques, 5, Barcelona, 1975.

Other industries. A classic work on the cork industry is R. Medir Jofra, Historia del gremio corchero, Madrid, 1953. The electricity supply industry is dealt with in F. Sintes Olives and F. Vidal Burdils, La industria eléctrica en España: estudio económico legal de la producción y consumo de electricidad y material eléctrico, Barcelona, 1938, and J. L. Martín Rodríguez and J. M. Ollé Romeu, Ayuntamiento de Barcelona, Documentos y Estudios, vol. 9, Orígenes de la industria eléctrica barcelonesa, Barcelona, 1961. On engineering and shipbuilding see the excellent work of A. de Castillo, La Maquinista Terrestre y Marítama, personaje histórico 1855–1955, Barcelona, 1955. For the naval industry of Vizcaya there is the still valuable work of T. Guiard, La industria naval vizcaína: anotaciones históricas y estadísticas desde sus orígenes hasta 1907 (second edition, revised and corrected by M. Basas Fernández), Bilbao, 1968.

Banking and Finance. There are some first-rate works on the banking sector: see especially El Banco de España: una historia económica, Madrid 1970; Servicio de Estudios del Banco de España, Ensayos sobre la economía española a mediados del siglo XIX, Madrid, 1970; G. Tortella, 'Spain, 1829–74', in R. E. Cameron, ed., Banking and Economic Development: Some Lessons of History, New York, 1972; G. Tortella, ed., La banca española en la Restauración, Madrid, 1974, 2 vols; and J. Sardá, La política monetaria y las fluctuaciones de la economía española en el siglo XIX, Barcelona, 1948. The following also deserve mention: R. de Santillán, Memoria histórica sobre los bancos de San Carlos, Español de San Fernando, Isabel II y de España, Madrid, 1865, 2 vols; J. A. Galvarriato, El Banco de España: constitución,

historia, vicisitudes y principales episodios en el primer siglo de su existencia,
Barcelona, 1932; J. G. Ceballos Teresi, Economía, finanzas, cambios: historia
económica, financiera y política de España en el siglo XX, Madrid, 1932, 7 vols; J.
M. Tallada Paulí, Historia de las finanzas españolas en el siglo XIX, Madrid, 1946;
R. Canosa, Un siglo de banca privada (1845–1945): apuntes para la historia de las
finanzas españolas, Madrid, 1945. One of the outstanding writers on Spanish
financial history is N. Sánchez Albornoz: among his many publications see especi-
ially Jalones en la modernización de España, Barcelona, 1975; España hace un
siglo: una economía dual, Barcelona, 1968; 'La crisis de 1866 en Madrid: la Caja de
Depósitos, las sociedades de crédito y la Bolsa', Moneda y Crédito, 100, 1967, 3–40;
and 'Los bancos y los sociedades de crédito en las provincias: 1856–1868', Moneda y
Crédito, 104, 1968, 39–68. On individual banks see: Banco Hispano Americano, El
primer medio siglo de su historia, Madrid, 1951, and Un siglo en la vida del Banco
de Bilbao: primer centenario, 1857–1957, Bilbao, 1957. The problems of the Catalan
banks are treated in P. Voltes Bou, La banca barcelonesa de 1840 a 1920, Barcelona,
1963; J. Sardá and L. Beltrán, Els problems de la banca catalana, Barcelona, 1933;
and F. Cabana, La banca a Catalunya: apunts per una historia, Barcelona, 1965. For
the Franco period see J. Muñoz, El poder de la banca en España, Madrid, 1969. The
stock exchanges of Barcelona and Bilbao are adequately covered in J. Fontana, La
vieja Bolsa de Barcelona, 1851–1914, Barcelona, 1961, and J. A. Torrente Fortuño,
Historia de la Bolsa de Bilbao, Bilbao, 1966.

Foreign investment in Spain. On the nineteenth century see A. Broder, 'Les inves-
tissements étrangers en Espagne au XIXᵉ siècle: méthodologie et quantification',
Revue d'Histoire Economique et Sociale, 1975, 29–63; R. E. Cameron, France and
the Economic Development of Europe, 1800–1914: Conquest of Peace and Seeds of
War, Princeton, 1961; and R. Anes Álvarez, 'Las inversiones extranjeras en España
de 1855 a 1880', in Ensayos sobre la economía española a mediados del siglo XIX.
For the renewal of foreign investment in the Franco period see M. Vázquez Montalbán, La penetración americana en España, Madrid, 1974; E. Bayo, El 'desafío' en
España, Madrid, 1970; and Stanford Research Institute, Las inversiones norteamericanas en España, Barcelona, 1972.

Transport. On the inadequacies of the Spanish roads before the railway age see D.
Ringrose, Transport and Economic Stagnation in Spain, 1750–1850, Durham, N.C.,
1970. The best study of the railways is A. Casares Alonso, Estudio histórico
económico de las construcciones ferroviarias españolas en el siglo XIX, Madrid,
1973. See also F. Waís San Martín, Historia general de los ferrocarriles españoles,
1830–1941, Madrid, 1967, and G. Tortella, 'Ferrocarriles, economía y revolución',
in C. E. Lida and I. M. Zavala, La revolución de 1868: historia, pensamiento,
literatura, New York, 1970. The development of the national market in the
nineteenth century is the subject of two recent articles: J. Fontana, ed., 'Formación
del mercado nacional y toma de conciencia de la burguesía', in Cambio económico y
actitudes políticas en la España del siglo XIX, Barcelona, 1973, and N. Sánchez
Albornoz, 'La integración del mercado nacional: España e Italia', in Jalones en la
modernización de España.

Foreign Trade. The collapse of Spain's trade with her American colonies is the
subject of an article by J. Fontana, 'Colapso y transformación del comercio exterior
español entre 1792 y 1827: un aspecto de la crisis de la economía del Antiguo
régimen', Moneda y Crédito, 115, 1970, 3–23. Colonial trade is also dealt with in the

second half of the proceedings of the first colloquium of Spanish economic historians: see J. Nadal and G. Tortella, *Agricultura, comercio colonial y crecimiento económico en la España contemporánea*, Barcelona, 1974. See also F. Rahola, *Comercio de Cataluña con América en el siglo XVIII*, Barcelona, 1931, and P. de Alzola, *Relaciones comerciales entre la Peninsula y las Antillas*, Madrid, 1895. Other works on Spanish foreign trade since the loss of the colonies include J. Plaza Prieto, 'El desarrollo del comercio exterior español desde principios del siglo XIX a la actualidad', *Revista de Economía Política*, 6, 1955, and V. Andres Álvarez, 'Historia y crítica de los valores de nuestra balanza de comercio', *Moneda y Crédito*, 3, 1945, 11–25.

Tariff policy. The best general accounts of Spain's tariff policy are both written by Catalans with a pronounced sympathy for protectionism; see G. Graell, *Historia del Fomento del Trabajo Nacional*, Barcelona, 1911, and M. Pugés, *Como triunfó el proteccionismo en España: la formación de la política arancelaria española*, Barcelona, 1931. See also: J. Illas y Vidal, *Memoria sobre los perjuicios que ocasionaría en España . . . la adopción del sistema del libre cambio*, Barcelona, 1849; L. Figuerola, *La reforma arancelaria de 1866*, Madrid, 1879; A. Cánovas del Castillo, 'La producción de cereales en España y los actuales derechos arancelarios', *Problemas Contemporáneos*, 3, Madrid, 1890; P. de Alzola, *La política económica mundial y nuestra reforma arancelaria*, Bilbao, 1906; M. Graell, *Las zonas neutrales: su importancia para Barcelona*, Barcelona, 1914; J. M. Tallada, 'La política comercial y arancelaria español en el siglo XIX', *Anales de Economía*, 3, 1943; and J. A. Castedo, *Referencias históricas y comentarios sobre la economía arancelaria española*, Madrid, 1958.

Social history, the labour movement. The best account of Spanish society in the eighteenth century is A. Domínguez Ortiz, *La sociedad española en el siglo XVIII*, Madrid, 1955. For the popular revolts which marked the final years of the *ancien régime* see P. Vilar, 'El motín de Esquilache y las crisis del Antiguo régimen', *Revista de Occidente*, 107, 1972, 199–249; L. Rodríguez, 'El motín de Madrid de 1766', *Revista de Occidente*, 121, 1973, 24–49; L. Rodríguez, 'Los motines de 1766 en provincias', *Revista de Occidente*, 122, 1973, 183–207; E. Moreu Rey, *Revolució a Barcelona el 1789*, Barcelona, 1967; I. Castells, 'Els rebomboris del pa de 1789 a Barcelona', *Recerques*, 1, Barcelona, 1970; and M. Ardit Lucas, 'Los alborotos de 1801 en el reino de Valencia', *Hispania*, 29, 1969, 526–42. There are three excellent works on Spain's rural disturbances in the nineteenth and early twentieth centuries: C. Bernaldo de Quirós, *El espartaquismo agrario andaluz*, new edn, Madrid, 1974; R. Pérez del Alamo, *Apuntes sobre dos revoluciones andaluzas*, new edn, Madrid, 1971; and J. Díaz del Moral, *Historia de las agitaciones campesinas andaluzas – Córdoba: antecedentes para una reforma agraria*, new edn, Madrid, 1973. On the birth of the industrial proletariat see J. Fontana, 'Nacimiento del proletariado industrial y primeras etapas del movimiento obrero', in *Cambio económico y actitudes políticas en la España del siglo XIX*, Barcelona, 1973. Recent publications on the Spanish labour movement are reviewed in J. P. Fusi, 'Algunas publicaciones recientes sobre la historia del movimiento obrero español', *Revista de Occidente*, 123, 1973, 358–68. The most satisfactory general account is M. Tuñón de Lara, *El movimiento obrero en la historia de España*, Madrid, 1972. On the First International there is little to compare with J. Termes, *Anarquismo y sindicalismo en España: La Primera Internacional, 1864–81*, Barcelona, 1972. Other works which deserve mention include F. Romeu, *Las clases trabajadores en España, 1898–1930*,

Madrid, 1970, and G. Meaker, *The Revolutionary Left in Spain, 1914–23*, Stanford, 1974, together with the older works: A. Lorenzo, *El proletariado militante*, Toulouse, 1949, 2 vols; M. Buenacasa, *El movimiento obrero español, 1886–1926: historia y crítica*, new edn, Paris, 1966; A. Marvaud, *La Question social en Espagne*, Paris, 1910; and R. Lamberet, *L'Espagne (1750–1936). Mouvements ouvriers et socialistes (chronologie et bibliographie)*, Paris, 1953. Catalonia is in general well treated by labour and social historians; see the bibliography of E. Giralt, J. Termes and A. Balcells, *Bibliografia dels moviments socials a Catalunya, País Valencià i les iles*, Barcelona, 1972, as well as C. Martí, *Orígenes del anarquismo en Barcelona*, Barcelona, 1959; A. Balcells, *El sindicalismo en Barcelona, 1916–23*, Barcelona, 1965; and J. Romero Maura, *La Rosa de Fuego: republicanos y anarquistas: la política de los obreros barceloneses entre el desastre colonial y la semana trágica, 1899–1909*, Barcelona, 1975. For the history of the labour movement in the Basque region at the onset of its industrialisation see J. P. Fusi, *Política obrera en el País Vasco (1880–1923)*, Madrid, 1975.

INDEX